AAT

WORKBOOK

Intermediate Units 4 & 5

Financial Accounting

August 1997 edition

The fifth edition of this Workbook contains the following features.

- Details of the format of the central assessment
- Graded practice exercises
- Devolved assessments for practice
- A trial run devolved assessment to attempt under timed conditions
- All AAT central assessments set so far up to and including June 1997
- Five trial run central assessments to attempt under timed conditions

FOR JUNE 1998 AND DECEMBER 1998 ASSESSMENTS

BPP Publishing
August 1997

First edition 1993
Fifth edition August 1997

ISBN 0 7517 6084 6 (previous edition 0 7517 6926 6)

British Library Cataloguing-in-Publication Data

A catalogue record for this book
is available from the British Library

Published by

BPP Publishing Limited
Aldine House, Aldine Place
London W12 8AW

All our rights reserved. No part of this publication may be reproduced, stored in a retrieval system or transmitted, in any form or by any means, electronic, mechanical, photocopying, recording or otherwise, without the prior written permission of BPP Publishing Limited.

We are grateful to the Lead Body for Accounting for permission to reproduce extracts from the Standards of Competence for Accounting and to the Association of Accounting Technicians for permission to reproduce Central Assessment tasks. The suggested solutions have been prepared by BPP Publishing Limited.

Printed by Ashford Colour Press, Gosport, Hants

©

BPP Publishing Limited
1997

Page

INTRODUCTION
(v)

How to use this Workbook - standards of competence
- assessment structure - further guidance - BPP meets the AAT

PRACTICE EXERCISES

ORDER FORMS

REVIEW FORM & FREE PRIZE DRAW

HOW TO USE THIS WORKBOOK

This Workbook covers Unit 4: *Recording capital transactions* and Unit 5: *Preparing financial accounts*. It is designed to be used alongside BPP's *Financial Accounting* Tutorial Text. The Workbook provides Practice Exercises on the material covered in the Tutorial Text, together with Devolved Assessments and Central Assessments.

As you complete each chapter of the Tutorial Text, work through the *Practice Exercises* in the corresponding section of this Workbook. Once you have completed all of the Sessions of Practice Exercises, you will be in a position to attempt the Devolved Assessments.

The tasks involved in a *Devolved Assessment* will vary in length and complexity, and there may be more than one 'scenario'. If you complete all of the Devolved Assessments in this Workbook, you will have gained practice in all parts of the elements of competence included in Units 4 and 5. You can then test your competence by attempting the Trial Run Devolved Assessment, which is modelled on the type of assessment actually set by the AAT.

Of course you will also want to practise the kinds of task which are set in the *Central Assessments*. The main Central Assessment section of this Workbook includes all the AAT Central Assessments set from December 1993 to December 1994, and by doing them you will get a good idea of what you will face in the assessment hall. When you feel you have mastered all relevant skills, you can attempt the five Trial Run Central Assessments. These consist of the Central Assessments from June 1995 to June 1997 inclusive. Provided you are competent, they should contain no unpleasant surprises, and you should feel confident of performing well in your actual Central Assessment.

Class Exercises and Class Assessments

Each session of this Workbook includes a number of exercises without solutions to be attempted in the classroom. There is also a Class Devolved Assessment and a Central Assessment without solutions. The answers to these and to the Class Exercises will be found in the BPP Lecturers' Pack for this Unit.

A note on pronouns

For reasons of style, it is sometimes necessary in our study material to use 'he' instead of 'he or she', 'him' instead of 'him or her' and so on. However, no prejudice or stereotyping according to sex is intended or assumed.

STANDARDS OF COMPETENCE

The competence-based Education and Training Scheme of the Association of Accounting Technicians (AAT) is based on an analysis of the work of accounting staff in a wide range of industries and types of organisation. The Standards of Competence for Accounting which students are expected to meet are based on this analysis.

The Standards identify the *key purpose* of the accounting occupation, which is to operate, maintain and improve systems to record, plan, monitor and report on the financial activities of an organisation, and a number of *key roles* of the occupation. Each key role is subdivided into *units of competence*. By successfully completing assessments in specified units of competence, students can gain qualifications at NVQ/SVQ levels 2, 3 and 4, which correspond to the AAT Foundation, Intermediate and Technician stages of competence respectively.

Intermediate stage key roles and units of competence

The key roles and unit titles for the AAT Intermediate stage (NVQ/SVQ level 3) are set out below.

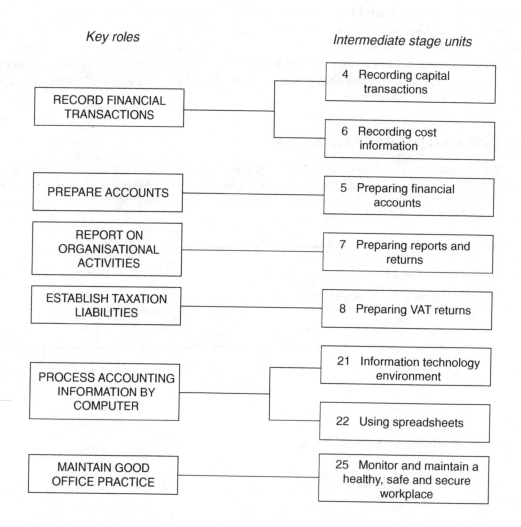

Units and elements of competence

Units of competence are divided into *elements of competence* describing activities which the individual should be able to perform.

Each element includes a set of *performance criteria* which define what constitutes competent performance. Each element also includes a *range statement* which defines the situations, contexts, methods etc in which the competence should be displayed.

Supplementing the standards of competence are statements of *knowledge and understanding* which underpin competent performance of the standards.

The elements of competence for Unit 4: *Recording capital transactions* and Unit 5: *Preparing financial accounts* are set out below. For each unit, the performance criteria are listed first, followed by the knowledge and understanding required for the unit as a whole. These are cross-referenced to sessions of exercises in this BPP Workbook, which correspond with chapters in the *Financial Accounting* Tutorial Text.

Unit 4: Recording capital transactions

4.1 Maintain records and accounts relating to capital expenditure

Performance criteria		Session(s)
1	Relevant details relating to specific items of capital expenditure are correctly entered in the appropriate records	4
2	The organisation's records agree with the physical presence of capital items	4
3	Any acquisition and disposal costs and revenues are correctly identified and recorded	4
4	Depreciation charges and other necessary entries and adjustments are correctly calculated and recorded in the appropriate ledger accounts	4
5	Where required, the records show clearly the prior authority for capital expenditure and indicate the approved method of funding	4
6	The organisation's policies, regulations, procedures and timescales are observed	4
7	Discrepancies, unusual features or queries are identified and either resolved or referred to the appropriate person	4

Range statement

1   Entries relating to tax allowances are excluded

2   Depreciation methods: straight line, reducing balance

3   Discrepancies, unusual features or queries include lack of agreement between physical items and records

Introduction

| Knowledge and understanding | Session(s) |

The business environment

- Types and characteristics of different types of asset — 4
- Main requirements of SSAP 12 or any relevant FRS — 4
- Relevant legislation and regulations (public sector organisations) — 4

Accounting techniques

- Methods of depreciation — 4

- Accounting treatment of capital items sold, scrapped or otherwise retired from service — 4

- Use of plant registers and similar subsidiary records — 4

- Use of transfer journal — 1

Accounting principles and theory

- Basic accounting concepts and principles: matching of income and expenditure within an accounting period, historic cost, accruals, consistency, prudence, materiality — 2

- Principles of double entry accounting — 1

- Distinction between capital and revenue expenditure, what constitutes capital expenditure — 4

The organisation

- Background understanding that the system of an organisation are affected by its organisational structure, its administrative systems and procedures and the nature of its business transactions — 4

Unit 5: Preparing financial accounts

5.1 Record income and expenditure

Performance criteria	Session(s)
1	Income and expenditure is correctly recorded in the appropriate ledger accounts	5, 9
2	Any accrued or prepaid income and expenditure is correctly identified and adjustments are made	6, 9
3	The organisation's policies, regulations, procedures and timescales are observed	5, 6, 9
4	Income and expenditure is analysed in accordance with defined requirements and appropriate information is passed to management	5, 6, 9
5	Discrepancies, unusual features or queries are identified and either resolved or referred to the appropriate person	5, 9

Range statement

1   Items of income and expenditure for an organisation, including capital receipts and payments

5.2 Prepare accounts from incomplete records

	Performance criteria	Session(s)
1	Essential accounts and reconciliations are correctly prepared	8
2	Existing primary information is accurately summarised	7, 9
3	Other relevant information is correctly identified and recorded	7, 9
4	Investigations into the client's business transactions are conducted with tact and courtesy	6
5	The organisation's policies, regulations, procedures and timescales are observed	7, 8, 9
6	Discrepancies, unusual features or queries are identified and either resolved or referred to the appropriate person	7, 8, 9

Range statement

1   Reconstructing any accounts from data in an unusual or incomplete form

2   Discrepancies, unusual features or queries include situations where insufficient data has been provided, where there are inconsistencies within the data

5.3 Prepare the extended trial balance

	Performance criteria	Session(s)
1	The trial balance is accurately extended and totalled	10
2	Totals from the general ledger or other records are correctly entered on the extended trial balance	
3	Any errors disclosed by the trial balance are traced and corrected	10
4	Any adjustments not dealt with in the ledger accounts are correctly entered on the extended trial balance	10
5	An agreed valuation of closing stock is correctly entered on the extended trial balance	10
6	The organisation's policies, regulations, procedures and timescales are observed	10
7	Discrepancies, unusual features or queries are identified and either resolved or referred to the appropriate person	10

Range statement

Relevant accounting policies include the treatment of depreciation and other provisions

Unit 5: Knowledge and understanding

The column headed *Elements* indicates the elements of Unit 5 under which the area of knowledge and understanding is listed in the Standards of Competence.

The business environment	*Elements*	*Session(s)*
• General function and status of SSAPs and FRSs	5.1, 5.2, 5.3	3
• Main requirements of SSAPs 2, 5, 9, 12, 13 and 21 as they affect this element and any relevant FRSs	5.2, 5.3	3 - 6
• Legal, VAT and tax requirements	5.2	3, 5
• Need to present accounts in the correct form	5.2	3, 6

Accounting techniques		
• Accounting treatment of accruals and prepayments	5.1, 5.2, 5.3	6, 9
• Use of transfer journal	5.1, 5.2, 5.3	5
• Methods of analysing income and expenditure	5.1	5, 9
• Methods of restructuring accounts from incomplete evidence	5.2	8
• Correction of different types of error	5.2, 5.3	8, 9, 10
• Making and adjusting provisions	5.2, 5.3	8, 9, 10

Accounting principles and theory		
• Principles of double entry accounting	5.1, 5.3	1
• Basic accounting concepts and principles - matching of income and expenditure within an accounting period, historic cost, accruals, consistency, prudence, materiality	5.1	2
• Function and form of accounts for income and expenditure	5.1	5
• Function and form of a trial balance	5.2, 5.3	1, 7, 8
• Basic principles of stock valuation: cost or NRV; what is included in cost	5.2, 5.3	7
• Objectives of making provisions for depreciation and other purposes	5.2, 5.3	4

The organisation		
• Background understanding that the system of an organisation is affected by its organisational structure, its administrative systems and procedures and the nature of its business transactions	5.1, 5.2, 5.3	5

ASSESSMENT STRUCTURE

Devolved and central assessment

The units of competence at the Intermediate stage are assessed by a combination of devolved assessment and central assessment.

Devolved assessment tests students' ability to apply the skills detailed in the relevant units of competence. Devolved assessment may be carried out by means of:

(a) simulations of workplace activities set by AAT-approved assessors; or
(b) observation in the workplace by AAT-approved assessors.

Central assessments are set and marked by the AAT, and concentrate on testing students' grasp of the knowledge and understanding which underpins units of competence.

The Intermediate Stage

Units of competence at the AAT Intermediate stage (NVQ/SVQ level 3) are tested by central assessment (CA) and devolved assessment (DA) as follows.

Unit number		Central assessment	Devolved assessment
4	Recording capital transactions		✓
5	Preparing financial accounts	✓	✓
6	Recording cost information	✓	✓
7	Preparing reports and returns	✓	✓
8	Preparing VAT returns		✓
21	Information technology environment		✓
22	Using spreadsheets		✓
25★	Monitor and maintain a healthy, safe and secure workplace		✓

Note. If you have covered Unit 25 Health, Safety and Security at Foundation level, you do not need to study it again. If not, a *Health and Safety at Work* booklet may be obtained from BPP (see the order form at the end of this Workbook).

Central Assessment (FA): Preparing Financial Accounts

The Central Assessment *Preparing Financial Accounts* covers underpinning knowledge and understanding for Unit 5 and can be expected to be divided into sections as follows.

Section 1   Extended trial balance exercise
Section 2   Short answer questions with some communication tasks
Section 3   Incomplete records exercise

All questions and tasks in all parts are to be attempted: none is optional. The time allowed is three hours.

The main topics to be assessed are: relevant accounting concepts and principles, the nature and classification of assets and liabilities, capital and revenue expenditure, objectives and principles of depreciation, and relevant accounting standards.

FURTHER GUIDANCE

In his *Assessment manual* the AAT has produced further guidance on the assessments for Units 4 and 5. Extracts are given below.

Central assessment: *Financial Accounting*

Part 1

Part 1 is an accounting exercise which gives a brief description of the business and a list of period-end accounts balances. A fair sample of the main types of account will be included although the scale of the tasks will not be as great as would be expected in a devolved assessment. Candidates will be required to prepare an extended trial balance and deal with adjustments such as accruals and prepayments, depreciation, provisions etc. Error corrections and other adjustments, possibly requiring journal entries, may also be a part of the exercise.

Part 2

This consists of a number of short-answer questions to test communication skills, knowledge and understanding. These may require brief explanations, calculations, accounting entries, selection from a number of given possible answers, or other similar responses. Some of the responses will be in the form of memos and/or draft letters. Examples of aspects which could be included are:

Depreciation
Stock valuation
Other year end adjustments
Function of trial balance
Accounting concepts and principles
Accounting standards (general function and effects)
Capital and revenue distinction
VAT regulations and entries

Part 3

There will be one or more practical accounting problems in non-standard form involving the processing or re-structuring of given data to produce the information required. This is to test the candidates' understanding of the inter-relationships within the data and the ability to handle less routine situations. Incomplete records problems are a strong possibility for inclusion but additionally or alternatively there could be problems involving aspects such as stock valuation, fixed asset transactions and depreciation, accruals and prepayments etc.

Devolved assessment

General principles

All students should collect evidence of competence in the relevant units at the Intermediate Stage and present this for assessment in the form of a portfolio of work. The portfolio might include evidence obtained from the workplace, simulations and projects undertaken at college or the workplace.

Specific guidance for each unit

The following examples are designed to suggest the types of evidence that students might collect for their portfolio at the Intermediate Stage. The list is not exhaustive, and assessors and mentors should use their own judgement in deciding on the relevance of a particular piece of evidence.

Recording capital transactions

Few students are likely to maintain capital records as part of their work experience. Most evidence will therefore be likely to be in the form of simulations. The portfolio should include at least one example of each of the exercises below.

Possible simulations:

(a) Record the purchase, sale and depreciation of assets in realistically designed asset registers (eg vehicle, plant registers)

(b) Exercise/case which includes dealing with a discrepancy between physical items and the records

(c) Problems on the straight line and reducing balance methods of depreciation

Preparing financial accounts

Workplace evidence can be presented, where possible, but it is unlikely that it will cover all aspects of the Standards except in the case of a small firm. The main object is to ensure that accounting exercises are realistic and include a sufficient number of contingencies. They should be competence-based rather than mechanical text book exercises. The portfolio should include a wide spread of relevant simulations (eg at least one of each type of exercise listed below), including a number which are computer-based.

Possible simulations:

(a) Incomplete records (a common form of simulated exercise, many good examples available)
(b) Long accounting exercises with accruals, pre-payments etc
(c) Trial balance with adjustments
(d) Correction of error exercises
(e) Exercises showing the analysis of income and expenditure

BPP MEETS THE AAT

On behalf of students, BPP keeps in touch with the AAT and seeks to determine the approach which should be followed in an assessment. On this page, we summarise the points in question and answer form.

What is the correct treatment for drawings of business stock for personal use?

The traditional view is

DEBIT	Drawings
CREDIT	Purchases

at cost price

However, the AAT's recommended treatment, according better with modern practice and the requirements of HM Customs and Excise, is as follows.

DEBIT	Drawings at selling price (including VAT)
CREDIT	Sales
CREDIT	VAT

In the March 1995 edition of the Education and Training Newsletter, acknowledging the variation in practice and between different VAT offices, the AAT stated that the traditional method would be accepted, but you should try to use the newer, recommended method if information on VAT is available.

Are manufacturing accounts assessed at the Intermediate Stage?

Yes, but only the basic principles. For example, as part of an incomplete records exercise manufacturing accounts could be assessed, but only to draw up a P&L account, *not* full-blown accounts. Students should know the principles. This approach is justified by the range statement under 5.2 which could cover *any account*.

The principles involved could be assessed, eg calculation of cost of stock, but there will be NO assessment of the 'fringe' areas.

Could club accounts be assessed?

Yes, club accounts could feature as part of an incomplete records question.

Are hire purchase transactions assessable (SSAP 21)

Yes, this is explicitly mentioned in the Standards of Competence (elements 5.2 and 5.3), but only very basic aspects would be tested, eg treatment, what might appear in financial accounts, not 'T' accounts. An example of the type of question set is task 2.3 from the December 1996 Central Assessment.

Is it correct that only a background knowledge of the nature of partnerships and companies is required?
You are right in your understanding that a background knowledge of the nature of partnerships and companies is required and that the detailed accounting aspects are not assessable until Technician Stage. If company extended trial balances are covered, clear guidance will be given to candidates and additional accounts (ie beyond share capital and profit and loss accounts) will not be included.

Practice exercises

1 Double entry bookkeeping: revision

Objectives of this session

This session tests knowledge and understanding of the following areas.

- **Double entry bookkeeping**

- **Books of prime entry**

- **Control accounts**

- **Assets and liabilities**

- **Bad and doubtful debts**

- **From ledger accounts to financial statements**

Exercise 1   Level: EASY

Which of the following records is not a book of prime entry?

A   Bank statements
B   Petty cash book
C   Journal
D   Sales returns day book

Exercise 2   Level: EASY

The extract below is taken from a book of prime entry.

Date	Narrative	Folio	Total £	Discounts allowed £	Sales ledger £	Sundry £
1.5.19X9	M James & Co	SL12	140.00	10.00	140.00	-

Which book of prime entry is represented here?

Exercise 3   Level: EASY

You have purchased a new item of equipment on credit for £100,000. What is the double entry necessary to record the transaction?

Exercise 4   Level: EASY

You are presented with the following nominal ledger entries to post.

DEBIT	Cash account	£150.55	
CREDIT	Debtors control		£150.55

(a)   What does this transaction probably represent?
(b)   What other accounting procedures might you have followed?

Exercise 5   Level: EASY

What transaction is represented by the following entries?

DEBIT	Rent account	£100	
CREDIT	Landlord		£100

Exercise 6   Level: EASY

The total cost of wages and salaries debited in a business's profit and loss account is equal to:

A   the total net pay received by all employees
B   the total gross pay earned by all employees
C   the total gross pay earned by all employees plus employees' NI and pension contributions
D   the total gross pay earned by all employees plus employer's NI and pension contributions

Exercise 7   Level: EASY

During the monthly payroll routine of Colossal plc it was found that employer's NI contributions amounted to £1,500,000. What entries should be made to record this sum in the company's accounts?

A   DEBIT   Wages and salaries control account
    CREDIT   Wages and salaries expense account

B   DEBIT   Wages and salaries expense account
    CREDIT   Wages and salaries control account

C   DEBIT   Wages and salaries control account
    CREDIT   NIC control account

D   DEBIT   Wages and salaries expense account
    CREDIT   NIC control account

Exercise 8
Level: MODERATE

Which of the following occurrences could *not* account for a credit balance on a trade debtor's account?

A   A sales invoice has been paid twice
B   A sales invoice has been posted to another customer's account in error
C   Returns outwards have not been taken into account
D   A cheque from the customer was made out in the wrong amount

Exercise 9
Level: MODERATE

In the first quarter of 19X3, a business had taxable outputs, net of VAT of £42,780, and taxable inputs, net of VAT of £30,360. All are subject to VAT at standard rate. At the end of the quarter, how much is payable to or recoverable from HM Customs & Excise?

Exercise 10
Level: MODERATE

Munificent Ltd offers a 5% trade discount to Pampered Ltd, a credit customer, and also 2½% of invoice value as settlement discount if Pampered Ltd pays within ten days. Pampered Ltd purchases goods for £15,000 before discounts on credit on 31 August and pays on 8 September.

What amount will be credited as a sale in Munificent Ltd's nominal ledger, and how much will be charged as discount allowed? (*Note.* VAT is not relevant to these transactions.)

Exercise 11
Level: MODERATE

A debtors control account contains the following entries.

	£
Balance brought forward at 1 January	21,400
Bank	102,000
Discounts allowed	8,125
Credit sales	120,100

There are no other entries in the account. What is the closing balance carried forward at 31 December?

Exercise 12
Level: MODERATE

A creditors control account contains the following entries.

	£
Bank	79,500
Credit purchases	83,200
Discounts received	3,750
Contra with debtors control account	4,000
Balance c/f at 31 December 19X8	12,920

There are no other entries in the account. What was the opening balance brought forward at 1 January 19X8?

Exercise 13
Level: MODERATE

Gordon Ltd has an accounting year ended 31 December 19X2. At that date, the balance on the sales ledger control account was £65,000, but the total of the individual accounts in the sales ledger came to £63,620. Upon investigation the following facts were discovered.

(a)   The sales day book total for week 44 had been overcast by £300.

(b)   A credit balance of £210 on Flash's account in the sales ledger had been incorrectly treated as a debit entry, when balancing off his account.

(c)   A purchase ledger contra of £1,500 had been entered in Ming's account in the sales ledger but no other entry had been made.

What are the adjusted totals of the sales ledger control account and the sales ledger balances?

Exercise 14   Level: MODERATE

A company's bank statement shows £715 direct debits and £353 investment income not recorded in the cash book. The bank statement does not show a customer's cheque for £875 entered in the cash book on the last day of the accounting period. If the cash book shows a credit balance of £610 what balance appears on the bank statement?

A   £97 overdrawn
B   £627 overdrawn
C   £1,123 overdrawn
D   £1,847 overdrawn

Exercise 15   Level: ADVANCED

The Lax Company began trading in 19X7 and makes all its sales on credit. The company suffers from a high level of bad debts and a provision for doubtful debts of 3% of all outstanding debtors is made at the end of each year.

Information for 19X7, 19X8 and 19X9 is as follows.

	Year to 31 December		
	19X7	*19X8*	*19X9*
	£	£	£
Outstanding debtors at 31 December	44,000	55,000	47,000
Bad debts written off during year	7,000	10,000	8,000

Tasks

(a) State the amount to be shown in the profit and loss account for bad debts and provision for doubtful debts for the years ended 31 December 19X7, 19X8 and 19X9.

(b) State the value of debtors which would be shown in the balance sheet as at 31 December each year.

Class Exercise 1   Level: EASY

On 1 January 19X3 a business has assets of £5,000 and liabilities of £3,000. What is the value of the owner's investment?

Class Exercise 2   Level: EASY

What is the principal difference between the balance sheet and the profit and loss account?

Class Exercise 3   Level: MODERATE

On 1 January 19X3, a business had assets of £10,000 and liabilities of £7,000. By 31 December 19X3 it had assets of £15,000, liabilities of £10,000. The owner had contributed capital of £4,000. How much profit had the business made over the year?

Class Exercise 4   Level: MODERATE

A company receives a purchase invoice from a supplier. Briefly describe how the data on the invoice is processed before appearing on the company's financial statements.

2 *Classification of assets and fundamental accounting concepts*

Objectives of this session

This session tests knowledge and understanding of the following areas.

- **Capital and revenue expenditure**

- **Assets and expenses**

- **Prudence**

- **Materiality**

- **Accruals**

- **Consistency**

- **Historical cost**

Practice exercises

Exercise 1
Level: EASY

What, briefly, is the difference between 'capital' and 'revenue' spending?

Exercise 2
Level: EASY

Accounting concepts never conflict. True or false? Explain your answer.

Exercise 3
Level: MODERATE

Compare the following two profit and loss accounts prepared for a sole trader who wishes to show them to the bank manager to justify continuation of an overdraft facility.

YEAR ENDED 31 DECEMBER 19X3

	£	£
Sales revenue		25,150
Less: production costs	10,000	
selling and administration	7,000	
		17,000
Gross profit		8,150
Less interest charges		1,000
Profit after interest		7,150

YEAR ENDED 31 DECEMBER 19X4

	£
Sales revenue less selling costs	22,165
Less production costs	10,990
Gross profit	11,175
Less administration and interest	3,175
Net profit	8,000

Which fundamental accounting concept is being ignored here? Justify your choice.

How do you think the changes in the format of these financial statements affect the quality of the accounting information presented?

Exercise 4
Level: MODERATE

You are in business in a small town, whose main source of economic prosperity is the tourist trade. On 25 March 19X2 the town celebrated the 1,000th anniversary of its existence. The town held a number of festivals to mark this occasion and to bring in more tourists.

Your business has had the good fortune to be involved in the event. You have made 1,000 commemorative mugs. These were all made by 31 December 19X1 to be ready at the beginning of the year. They cost 40 pence each to make and during the anniversary year they were for sale at 75 pence each. At the end of the anniversary year, there are 200 still unsold. You estimate that you are unlikely to sell any more at 75 pence, but you might be able to sell them at 30 pence each.

Task

Which fundamental accounting concepts will you consider when assessing a value for the mugs in your balance sheets:

(a) at the end of 19X1;
(b) at the end of 19X2?

On the basis of your considerations, note down the value of the mugs you would include in the balance sheet at 31 December 19X1 and 31 December 19X2.

Exercise 5
Level: MODERATE

Note down which of the following would be an asset on the balance sheet, which would be an expense in a period end profit and loss account and which would be neither (in which case, have a stab at saying what it is).

(a) A company car

(b) Interest on a bank overdraft

(c) A bank loan repayable in five years

(d) Petty cash of £25

(e) The portion of uniform business rate paid covering the period after the balance sheet date

(f) Freehold property

(g) Payment of wages for a director with a two year service contract

(h) Payments into a pension fund

(i) A debtor who will pay in 18 months time

(j) A bad debt written off

(k) A patent

Exercise 6   Level: MODERATE

You work for a multinational company and you are preparing two accounting documents:

(a) a statement for a customer, listing invoices and receipts, and detailing the amounts owed;

(b) a report sent to the senior management of a division, who want a brief comparative summary of how well the firm is doing in the UK and in France.

How would considerations of *materiality* influence your preparation of each document?

Class Exercise 1   Level: MODERATE

What is historical cost accounting?

Class Exercise 2   Level: ADVANCED

You make widgets for a living. Each widget has two components: a Wid and a Jet. Each Wid costs £1 and each Jet costs 50 pence. Widgets sell for £5.00 each.

In January 19X3 you sell 30 widgets, although the money for ten will not be received until February. You have acquired 40 Jets which you paid for at the beginning of the month, and 50 Wids which do not have to be paid for until March.

What is the surplus for January on the basis of:

(a) cash accounting;
(b) accrual accounting?

3 The general function and status of SSAPs and FRSs

Objectives of this session

This session tests knowledge and understanding of the following areas.

- **The development and status of accounting standards**

- **SSAPs**

- **FRSs**

Exercise 1 Level: EASY

What is an accounting standard?

Exercise 2 Level: EASY

Accounting standards are not enforceable in law.

True ☐

False ☐

Exercise 3 Level: EASY

What do the following acronyms stand for?

(a) SSAP
(b) FRS
(c) ED
(d) DD
(e) FRED
(f) ASB
(g) IASC
(h) CCAB
(i) FRC

Class Exercise 1 Level: MODERATE

Accounting standards never conflict with Companies Act requirements.

True ☐

False ☐

Class Exercise 2 Level: MODERATE

What are the functions of SSAPs and FRSs?

4 Unit 4: Recording capital transactions

Objectives of this session

This session provides practice in the following skills and techniques.

- **The basic principles relating to fixed assets**

- **Understanding and accounting for depreciation**

- **Understanding and accounting for purchase and sale of fixed assets**

- **The importance of the fixed assets register**

- **Authorisation and control**

Exercises 1 and 2 test your knowledge and understanding of some basic facts about fixed assets.

Exercise 1   Level: EASY

(a) Define briefly the following terms.

    (i)   Capital expenditure
    (ii)   Revenue expenditure

(b) Explain briefly the effect on the final accounts if:

    (i)   capital expenditure is treated as revenue expenditure;
    (ii)   revenue expenditure is treated as capital expenditure.

Exercise 2   Level: EASY

Would you capitalise the following items in the accounts of a company:

(a)   a box file;
(b)   a computer;
(c)   a small plastic display stand?

Exercises 3 and 4 test your understanding of the concept of depreciation.

Exercise 3   Level: EASY

What does depreciation do and why is it necessary?

Exercise 4   Level: MODERATE

Briefly explain, without numerical illustration, how the straight line and reducing balance methods of depreciation work. What different assumptions does each method make?

Exercise 5   Level: MODERATE

This exercise tests your ability to calculate depreciation using the straight line and reducing balance method.

On 1 January 19X1 a business purchased a laser printer costing £1,800. The printer has an estimated life of 4 years after which it will have no residual value.

Task

Calculate the annual depreciation charges for 19X1, 19X2, 19X3 and 19X4 on the laser printer on the following bases:

(a)   the straight line basis; and
(b)   the reducing balance method at 60% per annum.

Note. Your workings should be to the nearest £.

Exercises 6 to 10 and Class Exercise 4 are calculations involving depreciation and purchases and sales of fixed assets.

Exercise 6   Level: MODERATE

Look back to the information in Exercise 5. Suppose that in 19X4 the laser printer were to be sold on 1 July for £200 and that the business had chosen to depreciate it at 60% per annum using the reducing balance method applied on a month by month basis.

Task

Reconstruct the following accounts for 19X4 *only*.

(a) The laser printer account
(b) The provision for depreciation - laser printer account
(c) The assets disposals account

Exercise 7   Level: MODERATE

The financial year of Holloway plc ended on 31 May 19X9.

At 1 June 19X8 the company owned motor vehicles costing £124,000 which had been depreciated by a total of £88,000.

On 1 August 19X8 Holloway plc sold motor vehicles, which had cost £54,000 and which had been depreciated by £49,000, for £3,900 and purchased new motor vehicles costing £71,000.

It is the policy of Holloway plc to depreciate its motor vehicles at 35% per annum using the reducing balance method. A full year's depreciation is charged on all motor vehicles in use at the end of each year. No depreciation is charged for the year on assets disposed of during that year.

Task

Show the following accounts as they would appear in the ledger of Holloway plc for the year ended 31 May 19X9 only.

(a) The motor vehicles account
(b) The provision for depreciation: motor vehicles account
(c) The assets disposals account

Exercise 8   Level: MODERATE

Jim Pentonville is the owner of a taxi business and his financial year runs from 1 July to 30 June. On 1 July 19X9 he had two vehicles used by his drivers, one a Ford purchased on 10 January 19X7 for £10,000 and the other a Toyota purchased on 12 August 19X7 for £8,000.

During November 19X9 Jim decided to replace the Ford and trade it in for a new Mercedes costing £15,500. Jim took delivery of the new car on 14 November. The garage accepted the Ford together with a cheque for £9,500 in payment.

Vehicles are depreciated at 10% per annum reducing balance method, with a full year's depreciation charged in the year of purchase and no depreciation charged in the year of disposal.

Task

(a) Calculate the value on 1 July 19X9 of both the Ford and the Toyota.

(b) Draw up the motor vehicles account, the provision for depreciation: motor vehicles account and the motor vehicles disposal account as they would appear in the ledger for the year ended 30 June 19Y0. Show clearly any transfers to or from the profit and loss account and any closing balances.

Exercise 9   Level: ADVANCED

The following information has been taken from the ledger of Annette Ltd as at 31 May 19X1.

	£
Land	80,000
Buildings	160,000
Fixtures and fittings	176,000
Motor vehicles	90,000
Provisions for depreciation	
Land and buildings	32,000
Fixtures and fittings	88,000
Motor vehicles	54,000

The above information is before taking the following into account.

(a) During the year ended 31 May 19X1 motor vehicles which had cost £30,000 and which had a net book value of £6,000 were sold for £9,000.

(b) Depreciation has yet to be provided for as follows.

On buildings	2% straight line method
On fixtures and fittings	25% reducing balance method
On motor vehicles	20% straight line method

No depreciation is charged on land.

Task

Prepare in so far as the above information permits the following ledger accounts for the year ended 31 May 19X1.

(a) Assets disposals
(b) Provision for depreciation: land and buildings
(c) Provision for depreciation: fixtures and fittings
(d) Provision for depreciation: motor vehicles

Exercise 10   Level: ADVANCED

Since 1 October 19X7, the Strange Ways Engineering Company Ltd has been building up its own customers' delivery service and accordingly has purchased the following vehicles.

19X7			
1 October	Van	E676TVX	costing £28,000.00
19X8			
1 January	Lorry	E438CBA	costing £36,000.00
19X9			
1 February	Van	E779GMS	costing £16,000.00
1 July	Van	F934KTA	costing £24,000.00

The following additional information is available.

(a) Lorry E438CBA proved to be unsuitable for the company's trade and was therefore sold on 31 December 19X8 to John Krim for £21,680.00.

(b) Van E779GMS was bought second hand. Before joining the company's transport fleet on 1 April 19X9 this van was converted to meet the company's requirements. The conversion work was carried out in the company's own workshops, the following costs being incurred.

	£
Direct labour	1,880.00
Direct materials	3,200.00
Variable overheads	1,370.00

Fixed overheads apportionment added at 25% of prime cost.

(c) It is the company's policy to provide depreciation on motor vehicles at the rate of 20% per annum on cost, time-apportioned where purchased during the year. No depreciation is charged in the year of disposal.

Task

Prepare the following accounts where relevant for each of the years ended 30 September 19X8 and 19X9 in the books of the Strange Ways Engineering Company Ltd.

Motor vehicles at cost
Motor vehicles provision for depreciation
Lorry E438CBA disposal

Class Exercise 1   Level: EASY

This exercise tests your understanding of the purpose of the fixed assets register.

(a) What would you expect to find in a fixed assets register?
(b) What events give rise to entries in a fixed assets register?

Class exercises 2 and 3 test your understanding of matters relating to authorisation and control.

Class Exercise 2   Level: EASY

What details would you expect to find on:

(a) the capital expenditure authorisation form; and
(b) the asset disposal authorisation form?

Class Exercise 3   Level: MODERATE

(a) Give reasons why the fixed assets register might not reconcile with the fixed assets actually present.

(b) What action should be taken when discrepancies are discovered?

Class Exercise 4   Level: MODERATE

On 1 January 19X1 Mr Floss purchased a candyfloss-making machine for his fairground stall. The machine cost £2,800 and has an estimated economic life of four years after which it will have no residual value. The financial year of the business ends on 31 December each year.

(a) Calculate the annual depreciation charges on the machine for each of the four years on each of the following bases.

   (i)   The straight line basis
   (ii) The reducing balance method at 55% per annum

Note. Your workings should be to the nearest £.

(b) Suppose that the business sold the machine half way through the third year for £1,000 and that depreciation had been provided for using the straight line method applied on a month for month basis.

Task

Reconstruct the following accounts for the third year only.

   (i)   The machine account
   (ii)   The provision for depreciation: machine account
   (iii) The assets disposals account

5 Final accounts and the accounting system

Objectives of this session

This session provides practice in the following skills and techniques.

- **Posting income and expenditure to the appropriate ledger accounts**

- **Analysing income and expenditure and passing the relevant information to management**

- **Observing the requirements of SSAP 5 *Accounting for value added tax*, SSAP 13 *Accounting for research and development* and SSAP 21 *Accounting for leases and hire purchase contracts***

- **Observing the organisation's policies, regulations, procedures and timescales**

- **Identifying discrepancies, unusual features or queries and either resolving them or referring them to the appropriate person**

Exercise 1
Level: EASY

List and briefly explain:

(a) the four fundamental accounting concepts contained in Statement of Standard Accounting Practice 2; and

(b) the fifth principle contained in the Companies Act 1985.

Exercise 2
Level: EASY

What are the main reasons for and purposes behind preparing accounts, for both limited companies and unincorporated bodies such as sole traders and partnerships?

Exercise 3
Level: EASY

Describe the form and function of the balance sheet and the profit and loss account of a limited company.

Exercise 4
Level: MODERATE

The following transactions were recorded in a company's books during one week of its trading year.

	£
Trade purchases (at list price)	4,500
Sales on credit (at list price)	6,000
Purchase of a van	10,460
Entertaining	360
Purchase of a car for a sales representative	8,600

A settlement discount of £300 is available on the sales. All figures are given exclusive of VAT at 17.5%. If the balance on the VAT account was £2,165 at the beginning of the week, what is the balance at the end of the week?

Exercise 5
Level: MODERATE

In a lessor's accounts (ie someone who has obtained or is renting an asset under a lease) why is an asset obtained under a finance lease put in the balance sheet whereas one obtained under an operating lease is not?

Class Exercise 1
Level: MODERATE

A trader, registered for VAT, undertook the following transactions during the year ended 31 March 19X8.

	£
Sales taxable at standard rate	500,000
Sales taxable at zero rate	25,000
Exempt sales	75,000
Expenses subject to input tax	300,000

Included in expenses is the purchase of a motor car for £8,000 and a delivery van for £10,000. All figures are given exclusive of VAT. No particular purchase is attributable to any particular sale.

How much input tax can be reclaimed by the trader?

Class Exercise 2
Level: MODERATE

Garner Ltd has incurred research and development costs of £117,000 during 19X8, which have been analysed as follows.

	£
Pure research	35,000
Development work for contract with Kay Ltd	15,000
Applied research	22,000
Project development costs (including market research £3,000)	45,000
	117,000

Task

State how the figures for R & D would be shown in the balance sheet and profit and loss account of Garner Ltd, according to the rules in SSAP 13.

6 Accruals and prepayments

Objectives of this session

This session provides practice in the following skills and techniques.

- **Identifying any accruals and prepayments required**

- **Calculating the accruals and prepayments to be made and posting them in the ledger accounts**

- **Investigating business transactions with tact and courtesy**

Exercise 1   Level: EASY

An electricity accrual of £375 was treated as a prepayment in preparing a company's profit and loss account.

What was the resulting effect on the profit of the company?

Exercise 2   Level: EASY

At 31 December 19X7 the accounts of a company show accrued rent payable of £250. During 19X8 the company pays rent bills totalling £1,275, including one bill for £375 in respect of the quarter ending 31 January 19X9.

What is the profit and loss charge for rent payable for the year ended 31 December 19X8?

Exercise 3   Level: MODERATE

A company is making up its accounts to 31 December 19X3. You have been asked to identify expense accruals and prepayments near the year end. You have found the following invoices relating to the telephone account from before and after the year end. Identify any accrual or prepayment which should be made at the year end.

Note. System rental is paid in advance, calls are paid in arrears.

```
┌─────────────────────────────────────────────────────────────────────────┐
│                                                                           │
│   ☎ NATIONAL            ┌─────────────────────────────────────┐          │
│     TELECOM             │     Telephone  Account              │          │
│                         └─────────────────────────────────────┘          │
│                         National Telecommunications plc VAT No. 234 5678 12│
│                                 Customer account number                   │
│   BELL HOUSE                                                              │
│   RINGROAD                          QQ 7724 5187 PPP1 A1                  │
│ ── LONDON                                        15/02/X4                 │
│   WE7 7TT                                       (TAX POINT)               │
│                                                                           │
│   BILL ENQUIRIES 0171-000 2222        Benson Limited                     │
│                                       Unit 5                              │
│   NOTIFICATION OF PAYMENT             Barkside Estate                     │
│   (24 HOURS) 01444 098765             NP7 0XS                            │
│  ─  ─  ─  ─  ─  ─  ─  ─  ─  ─  ─                                         │
│                                                                           │
│   SALES/GENERAL                                                           │
│   ENQUIRIES      0171-000 3333                                            │
│                                                                           │
└───────────────────────────────────────────────────────────────────────  │
```

CHARGES FOR TELEPHONE SERVICE ON 0171-000 3333

	£	£
CURRENT CHARGES		
Rental-System 16/02/X4 to 15/05/X4	660.00	
Dialled Calls		
Meter Reading 16/11/X3 209,363		
Meter Reading 16/02/X4 238,080		
Number of units @ 4.20p 28,717	1,206.114	
Low User Rental Rebate		
Total of Current Charges (Excl VAT)	1,866.11	
Value Added Tax at 17.50%	326.57	
Total of Current Charges (Incl VAT)		2,192.68
		£ 2,192.68

Total Amount Due

PLEASE SEE OVERLEAF FOR PAYMENT AND CUSTOMER SERVICE INFORMATION

G Girobank	PAYMENT SLIP	**Bank Giro Credit**
Customer account number	Credit account number Amount	By transfer from Girobank a/c no.
Q7724 3187 PPP1A1	149227 £ 2,192.68	

Cashiers Stamp and initials

Signature _____ Date _____   CASH

CHEQ

43-80-63 MIDLAND BANK plc
Head Office Collection Account   £

☎ NATIONAL TELECOM

Items   Fee   Please do not write or mark below this line or fold this payment slip

---

Exercise 4   Level: MODERATE

A company makes up accounts each year to 31 May. The rent on the company premises is payable quarterly in advance on 1 January, 1 April, 1 July and 1 October. The Uniform Business Rate (UBR) is set by the local authority in respect of a year running from 1 April to 31 March. It is paid each year in two equal instalments in advance on 1 April and 1 October.

The annual rental for the calendar years 19X6 and 19X7 was £6,600 and £7,200 respectively, but on 1 January 19X8 it was increased to £7,800 per annum. The UBR for the last three years has been as follows.

19X6/X7	£4,800
19X7/X8	£5,400
19X8/X9	£6,000

What is the charge for rent and the UBR in the profit and loss account for the year ended 31 May 19X8? What accruals or prepayments will be carried forward at the year end?

Exercise 5

Level: ADVANCED

You are acting as an assistant to the accountant of Hilyard Ltd as the accounts are being prepared for the year ended 31 March 19X5. The accountant has asked you to review the invoices received during the month after the year end as part of the procedure for identifying accruals. You carry out your review and discover the following invoices.

National Gas plc
South Eastern
Helium House
Nitrogen Road
LONDON SE11 1AA

If you have an enquiry about this bill please ring
0181-666 9999

Calls are charged at local call rate.
For other enquiries look in the telephone directory under 'GAS'.

VAT Registration Number
222 6789 21

Please send enquiries to above address - for payment see overleaf

HILYARD LIMITED
UNIT 7
TOTTING ESTATE
LONDON N6 3PT

Customer reference number
1576 2931 00 7
Date of bill (tax point)
20 APRIL 19X5
Calorific Value
38.30 MJ/m³..
1027
Btu's per cubic foot

date of meter reading	Meter reading (see below for key)		Gas supplied			Charges
	Present	Previous	100's cubic feet	Therms	Vat %	
20 APRIL	**017898**	**016971**	**927**	**952.029**	**17.5**	**436.98**
STANDING CHARGE 19.01.X5 TO 20.04.X5					**17.5**	**27.63**
092 DAYS AT 30.03p PER DAY						
			45.90 Pence per Therm			**464.61**

CREDIT
TARIFF
If the present meter reading is an estimate (E) and you would like us to use your own meter reading, please write your reading on the back of the bill and send it to us as soon as possible. Or telephone and tell us your reading.

Thank you.

VAT	**81.31**
TOTAL £	**545.92**

METER LOCATED AT UNIT 7, TOTTING ESTATE
LONDON N6

Key
to types of meter reading
E Estimated reading
C Customer's reading
X Exchange meter

Girobank   PAYMENT SLIP   **Bank Giro Credit**

By transfer from Girobank a/c no.

135
205

Customer account number
1576 2931 007

Credit account number
3437957

Amount
£ 545.92

Cashiers Stamp and initials

Signature _____ Date _____

43-80-63   MIDLAND BANK plc
Head Office Collection Account

CASH
CHEQ
£

HILYARD LIMITED
UNIT 7
TOTTING ESTATE
LONDON N6 3PT

National Gas SOUTH EASTERN

Items   Fee   Please do not write or mark below this line or fold this payment slip

NATIONAL
ELECTRICITY

YOUR CUSTOMER SERVICES OFFICE IS:	YOU CAN PHONE US ON:
POWER ROAD LONDON E2 9AJ	0171 123 1234

HILYARD LTD
UNIT 7
TOTTING ESTATE
LONDON N6 3PT

WHEN TELEPHONING
We have a call queuing system. When you hear the ringing tone please wait for a reply as calls are answered in strict rotation.
BUSY TIMES
Please try to avoid 9-30AM - 10-30 AM and 2 PM to 3 PM

METER READING		UNITS USED	UNIT PRICE (pence)	V.A.T code	AMOUNT £
PRESENT	PREVIOUS				
48587	41132	7455	7.470	1	556.89
STANDING CHARGE				1	42.80
TOTAL CHARGE (EXCLUDING VAT)					599.69
VAT 1 **£599.69** @ 17.5% COMMERCIAL					104.95

MAKE YOUR BILLS EASIER TO SWALLOW. SEE PAGE 4 OF SOURCE FOR BUDGET SCHEME APPLICATION.

E=Estimated reading. Please read carefully the advice given on the back of this bill
C=Your own reading

BALANCE TO PAY	704.64
VAT CHARGE THIS BILL	104.95

YOUR ACCOUNT NUMBER	BILL DATE/TAX POINT	READING DATE	NON-DOMESTIC USE
C/132.4494/011.813	29 APRIL 19X5	29 April 19X5	100%

G' Girobank   PAYMENT SLIP   **Bank Giro Credit**

135 205	Customer account number	Credit account number	Amount	By transfer from Girobank a/c no.
	1324494011813	543 8063	£ 704.64	

Cashiers Stamp and initials

Signature _____   Date _____

43-80-63

MIDLAND BANK plc
Head Office Collection Account

HILYARD LTD
UNIT 7
TOTTING ESTATE
LONDON N6 3PT

CASH
CHEQ
£

NATIONAL
ELECTRICITY

Items   Fee   Please do not write or mark below this line or fold this payment slip

Task

Calculate the accruals which should be made in relation to these invoices.

Note. The previous reading date for the electricity was 6 January 19X5.

Exercise 6   Level: ADVANCED

The prepayment brought forward on the water rates account on 1 January 19X2 was £492.50. The bill shown below was received and paid in full on the date shown.

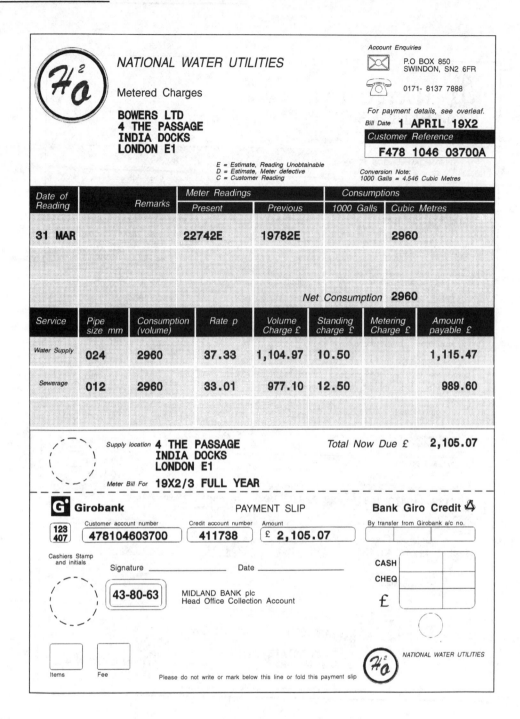

Task

Draw up the ledger account for water rates for the year ended 31 December 19X2.

Class Exercise 1 Level: MODERATE

Ratsnuffer is a business dealing in pest control. Its owner, Roy Dent, employs a team of eight who were paid £12,000 per annum each in the year to 31 December 19X5. In the following year 19X6 he raised salaries by 10% to £13,200 per annum each. On 1 July 19X6, he hired a trainee at a salary of £8,400 per annum. He pays his work force on the first working day of every month, one month in arrears, so that his employees receive their salary for January on the first working day in February, and so on.

Tasks

(a) Calculate the cost of salaries which would be charged in the profit and loss account of Ratsnuffer for the year ended 31 December 19X6.

(b) Calculate the amount actually paid in salaries during the year (the amount of cash received by the workforce).

(c) State the amount of accrued charges for salaries which would appear in the balance sheet of Ratsnuffer as at 31 December 19X6.

Class Exercise 2   Level: ADVANCED

The Batley Print Shop rents a photocopying machine from a supplier for which it makes a quarterly payment as follows:

(a) three months rental in advance;
(b) a further charge of 2 pence per copy made during the quarter just ended.

The rental agreement began on 1 August 19X4 and the first six quarterly bills were as follows.

Bills dated and received	Rental	Costs of copies taken	Total
	£	£	£
1 August 19X4	2,100	0	2,100
1 November 19X4	2,100	1,500	3,600
1 February 19X5	2,100	1,400	3,500
1 May 19X5	2,100	1,800	3,900
1 August 19X5	2,700	1,650	4,350
1 November 19X5	2,700	1,950	4,650

The bills are paid promptly, as soon as they are received.

Tasks

(a) Calculate the charge for photocopying expenses for the year to 31 August 19X4 and the amount of prepayments and/or accrued charges as at that date.

(b) Calculate the charge for photocopying expenses for the following year to 31 August 19X5, and the amount of prepayments and/or accrued charges as at that date.

7 The trial balance and stocks

Objectives of this session

This session provides practice in the following skills and techniques.

- **Appreciating the function and form of the trial balance**

- **Calculating the cost of goods sold and allocating expenditure correctly**

- **The requirements of SSAP 9 *Stocks and long-term contracts* in relation to stock counts and valuation**

Practice exercises

Exercise 1

Level: EASY

The following amounts appear in the books of Dearden Ltd at the end of the financial year.

	£
Opening stock	5,700
Closing stock	8,540
Carriage outwards	6,220
Purchases	75,280
Returns inwards	5,540
Carriage inwards	3,680

Task

Calculate the figure for cost of sales for the trading account.

Exercise 2

Level: MODERATE

You have been given the following list of balances from the accounts of Pooley Ltd as at 31 December 19X7.

	Dr	Cr	£
Stock as at 1 January 19X7	22000		22,000
Purchases	223000		223,000
Sales		340,700	340,700
Discounts allowed	4600		4,600
Discounts received		5500	5,500
Returns in	6700		6,700
Returns out		5600	5,600
Wages and salaries	34500		34,500
Bad debts	3100		3,100
Carriage in	1400		1,400
Carriage out	2200		2,200
Other operating expenses	24500		24,500
Trade debtors	34000		34,000
Trade creditors		21600	21,600
Provision for bad debts		450	450
Cash on hand	800		800
Bank overdraft		23400	23,400
Profit and loss account at 1 January 19X7		8550	8,550
Share capital		30000	30,000
Property	50000		50,000
Equipment	64000		64,000
Provisions for depreciation at 1 January 19X7			
Property		10000	10,000
Equipment		25000	25,000
	470,800	470,800	

Task

Lay out the trial balance and add up the debit and credit columns.

Exercise 3

Level: MODERATE

Jackson Ltd's draft balance sheet includes a stock figure of £28,850. On further investigation the following facts are discovered.

(a) One stock sheet has been over-added by £212 and another under-added by £74.

(b) Goods included at their cost of £460 had deteriorated. They could still be sold at their normal selling price (£800) once repair work costing £270 was complete.

(c) Goods costing £430 sent to customers on a sale or return basis had been included in stock at their selling price of £665.

32 BPP Publishing

Task

Calculate the revised stock figure.

Dean Ltd's stock includes three items for which the following details are available.

	Supplier's list price £	Net realisable value £
Product A	3,600	5,100
Product B	2,900	2,800
Product C	4,200	4,100
	10,700	12,000

The company receives a 2½% trade discount from its suppliers and it also takes advantage of a 2% discount for prompt payment.

Task

Calculate the total value of products A, B and C which should be shown in stock in the balance sheet.

On 28.2.19X8, which is one month before the end of his financial year, the ledger accounts of A Hubble were as follows.

CASH

	£		£
Capital	9,500	Rent	2,750
Bank loan	3,000	Creditors	700
Sales	11,200	Interest	350
Debtors	400	Electricity	400
		Telephone	180
		Drawings	1,300

CAPITAL

	£		£
		Cash	9,500

BANK LOAN

	£		£
		Cash	3,000

SALES

	£		£
		Cash	11,200
		Debtors	4,600

DEBTORS

	£		£
Sales	4,600	Cash	400

RENT

	£		£
Cash	2,750		

PURCHASES

	£		£
Creditors	2,100		

CREDITORS

	£		£
Cash	700	Purchases	2,100

INTEREST

	£		£
Cash	350		

ELECTRICITY

	£		£
Cash	400		

TELEPHONE

	£		£
Cash	180		

DRAWINGS

	£		£
Cash	1,300		

During the last month of his financial year, A Hubble recorded the following transactions.

(a) He bought goods for £2,000, half for credit and half for cash.

(b) He paid the following:

    (i)   interest £20;
    (ii)   electricity £25;
    (iii) telephone £12.

(c) He made sales of £3,500 of which £500 were for cash.

(d) He received £220 from debtors.

Tasks

(a) Post the transactions for March 19X8 into the ledger accounts.

(b) Balance off the ledger accounts and draw up a trial balance.

(c) Prepare a balance sheet as at 31.3.19X8 and a trading, profit and loss account for the year ended 31.3.19X8.

Class Exercise　　　　　　　Level: MODERATE

Swallow Ltd is a manufacturer of chipboard. During the stocktake it is discovered that a quantity of the large standard size chipboard has been damaged. Only the edges of the sheets are affected, so it would be possible to cut the wood down to the smaller standard size.

The production cost of this quantity of large chipboard was £25,500 and it would normally sell for £42,000. The same number of sheets of the smaller chipboard would normally cost £18,000 to produce and they would sell for £27,000.

The company's selling and distribution costs are calculated as 5% of selling price. The estimated cost of reducing the damaged wood to the smaller size is £750.

Task

Calculate the balance sheet value of this stock item.

8 *Incomplete records*

Objectives of this session

This session provides practice in the following skills and techniques.

- **Preparing reconciliations of essential accounts**

- **Accurately summarising existing primary information**

- **Identifying and recording any other relevant information**

- **Reconstructing any accounts from data in an unusual or incomplete form**

- **Resolving or reporting discrepancies, unusual features or queries including situations where insufficient data has been provided and where there are inconsistencies within the data**

Exercise 1
Level: EASY

A debtors control account contains the following entries:

	£
Balance b/f 1 January	42,800
Bank	204,000
Discounts allowed	16,250
Credit sales	240,200

Assuming there are no other entries into the account, what is the closing balance at 31 December?

Exercise 2
Level: MODERATE

The balances in a company's sales ledger at 31 December 19X2 were totalled and their sum was found to be £251,385. At the same date, the debit balance on the company's debtor control account was found to be £247,533. Upon investigation the following facts were discovered.

(a) One customer, whose balance was £1,260 credit, had been omitted from the list of sales ledger balances.

(b) A bad debt of £1,500 had not been entered in the nominal ledger.

(c) Cash received of £840 had been debited to the customer's personal account.

(d) A customer's cheque for £2,412 had been dishonoured by the bank, but no adjustment had been made in the control account.

Task

Reconcile the debtors control account with the list of balances as at 31 December 19X2.

Exercise 3
Level: MODERATE

The following information is available in respect of Higgins Ltd.

	£
Balances at 1 June 19X6	
PAYE control account	89,944
NIC control account	58,924
Wages and salaries summary for June 19X6	
Total gross pay	217,640
PAYE	55,720
Employees' NIC	17,240
Employer's NIC	35,000
Employees' savings deductions	5,080
Payments to the Inland Revenue during June 19X6	
In respect of PAYE	35,680
In respect of NIC	32,960

Tasks

(a) State the amount of net pay received by employees in June 19X6.
(b) Produce the PAYE and NIC control accounts, showing a closing balance.

Exercise 4
Level: MODERATE

Clinton Ltd has not kept a proper set of accounting records during 19X3 due to the prolonged illness of the bookkeeper. However, the following information is available.

	£
Cash purchases in year	5,850
Cash paid for goods supplied on credit	41,775
Creditors at 1 January 19X3	1,455
Creditors at 31 December 19X3	1,080

Task

Calculate Clinton Ltd's purchases figure for the trading account for 19X3.

Exercise 5   Level: MODERATE

An extract from a company's trading account stood as follows for the year ended 31 March 19X2.

	£	£
Sales		150,000
Opening stock	12,000	
Purchases	114,500	
	126,500	
Closing stock	14,000	
		112,500

Tasks

(a) Calculate the gross profit as a percentage of cost of sales.
(b) Calculate the gross profit as a percentage of sales.

Exercise 6   Level: MODERATE

Jennings Ltd had opening stock of £71,300. Purchases and sales for 19X7 were £282,250 and £455,000 respectively. The gross profit margin is a constant 40% on sales. On 31 December 19X7 a fire destroyed all the stock on Jennings Ltd's premises, except for small sundry items with a cost of £1,200.

Task

Calculate the cost of the stock destroyed.

Class Exercise 1   Level: MODERATE

Blissetts Ltd is a retail company and sales are all on cash terms. During 19X4 their bank account shows cash banked of £142,950 which included £660 in respect of the repayment of a director's loan. About £450 was taken from the till every month for wages and £60 was taken weekly for sundry expenses. The cash in the till amounted to £930 on 1 January 19X4 and £780 on 31 December 19X4.

Task

Calculate the sales figure for Blissetts Ltd for 19X4.

Class Exercise 2   Level: ADVANCED

The following trading account was produced by Arnold Ltd for the year ended 31 March 19X6.

	£	£
Sales		645,000
Opening stock	75,000	
Purchases	468,750	
	543,750	
Closing stock	57,000	
Cost of sales		486,750
Gross profit		158,250

The following figures have been extracted from Arnold Ltd's balance sheet as at 31 March 19X6.

	£
Trade debtors	90,000
Prepayments	6,000
Cash in hand	9,000
Bank overdraft	12,000
Trade creditors	60,000
Accruals	4,500
Proposed dividend	7,500

Tasks

Calculate:

(a) the stock turnover period in days;
(b) the debtors' collection period in days;
(c) the creditors' payment period in days;
(d) the current ratio at 31 March 19X6;
(e) the quick ratio (or acid test ratio) at 31 March 19X6.

9 Club accounts and manufacturing accounts

Objectives of this session

This session provides practice in the following skills and techniques.

- **Subscriptions in the income and expenditure account**

- **Calculating the accumulated fund**

- **Life membership subscription**

- **Preparation of income and expenditure account and balance sheet**

- **Types of cost in a manufacturing account**

- **Provision for unrealised profit**

- **Preparation of a manufacturing account**

Practice exercises

Exercise 1
Level: EASY

The following information relates to a sports club.

	£
19X4 subscriptions unpaid at beginning of 19X5	410
19X4 subscriptions received during 19X5	370
19X5 subscriptions received during 19X5	6,730
19X6 subscriptions received during 19X5	1,180
19X5 subscriptions unpaid at end of 19X5	470

The club takes credit for subscription income when it becomes due, but takes a prudent view of overdue subscriptions. What amount should be credited to the income and expenditure account for 19X5?

Exercise 2
Level: EASY

Which one of the following costs would *not* be shown as a factory overhead in a manufacturing account?

A The cost of insurance on a factory
B The cost of an extension to a factory
C The cost of depreciation on a factory
D The cost of rent on a factory

Exercise 3
Level: EASY

Which one of the following costs would be included in the calculation of prime cost in a manufacturing account?

A Factory rent
B Office wages
C Direct production wages
D Depreciation on machinery

Exercise 4
Level: MODERATE

(a) A club takes credit for subscriptions when they become due. On 1 January 19X5 arrears of subscriptions amounted to £38 and subscriptions paid in advance were £72. On 31 December 19X5 the amounts were £48 and £80 respectively. Subscription receipts during the year were £790.

What amount would be shown for income from subscriptions in the income and expenditure account for 19X5?

(b) A club takes no credit for subscriptions due until they are received. On 1 January 19X5 arrears of subscriptions amounted to £24 and subscriptions paid in advance were £14. On 31 December 19X5 the amounts were £42 and £58 respectively. Subscription receipts during the year were £1,024.

What amount would be shown for income from subscriptions in the income and expenditure account for 19X5?

Exercise 5
Level: MODERATE

The following balances were extracted from the books of the Grand Slam Bridge Club as at 31 December 19X5.

	£
Tables and chairs	380
Playing cards and other accessories	102
Stock of reference books	130
Subscriptions in advance	80
Subscriptions in arrears	27
Life membership fund	300
Deficit for the year	117

Life membership funds are accounted for by crediting them to a life membership account, where they remain until the death of the member.

The only movement on the life membership account in 19X5 arose from the death of one of the five life members during the year. His subscription had been transferred to the accumulated fund before the above balances had been extracted.

(a) What was the balance on the accumulated fund at 31 December 19X5?
(b) What was the balance on the accumulated fund at 1 January 19X5?

Exercise 6   Level: MODERATE

For many years, life membership of the Tipton Poetry Association cost £100, but with effect from 1 January 19X5 the rate has been increased to £120. The balance on the life membership fund at 31 December 19X4 was £3,780 and membership details at that date were as follows.

	No of members
Joined more than 19 years ago	32
Joined within the last 19 years	64
	96

The Association's accounting policy is to release life subscriptions to income over a period of 20 years beginning with the year of enrolment.

During 19X5, four new members were enrolled and one other member (who had joined in 19X1) died.

What is the balance on the life membership fund at 31 December 19X5?

Exercise 7   Level: MODERATE

The following details are available in respect of a company's manufacturing operations during 19X5.

		£
Work in progress:	opening stock	42,920
	closing stock	39,610
Raw materials:	opening stock	12,940
	purchases in year	213,680
	closing stock	14,550
Carriage inwards		3,970
Carriage outwards		4,200
Wages and salaries:	factory supervisor	12,490
	direct production staff	96,380
	other factory staff	18,330
	administration staff	21,520
Other factory costs		63,310

The company transfers goods from factory to warehouse at a price which represents a profit to the factory of 15% on the transfer price.

Task

Prepare the company's manufacturing account for 19X5, showing the following.

(a) Prime cost of production in 19X5
(b) Factory cost of finished goods produced in 19X5
(c) Factory profit on goods transferred to the warehouse in 19X5

Exercise 8   Level: MODERATE

A manufacturing company transfers finished goods from factory to warehouse at cost plus 5%. At 31 December its stocks of finished goods, valued at transfer prices, have been as follows.

19X5 £4,620
19X6 £5,460
19X7 £3,780

Tasks

(a) Calculate the adjustment for unrealised profit in the profit and loss account for the year ended 31 December 19X6.

(b) Calculate the adjustment for unrealised profit in the profit and loss account for the year ended 31 December 19X7.

Exercise 9   Level: ADVANCED

Tutorial note. The AAT has stated that club accounts could come up as part of an incomplete records problem. So far there have been no instances of this, but this exercise tests the type of problem that might come up.

On 1 January 19X5 a club owed its suppliers £435 in respect of bar stocks; on 31 December 19X5 the amount was £363. The cash book showed payments to suppliers of £5,685 during the year. Opening stock amounts to £390. Bar sales are mostly on cash terms, though IOUs are occasionally accepted from members. IOUs outstanding at 1 January 19X5 amounted to £12; on 31 December 19X5 the figure was £8. The cash book shows that till receipts lodged in the bank during the year amounted to £6,064, but this was after paying the barman's wages of £20 per week in cash. Bar prices are fixed so as to earn a constant mark-up of 25% on cost.

Tasks

(a) Calculate the cost of closing stock at 31 December 19X5.

(b) What is the net profit on bar trading disclosed in the club's income and expenditure account for 19X5?

Class Exercise 1   Level: ADVANCED

The treasurer of the Giltan Golf Club has prepared the following receipts and payments account for the year ended 31 March 19X8:

	£		£
Balance at 1 April 19X7	682	Functions	305
Subscriptions	2,930	Repairs	146
Functions	367	Telephone	67
Sale of land	1,600	Extensions to clubhouse	600
Bank interest	60	Furniture	135
Bequest	255	Heat and light	115
Sundry income	46	Salary and wages	2,066
		Sundry expenses	104
		Balance c/d:	
		Bank 2,300	
		Cash 102	
			2,402
	5,940		5,940

Task

Prepare an income and expenditure account for the year ended 31 March 19X8 and a balance sheet at that date. The treasurer has supplied the following additional information.

(a) Subscriptions received included £65 which had been in arrears at 31 March 19X7 and £35 which had been paid for the year commencing 1 April 19X8.

(b) Land sold had been valued in the club's books at cost £500.

(c) Accrued expenses are as follows.

	31 March 19X7 £	31 March 19X8 £
Heat and light	32	40
Wages	12	14
Telephone	14	10
	58	64

(d) Depreciation is to be charged on the original cost of assets appearing in the books at 31 March 19X8 as follows.

Buildings	5 per cent
Fixtures and fittings	10 per cent
Furniture	20 per cent

(e) The following balances are from the club's books at 31 March 19X7.

	£
Land at cost	4,000
Buildings at cost	3,200
Buildings provision for depreciation	860
Fixtures and fittings at cost	470
Fixtures and fittings provision for depreciation	82
Furniture at cost	380
Furniture provision for depreciation	164
Subscriptions in arrears (including £15 from a lapsed member who had emigrated)	80
Subscriptions in advance	30
Accrued expenses	58
Bank	600
Cash	82
Accumulated fund	7,618

Class Exercise 2 — Level: ADVANCED

The following balances were taken from the books of the Improvident Actuaries Society Golf Club as at 1 January 19X5.

	£	£
Course at cost		70,000
Clubhouse at cost		15,000
Building fund - represented by investments:		
£20,000 4% consolidated stock	7,400	
Deposit with building society	10,000	
		17,400
Subscriptions in advance (19X5)		400
Creditors for bar supplies		350
Life membership fund		4,000
Subscriptions in arrears		600
Bar stock		4,800
Clubhouse equipment at cost		3,200
Cash in hand	100	
Cash at bank	850	
		950

An analysis of the bank account operated by the club showed the following summary of receipts and payments during the year ended 31 December 19X5.

Receipts	£
Subscriptions	25,000
Life members	2,000
Sale of instruction manuals	700
Green fees	300
Sale of old carpet from clubhouse	22
Bar takings	28,500
Consolidated stock interest	800

Payments	£
Upkeep of course	16,150
General clubhouse expenses (including bar wages of £4,200)	12,150
Petty cash (expenses paid to treasurer)	1,550
Bar supplies	23,150
Purchase of instruction manuals	250
Piano	500
Deposited with building society	800
Replacement carpet for clubhouse	1,260

The following information is significant for the preparation of the club's accounts.

(a) The club maintains a building fund separate from the capital fund and life membership fund. The building fund is invested in consolidated stock and a building society, whilst the capital fund and life membership fund are represented by the general assets of the club.

(b) The building society has been instructed to credit the interest on the club's account direct to the account at each half year. The society computes interest half yearly on 30 June and 31 December. This year the interest amounted to £740. Interest paid on the consolidated stock is also added to the building fund by paying it into the building society account.

(c) There were four life members at the beginning of the year, one of whom has since died. Two other life members have, however, joined the club.

(d) Renewals of clubhouse furnishings are to be treated as revenue expenditure.

(e) Outstanding at 31 December 19X5 were:

	£
Creditors for bar supplies	1,600
Subscriptions in advance (19X6)	900
Subscriptions in arrear (19X5)	300
Bar chits not yet settled	35

(f) Bar stocks at 31 December 19X5 were valued at £4,300.

(g) It is a rule of the club that a cash float of £100 shall be maintained in the treasurer's hands. To this end an imprest petty cash account is operated.

(h) An insurance premium of £480 has been paid by cheque during 19X5 for the year to 31 March 19X6.

Tasks

(a) Prepare an income and expenditure account for the year ended 31 December 19X5.
(b) Prepare a balance sheet as at that date.

Class Exercise 3   Level: ADVANCED

From the information given below your task is to prepare the manufacturing, trading and profit and loss account of Abcoll Ltd for the year ended 31 December 19X5.

Balances at 31 December 19X4

	£
Authorised and issued share capital	
Ordinary shares of £1 each fully paid	100,000
Reserves	1,000
Creditors	57,400
Fixed assets (cost £60,000)	39,000
Stocks	
Raw materials	25,000
Work in progress, valued at prime cost	5,800
Finished goods	51,000
Debtors	35,000
Cash at bank	2,000
Administration expenses prepaid	600

The following transactions occurred during 19X5.

Invoiced sales, less returns	243,000
Cash received from debtors	234,700
Discounts allowed	5,400
Bad debts written off	1,100
Invoiced purchases of raw materials, less returns	80,000
Payments to creditors	82,500
Discounts received	1,700
Factory wages paid	33,300
Manufacturing expenses paid	61,900
Administration expenses paid	16,200
Selling and distribution expenses paid	16,800
Payment for purchase of fixed assets	30,000

Balances at 31 December 19X5

	£
Fixed assets (cost £90,000)	60,000
Stocks	
Raw materials	24,000
Work in progress	5,000
Finished goods	52,000
Administration expenses accrued	1,100
Factory wages accrued	700
Selling and distribution expenses prepaid	1,200

The following information is given.

(a) Depreciation of fixed assets is to be apportioned between manufacturing, administration and selling in the proportions of 7: 2: 1.

(b) Discounts allowed and bad debts written off are to be regarded as selling and distribution expenses.

(c) Discounts received are to be credited to administration expenses.

(d) Taxation is to be ignored.

Tutorial notes

1   A manufacturing account is a detailed breakdown of what would be the 'Purchases' line in cost of sales in a non-manufacturing organisation. Your aim is to set out how raw materials, work in progress, direct wages and indirect factory expenses are gathered together to arrive at the 'Factory cost of finished goods produced'.

2   Most of the figures can be taken straight from the figures given, but don't forget accruals and depreciation.

3   Once you have the figure for finished goods produced you can prepare the trading and profit and loss account in the normal way.

4   Beware! You do not need all of the figures you are given in this question.

10 Extended trial balance

Objectives of this session

This session provides practice in the following skills and techniques.

- **Accurately extending and totalling the trial balance**

- **Entering totals from the general ledger or other records correctly on the extended trial balance**

- **Entering any adjustments not dealt with in the ledger accounts on the extended trial balance**

- **Entering the agreed valuation of closing stock on the extended trial balance**

- **Following relevant accounting policies when dealing with items on the extended trial balance, including making and adjusting provisions**

Folio	Account	Trial balance		Adjustments		Accrued	Prepaid	Profit and loss a/c		Balance sheet	
		Debit	Credit	Debit	Credit			Debit	Credit	Debit	Credit
		£	£	£	£	£	£	£	£	£	£
	SUB-TOTAL										
	Profit for the year										
	TOTAL										

Tutorial note. All the solutions to the exercises in this chapter should be shown on the extended trial balance shown on the previous page. The solutions to all the exercises in this section are shown on one ETB, so don't look at the solution until you have finished the entire session. It would be advisable to work in pencil for the time being.

In these exercises you should ignore VAT.

Exercise 1

Level: EASY

You are assisting the accountant of Justin & West Ltd in the preparation of the accounts for the year ending 31 December 19X4. The following list of balances has been extracted from the ledgers.

	£
Land and buildings (freehold)	120,000.00
Share capital	100,000.00
Sales	471,384.22
Purchases	245,897.44
Stock at 1.1.19X4	79,533.51
Returns in	388.59
Returns out	1,768.62
Discounts allowed	3,978.89
Discounts received	2,115.27
Uniform business rate	27,450.82
Motor expenses	12,245.90
Salaries	103,228.19
Insurance	9,486.30
Trade debtors	32,381.45
Trade creditors	17,862.29
Carriage in	4,197.80
Carriage out	2,557.36
Motor vehicles	65,149.25
Bank balance (in credit at the bank)	7,826.88
Provision for depreciation	
Buildings	4,000.00
Motor vehicles	21,371.42
Bad debts	604.00
Profit and loss account 1.1.19X4	107,906.85

Task

Enter the trial balance on the ETB and add it up.

Exercise 2

Level: MODERATE

You should have realised by now that there is a difference on the trial balance. You should enter the difference in a suspense account.

On investigation, the following errors and omissions are found to have occurred.

(a) An invoice for £3,217.20 for general insurance has been posted to cash but not to the ledger account.

(b) A customer went into liquidation just before the year end, owing Justin & West £1,425.53. The amount was taken off debtors but the corresponding entry to expense the bad debt has not been made.

(c) A cheque paid for purchases has been posted to the purchases account as £4,196.29, when the cheque was made out for £4,916.29.

(d) A van was purchased during the year for £3,059.78, but this amount was credited to the motor vehicles account.

Task

Show the journal which will clear the suspense account, by dealing with the points noted above. Enter the journal on to the ETB.

Exercise 3   Level: MODERATE

No adjustments have yet been made for accruals or prepayments. The accountant asks you to search for any required accruals and prepayments and you find the following information.

(a) The bill for the Uniform Business Rate was received and paid on 1 April 19X4. The bill covers the period 1 April 19X4 to 31 March 19X5.

BLACKLEY FINANCE - NATIONAL NON-DOMESTIC RATE 19X4/X5

Date 01APRX4

> THIS NOTICE AND THE ENCLOSED BOOKLET COSTITUTE THE DEMAND NOTICE. THE BOOKLET PROVIDES INFORMATION WHICH YOU SHOULD READ.

JUSTIN & WEST LTD

Working Group	Account Reference	Total Charge
001	6019-500-1	21,610.18

Property Reference
19720001200001

Rateable value
54800

Multiplier
0.402

UNITS 1 - 3   OCC PERIOD 01-APRX4-31MARX5   22,029.60
WRIGHT ESTATE   TRANSITIONAL ADJUSTMENT   419.42 CR
BLACKLEY   TOTAL LIABILITY   21,610.18
                                                        21,610.18

Warehouse

• IN ACCORDANCE WITH GOVERNMENT REGULATIONS •
THIS DEMAND DOES NOT INCLUDE ANY AMOUNTS
THAT MAY BE OUTSTANDING FOR OTHER YEARS

TRANSITION CALCULATION

NOTIONAL CHARGE PER DAY (NC)
60.35506849
BASE LIABILITY PER DAY (BL)
49.45623542
APPROPRIATE FRACTION (AF) 19X4-X5
115.00/100 X 134.60/129.30 = 1.19713943
AMOUNT PAYABLE (AF X BL X 365)

                    =   21,610.18
TRANSITIONAL ADJUSTMENT =   419.42 CR

PLEASE QUOTE
ACCOUNT REFERENCE ———► | 60195001 |

Enquiries in connection with this account
should be addressed to:-
DIRECTOR OF FINANCE, BUSINESS RATE SECTION
MUNICIPAL OFFICES, 19 FLEET ROAD, BLACKLEY
B53 2NR
TEL: 01327-525 5000

BLACKLEY FINANCE

**BLACKLEY FINANCE CANNOT TAKE RESPONSIBILITY FOR RATEPAYERS
FAILING TO NOTE IMPORTANT INFORMATION CONTAINED ON THIS DEMAND AND IN THE BOOKLET-
PLEASE READ BOTH CAREFULLY**

(b) The insurance bill which had originally been posted to the suspense account was for motor insurance.

0013479

CR CAIN & Co
INSURANCE BROKERS

3, Green Avenue
Blackley
01327 41792

Tax Point
1 December 19X4

DEBIT NOTE

To:

Motor Insurance per attached schedule
1 December 19X4 to 30 November 19X5

£ 3,217 - 20

Member of Fimbra and Lautro

(c)   An invoice for carriage outwards was received after the year end.

MASON HAULAGE CO LTD 41 Breach Street Manchester To: Justin & West Ltd Units 1-3 Wright Estates Blackley	Tax point 31.01.X5 Invoice No. 1011732	
	VAT	**Amount**
Weekly trips Blackley - London 1 November 19X4 - 31 January 19X5	135.10	772.00
TOTAL VAT		772.00 135.10 907.10

Task

Calculate the necessary accruals or prepayments and enter them on the ETB.

Exercise 4   Level: MODERATE

The accountant tells you that the following adjustments need to be made.

(a)   Depreciation is to be provided as follows.

Freehold buildings	2% on cost
Motor vehicles	20% on cost

The buildings element of the figure for freehold land and buildings is £40,000.00. A full year of depreciation is charged in the year of acquisition of any asset.

(b)   A general provision for bad debts is to be made, at 1% of net trade debtors.

(c)   The closing stock figure was agreed at £81,749.22.

Task

Enter the necessary adjustments for the above items on to the ETB.

Exercise 5   Level: MODERATE

Extend and total the ETB.

Exercise 6   Level: ADVANCED

Attempt to produce a basic balance sheet and a trading, profit and loss account from the ETB.

Practice exercises

Class Exercise 1   Level: EASY

What is the purpose of the extended trial balance?

Class Exercise 2   Level: EASY

How do the journal and the extended trial balance interact?

Solutions
to
practice
exercises

SOLUTIONS TO SESSION 1 PRACTICE EXERCISES

Note. Suggested solutions to Exercises 1 to 15 in this session are set out below. There are often different ways to reach a satisfactory solution to an exercise and there may be no single right answer. Having completed the exercises for yourself, compare your approach to ours and identify any errors you may have made.

Solution to Exercise 1

A. Bank statements are not a book of prime entry for an organisation, as they are produced by the bank, not the organisation. They are useful, however, in that they enable an organisation to compare the bank's records with its own (the cash book).

Solution to Exercise 2

The cash book is represented here, recording a cash receipt of £140 from a credit customer who received a discount of £10.

Solution to Exercise 3

To record the purchase of a fixed asset costing £100,000 on credit you would:

DEBIT	Fixed assets	£100,000	
CREDIT	Creditors		£100,000

Solution to Exercise 4

(a) This probably represents cash received from a customer to reduce a debt. Alternatively (although much less likely), it might be cash received in advance posted to the customer's account in the debtors ledger, thus leaving it with a credit balance.

(b) If you maintained a sales ledger (ie a memorandum account) you will have noted the cash receipt against the customer's sales ledger account. The receipt might also have been noted in the cash book.

Solution to Exercise 5

The represents the receipt of a bill for rent from the landlord. The rent account is an expense account. The landlord is a creditor account.

Solution to Exercise 6

D. Total wages and salaries costs includes the gross amount paid to employees plus employer's NI and pension contributions. This you should remember from Unit 3 at Foundation level.

Solution to Exercise 7

D. Again, you should have had no difficulty in answering this question if you remembered what you learned at Unit 3.

Solution to Exercise 8

C. Returns outwards relate to purchases and creditors, and so would not affect a debtor's account.

Solution to Exercise 9

		£
Output VAT	£42,780 × 17½%	7,486.50
Input VAT	£30,360 × 17½%	5,313.00
Net payable		2,173.50

Solution to Exercise 10

Sales are booked net of trade discounts.

	£
Sale: £15,000 × (100% – 5%)	14,250

The settlement discount is calculated on net invoiced amount (ie on £14,250).

	£
Discount allowed: £14,250 × 2½%	356.25

Solution to Exercise 11

	£
Brought forward	21,400
Credit sales	120,100
Cash received	(102,000)
Discounts allowed	(8,125)
Closing balance	31,375

Solution to Exercise 12

	£
Opening balance	?
Credit purchases	83,200
Discounts received	(3,750)
Payment	(79,500)
Contra	(4,000)
Carried forward	12,920

Working backwards, we can see that the opening balance is £16,970.

Solution to Exercise 13

Once the reconciling items have been put through the books, both should equal £63,200. Let us see how this is done.

	£
Control account balance	65,000
Adjust for overcast of daybook	(300)
Adjust for contra	(1,500)
	63,200

	£
Sales ledger balances	63,620
Corrections of Flash error (2 × £210)	(420)
	63,200

The sales day book totals have nothing to do with the sales ledger, as they are posted to the sales ledger control account. The sales ledger control account needs to be adjusted for a contra already in the sales ledger. The error of £210 needs correcting to convert a debit balance into a credit balance. The difference between DR £210 and CR £210 is £420.

Solution to Exercise 14

D.

	£
Cash book balance	(610)
Automated payments	(715)
Investment income	353
Unprocessed cheque from customer	(875)
Balance per bank statement	(1,847)

Solution to Exercise 15

(a) *Initial working: provision for doubtful debts*

		£	£
31 December			
19X7	Provision required = £44,000 × 3%	1,320	
19X8	Provision required = £55,000 × 3%	1,650	
Increase in provision - charge to P & L			330
19X9	Provision required = £47,000 × 3%	1,410	
Decrease in provision - credit to P & L			(240)

Profit and loss account charge
Year ended 31 December

	19X7	19X8	19X9
	£	£	£
Bad debts	7,000	10,000	8,000
Provision for doubtful debts	1,320	330	(240)

(b)

Balance sheet extracts
as at 31 December

	19X7	19X8	19X9
	£	£	£
Debtors	44,000	55,000	47,000
Less provision for doubtful debts	1,320	1,650	1,410
Balance sheet value	42,680	53,350	45,590

SOLUTIONS TO SESSION 2 PRACTICE EXERCISES

Note. Suggested solutions to Exercises 1 to 6 in this session are set out below. There are often different ways to reach a satisfactory solution to an exercise and there may be no single right answer. Having completed the exercises for yourself, compare your approach to ours and identify any errors you may have made.

Solution to Exercise 1

Capital spending is expenditure on assets which are balance sheet items. Revenue spending is taken to the profit and loss account.

Solution to Exercise 2

False. The prudence concept may sometimes conflict with the accruals or matching concept, in which case, following SSAP 2, the prudence concept prevails. For example, if stock is held which is expected to be sold for less than it cost to buy or make, then that 'loss' on the value of the stock (cost less selling price) should be recognised immediately. Under the accruals concept, the loss would only be recognised when the sale is made.

Solution to Exercise 3

The fundamental accounting concept breached here is that of *consistency*. This concept holds that accounting information should be presented in a way that facilitates comparisons from period to period.

In the profit and loss account for 19X3 sales revenue is shown separately from selling costs. Also interest and administration charges are treated separately.

The new format is poor in itself, as we cannot know whether any future change in 'sales revenue less selling costs' is due to an increase in sales revenue or a decline in selling costs. A similar criticism can be levelled at the lumping together of administration costs and interest charges. It is impossible to divide the two.

It is not possible to 'rewrite' 19X3's accounts in terms of 19X4, because we do not know the breakdown in 19X3 between selling and administration costs.

The business's bank manager will not, therefore, be able to assess the business's performance, and might wonder if the sole trader has 'something to hide'. Thus the value of this accounting information is severely affected.

Solution to Exercise 4

The fundamental accounting concepts mainly involved are *accruals* and *prudence*.

The accruals concept states that income and expenditure should be matched in the same period if reasonably possible, whereas the prudence concept dictates that revenue should not be anticipated. However, you are reasonably certain of selling the mugs, so you would value them in the balance sheet at the beginning of the year at *cost*, as an *asset* (rather than treating them as an expense in the profit and loss account for that earlier year).

At 31 December 19X2 you have 200 spare, whose selling price is less than the cost of making them. The prudence concept would dictate therefore that they are valued in the balance sheet at the lower of these two amounts (ie sales value if it is lower than cost).

You could argue that valuing them at a lower amount means a conflict with the accruals concept, because the loss is accounted for before the sale. This is true. Normally, when accruals and prudence conflict, prudence should prevail.

As a consequence, at 1 January 19X2, the mugs would be valued at 40 pence each. At 31 December 19X2, the remaining mugs would be valued at 30 pence each.

Solution to Exercise 5

(a) Asset
(b) Expense
(c) Neither - it is a (long-term) liability
(d) Asset
(e) Asset - it relates to a future period and so is a 'prepayment'
(f) Asset
(g) Expense
(h) Expense
(i) Asset
(j) Expense
(k) Asset

Solution to Exercise 6

Materiality as a 'fundamental accounting concept' does have strict limitations. It refers primarily to financial *reporting*, but has no bearing at all on detailed procedural matters such as bank reconciliations or statements of account sent to customers.

Consequently, the statement sent to the customer, described in option (a), must be accurate to the last penny, however large it is. After all, if you receive a bill from a company for £147.50, you do not 'round it up' to £150 when you pay. Nor will the company billing you be prepared to 'round it down' to £145. A customer pays an agreed price for an agreed product or service. Paying more is effectively giving money away, and if you are going to do that, there might be worthier beneficiaries of your generosity. Paying less exposes your creditor to an unfair loss.

On the other hand, if you are preparing a performance report comparing how well the company is doing in the UK and France, entirely different considerations apply.

There is little point in being accurate to the last penny or centime (and inconsistencies might occur from the choice of currency rate used). This is because senior management are interested in the broad picture, and they are looking to identify comparisons between the overall performance of each division.

Assume that UK profits were £1,233,750.57 and profits in France were £1,373,370.75.

France	UK
£	£
1,373,370.75	1,233,750.57
or	*or*
£'000	£'000
1,373	1,234

The rounded figures are much easier to understand, and so the relative performance is easier to compare. Considerations of materiality would allow you to ignore the rounding differences, because they are so small and the information is used for comparative purposes only.

SOLUTIONS TO SESSION 3 PRACTICE EXERCISES

Note. Suggested solutions to Exercises 1 to 3 in this session are set out below. There are often different ways to reach a satisfactory solution to an exercise and there may be no single right answer. Having completed the exercises for yourself, compare your approach to ours and identify any errors you may have made.

Solution to Exercise 1

An accounting standard is a set of rules which prescribes the method or methods by which accounts should be prepared and presented. These 'working regulations' are issued by a national or international body of the accounting profession.

Solution to Exercise 2

False. Limited companies are required to disclose in their annual financial statements if they have complied with accounting standards, and, if not, why not. Accounts can be altered if non-compliance is not justified.

Solution to Exercise 3

(a) Statement of Standard Accounting Practice
(b) Financial Reporting Standard
(c) Exposure Draft
(d) Discussion Draft
(e) Financial Reporting Exposure Draft
(f) Accounting Standards Board
(g) International Accounting Standards Committee
(h) Consultative Committee of Accountancy Bodies
(i) Financial Reporting Council

SOLUTIONS TO SESSION 4 PRACTICE EXERCISES

Note. Suggested solutions to Exercises 1 to 10 in this session are set out below. There are often different ways to reach a satisfactory solution to an exercise and there may be no single right answer. Having completed the exercises for yourself, compare your approach to ours and identify any errors you may have made.

Solution to Exercise 1

(a) (i) *Capital expenditure* is expenditure which results in the acquisition of fixed assets or an improvement in their earning capacity.

    (ii) *Revenue expenditure* is expenditure for the purpose of the trade of the business, for example selling and distribution expenses or finance charges. In addition, revenue expenditure is incurred in maintaining the existing earning capacity of fixed assets.

(b) (i) If capital expenditure is treated as revenue expenditure, profits will be understated in the profit and loss account and fixed assets will be understated in the balance sheet.

    (ii) If revenue expenditure is treated as capital expenditure, then the profits for the period will be overstated in the profit and loss account and fixed assets will be overstated in the balance sheet.

Solution to Exercise 2

(a) No. You would write it off to the profit and loss account as an expense.

(b) Yes. You would capitalise the computer and charge depreciation on it.

(c) Your answer depends on the size of the company and whether writing off the item has a material effect on its profits. A large organisation might well write this item off under the heading of advertising expenses, while a small one would capitalise it and depreciate it over time.

Solution to Exercise 3

Depreciation is a measure of the wearing out of a fixed asset through use, time or obsolescence. It is charged in order to match revenue and expenses with one another in the same accounting period so that profits are fairly and consistently calculated. If the cost of fixed assets was not written off over time, there would be incomplete matching of revenue and expenses.

Solution to Exercise 4

In both cases, the depreciable amount is calculated first: cost or valuation less estimated residual value.

The *straight line method* charges the depreciable amount of an asset against profit in equal instalments over its estimated economic life. This method is therefore appropriate when an asset is expected to be equally useful throughout its economic life.

The *reducing balance method* charges a fixed percentage of the depreciable amount in the first year in which the asset is depreciated. In subsequent years, the fixed percentage is applied to the net book value of the asset. Each year, therefore, the charge reduces. This method is appropriate when there is expected to be a fairly long economic life with a rapid loss of efficiency in the early years.

Solution to Exercise 5

(a) Straight line depreciation will give the same charge each year for the four years of economic life, as follows.

$$\text{Annual depreciation} = \frac{\text{Cost minus residual value}}{\text{Estimated economic life}}$$

Annual depreciation $= \dfrac{£1,800 - £0}{4 \text{ years}}$

Annual depreciation $= \underline{£450}$

Annual depreciation charges are therefore £450 for each year from 19X1 to 19X4 inclusive.

(b) The reducing balance method at 60% per annum involves the following calculations.

	£	
Cost at 1.1.19X1	1,800	
Depreciation 19X1	1,080	60% × £1,800
Book value 1.1.19X2	720	
Depreciation 19X2	432	60% × £720
Book value 1.1.19X3	288	
Depreciation 19X3	173	60% × £288
Book value 1.1.19X4	115	
Depreciation 19X4 (Note)	115	(balance remaining)
Residual value at end of estimated economic life	-	

Annual depreciation charges are therefore 19X1: £1,080, 19X2: £432, 19X3: £173, 19X4: £115.

Note. At some point it will usually be considered a waste of time to carry on the depreciation calculations as the amounts involved will be immaterial. (Sometimes the asset is maintained in the books at £1.)

Solution to Exercise 6

(a)

LASER PRINTER ACCOUNT

		£			£
1.1.19X4	Bal b/f	1,800	1.7.19X4	Assets disposals a/c	1,800

(b)

PROVISION FOR DEPRECIATION: LASER PRINTER ACCOUNT

		£			£
			1.1.19X4	Bal b/f ie £1,080 + £432 + £173	1,685
1.7.19X4	Assets disposals a/c	1,743	1.7.19X4	Depreciation a/c ie 6 mths @ £115 pa	58
		1,743			1,743

(c)

ASSETS DISPOSALS ACCOUNT

		£			£
1.7.19X4	Laser printer account	1,800	1.7.19X4	Bank a/c	200
31.12.19X4	Profit and loss depreciation: (profit on disposal)	143	1.7.19X4	Provision for depreciation (laser printer a/c)	1,743
		1,943			1,943

Proof of profit on disposal £

	£
Received from sale of laser printer	200
Net book value at date of disposal = cost less accumulated depreciation = £1,800 − £1,743	57
Profit on disposal	143

Solution to Exercise 7

MOTOR VEHICLES: COST

		£			£
1.6.X8	Balance b/d	124,000	1.8.X8	Disposals	54,000
1.8.X8	Bank	71,000	31.5.X9	Balance c/d	141,000
		195,000			195,000

MOTOR VEHICLES - PROVISION FOR DEPRECIATION

		£			£
1.8.X8	Disposals	49,000	1.6.X8	Balance b/d	88,000
31.5.X9	Balance c/d	74,700	31.5.X9	Depreciation (P&L) (W)	35,700
		123,700			123,700

DISPOSAL OF FIXED ASSETS

		£			£
1.8.X8	Motor vehicles: cost	54,000	1.8.X8	Motor vehicles: dep'n	49,000
			1.8.X8	Bank	3,900
			31.5.X9	Loss on disposal (P&L)	1,100
		54,000			54,000

Working: depreciation charge

	£
Assets bought in earlier years:	
Cost b/f	124,000
Less assets sold in year	54,000
Still owned at year end	70,000
Depreciation b/f	88,000
Less assets sold in year	49,000
	39,000
Net book value at 31.5.X9	31,000
Assets acquired in the year	71,000
	102,000
Depreciation for the year at 35%	35,700

Solution to Exercise 8

(a)

		Ford £	Ford £	Toyota £	Toyota £
Cost			10,000		8,000
Depreciation:	year to June 19X7	1,000		-	
	year to June 19X8	900		800	
	year to June 19X9	810		720	
			(2,710)		(1,520)
Value as at 1 July 19X9			7,290		6,480

(b)

MOTOR VEHICLES ACCOUNT

		£			£
1 July 19X9	Balance b/f	18,000	14 Nov 19X9	Disposals	10,000
14 Nov 19X9	Purchase of Mercedes	15,500	30 June 19Y0	Balance c/d	23,500
		33,500			33,500
1 July 19Y0	Balance b/f	23,500			

PROVISION FOR DEPRECIATION: MOTOR VEHICLES

		£			£
14 Nov 19X9	Disposals	2,710	1 July 19X9	Balance b/f	4,230
30 Jun 19Y0	Balance c/d	3,718	30 June 19Y0	Profit and loss	2,198
		6,428			6,428

MOTOR VEHICLES DISPOSALS

		£			£
14 Nov 19X9	Motor vehicles	10,000	14 Nov 19X9	Provision for depreciation	2,710
			14 Nov 19X9	Motor vehicles	6,000
			30 June 19Y0	P & L a/c	1,290
		10,000			10,000

Solution to Exercise 9

(a)

ASSETS DISPOSALS

		£			£
31.5.X1	Motor vehicles	30,000	31.5.X1	Provision for depreciation	24,000
31.5.X1	Profit and loss a/c	3,000	31.5.X1	Cash	9,000
		33,000			33,000

(b)

PROVISION FOR DEPRECIATION: LAND AND BUILDINGS

		£			£
31.5.X1	Balance c/f	35,200	1.6.X0	Balance b/f	32,000
			31.5.X1	Profit and loss a/c	3,200
		35,200			35,200

(c)

PROVISION FOR DEPRECIATION: FIXTURES AND FITTINGS

		£			£
31.5.X1	Balance c/f	110,000	1.6.X0	Balance b/f	88,000
			31.5.X1	Profit and loss a/c*	22,000
		110,000			110,000

* Depreciation is calculated using the reducing balance method, ie 25% × £(176,000 − 88,000) = £22,000.

(d)

PROVISION FOR DEPRECIATION: MOTOR VEHICLES

		£			£
31.5.X1	Assets disposals	24,000	1.6.X0	Balance b/f	54,000
31.5.X1	Balance c/f	42,000	31.5.X1	Profit and loss a/c	12,000
		66,000			66,000

Solution to Exercise 10

MOTOR VEHICLES: COST

19X7/8		£	19X7/8		£
1.10	Bank	28,000	30.9	Balance c/d	64,000
1.1	Bank	36,000			
		64,000			64,000
19X8/9			19X8/9		
1.10	Balance b/d	64,000	31.12	Disposal of lorry	36,000
1.2	Bank	16,000	30.9	Balance c/d	75,720
1.4	Journal (W1)	7,720			
1.7	Bank	24,000			
		111,720			111,720

MOTOR VEHICLES: DEPRECIATION PROVISION

19X7/8		£	*19X7/8*		£
			30.9	Depreciation expense (W2)	
30.9	Balance c/d	11,000			11,000
19X8/9			*19X8/9*		
31.12	Disposal of lorry (W2)	5,400	1.10	Balance b/d	11,000
			30.9	Depreciation	
30.9	Balance c/d	14,772		expense (W2)	9,172
		20,172			20,172

DISPOSAL OF LORRY - E438 CBA

19X8/9		£	*19X8/9*		£
31.12	Motor vehicles: cost	36,000	31.12	Motor vehicles: dep'n provision	5,400
			31.12	Bank	21,680
			30.9	P & L a/c: loss on disposal	8,920
		36,000			36,000

Workings

1 *Van E779 GMS*

	£
Direct labour	1,880
Direct materials	3,200
Prime cost	5,080
Fixed overheads apportionment (@ 25% of prime cost)	1,270
Variable overheads	1,370
Total costs to be capitalised	7,720

2 *Depreciation charges*

19X7/8	£
Van E676 TVX: £28,000 × 20% × $^{12}/_{12}$	5,600
Lorry E438 CBA: £36,000 × 20% × $^{9}/_{12}$	5,400
Charge for the year	11,000

19X8/9	£
Van E676 TVX: as 19X7/8	5,600
Lorry E438 CBA: no charge, year of disposal	-
Van E779 GMS: (£16,000 + £7,720) × 20% × $^{6}/_{12}$	2,372
Van F934 KTA: £24,000 × 20% × $^{3}/_{12}$	1,200
	9,172

SOLUTIONS TO SESSION 5 PRACTICE EXERCISES

Note. Suggested solutions to Exercises 1 to 4 in this session are set out below. There are often different ways to reach a satisfactory solution to an exercise and there may be no single right answer. Having completed the exercises for yourself, compare your approach to ours and identify any errors you may have made.

Solution to Exercise 1

(a) The following fundamental accounting concepts are described by SSAP 2.

Accruals or matching concept. Revenue earned must be matched with the expenditure incurred in earning it. Both revenue and expenditure should be dealt with in the profit and loss account of the period to which they relate.

Prudence concept. Revenues and profits should not be recognised until it is certain that they will be realised in cash. All losses and expenses should be provided for as soon as they become apparent.

Going concern concept. The business will continue in its present state for the foreseeable future, there being no intention to put the company into liquidation or severely curtail its operations. The assets of the business should not be valued at their 'break-up' value.

Consistency concept. Similar items within a single set of accounts should be given similar accounting treatment. The same treatment should be applied from one period to another in accounting for similar items.

(b) The Companies Act 1985 also describes a fifth 'principle' (as it calls the accounting concepts). The *separate valuation principle* states that, in determining the amount to be attributed to an asset or liability in the balance sheet, each component item of the asset or liability must be determined separately.

Solution to Exercise 2

These are some of the main reasons for preparing accounts.

(a) Most businesses are continuous, but periodic reports are needed to assess whether their trading activities are successful or not.

(b) Many businesses are managed by people other than their owners. The owners will wish to see how well their managers are performing. In the case of a limited company, the managers will be the directors and the owners will be the shareholders.

(c) Limited companies are obliged by law to prepare a set of accounts on a yearly basis and file them with a company report at Companies House with the Registrar of Companies, ie there is a statutory reason for preparing accounts.

(d) Accounting profit is used as the basis for the calculation of tax due and also to calculate other important numbers such as the profit due to individual partners in a partnership or the bonus due to managers.

Solution to Exercise 3

A balance sheet is a list of the assets, liabilities and capital of a business at a given moment. Assets are divided into fixed assets and current assets. Liabilities may be current or long term.

A profit and loss account matches the revenue earned in a period with the costs incurred in earning it. It is usual to distinguish between a gross profit (sales revenue less the cost of goods sold) and a net profit (being the gross profit less the expenses of selling, distribution, administration and so on).

Solution to Exercise 4

The ledger account will look like this.

VAT CONTROL ACCOUNT

	£		£
Creditors (purchases)		Balance b/f	2,165.00
17.5% × £4,500	787.50	Debtors (sales)	
Creditors (van)		17.5% × £(6,000 – 300)	997.50
17.5% × £10,460	1,830.50		
Balance c/f	544.50		
	3,162.50		3,162.50

Solution to Exercise 5

The acquisition of an asset under a finance lease is almost the same as buying the asset but taking out a loan to do so; the asset should be treated the same way, so it is put in the balance sheet.

Acquiring an asset under an operating lease is more like renting an asset which can be returned to the owner at any time. The rent charges should therefore go though the profit and loss account with no asset in the balance sheet.

SOLUTIONS TO SESSION 6 PRACTICE EXERCISES

Note. Suggested solutions to Exercises 1 to 6 in this session are set out below. There are often different ways to reach a satisfactory solution to an exercise and there may be no single right answer. Having completed the exercises for yourself, compare your approach to ours and identify any errors you may have made.

Solution to Exercise 1

By classifying a liability as an asset the company has improved its profit figure. The amount of £375 has been treated as an increase in profit, instead of a £375 deduction from profit. The net effect is to overstate profit by £750.

Solution to Exercise 2

The profit and loss account charge for the year is £900, as the ledger account shows.

RENT PAYABLE

19X8		£	19X8		£
31 Dec	Bank: paid in year	1,275	1 Jan	Balance b/f	250
			31 Dec	Balance c/f	
				(prepaid: 1/3 × £375)	125
				P & L account	900
		1,275			1,275

Solution to Exercise 3

In this case both a prepayment and an accrual should strictly be made as follows.

$$\text{Rental prepayment} = \frac{46 \text{ days}}{92 \text{ days}} \times £627.50 = £313.75$$

$$\text{Calls accrual} = \frac{46 \text{ days}}{92 \text{ days}} \times £1,206.11 = £603.06$$

Solution to Exercise 4

The charge for the year for rent and the UBR will be as follows.

Rent = (£7,200 × $^7/_{12}$) + (£7,800 × $^5/_{12}$) = £7,450

UBR = (£5,400 × $^{10}/_{12}$) + (£6,000 × $^2/_{12}$) = £5,500

The prepayments are shown in the ledger accounts as follows.

RENT

	£		£
Balance b/f ($^1/_{12}$ × £7,200)	600	P & L account (balance)	7,450
Bank (2 × £1,800) + (2 × £1,950)	7,500	Balance c/f ($^1/_{12}$ × £7,800)*	650
	8,100		8,100

* ie 1/3 of the quarter's rent is prepaid

UBR

	£		£
Balance b/f ($^4/_{12}$ × £5,400)	1,800	P & L account (balance)	5,500
Bank (£2,700 + £3,000)	5,700	Balance c/f ($^4/_{12}$ × £6,000)*	2,000
	7,500		7,500

* ie 1/3 of the half year's UBR is prepaid

Solution to Exercise 5

The accruals required for the invoices are calculated as follows.

Gas bill, standing charge and consumption:

$$\frac{72\ \text{days}}{92\ \text{days}} \times £464.61 = £363.61$$

Electricity bill, standing charge and consumption:

$$\frac{84\ \text{days}}{113\ \text{days}} \times £599.69 = £445.79$$

Solution to Exercise 6

The ledger account will look like this.

WATER RATES

	£		£
Balance b/f	492.50	P & L account (balance)	2,071.30
Cash	2,105.07	Balance c/f (prepaid: $^3/_{12} \times £2,105.07$)	526.27
	2,597.57		2,597.57

SOLUTIONS TO SESSION 7 PRACTICE EXERCISES

Note. Suggested solutions to Exercises 1 to 5 in this session are set out below. There are often different ways to reach a satisfactory solution to an exercise and there may be no single right answer. Having completed the exercises for yourself, compare your approach to ours and identify any errors you may have made.

Solution to Exercise 1

Returns inwards are a reduction in sales and do not affect cost of sales. Carriage outwards is a distribution expense in the profit and loss account and is therefore irrelevant here.

Cost of sales

	£
Opening stock	5,700
Purchases	75,280
Carriage inwards	3,680
	84,660
Closing stock	(8,540)
	76,120

Solution to Exercise 2

The trial balance of Pooley Ltd will appear as follows at 31 December 19X7.

	Debit £	*Credit* £
Stock as at 1 January 19X7	22,000	
Purchases	223,000	
Sales		340,700
Discounts allowed	4,600	
Discounts received		5,500
Returns in	6,700	
Returns out		5,600
Wages and salaries	34,500	
Bad debts	3,100	
Carriage in	1,400	
Carriage out	2,200	
Other operating expenses	24,500	
Trade debtors	34,000	
Trade creditors		21,600
Provision for bad debts		450
Cash on hand	800	
Bank overdraft		23,400
Profit and loss account at 1 January 19X7		8,550
Share capital		30,000
Property	50,000	
Equipment	64,000	
Provisions for depreciation at 1 January 19X7		
Property		10,000
Equipment		25,000
	470,800	470,800

Solution to Exercise 3

	£
Draft stock figure	28,850
(a) Overstatement due to wrong addition £(212 – 74)	(138)
(b) No change (note 1)	-
(c) Reduction to cost £(665 – 430) (note 2)	(235)
	28,477

Notes

1   A comparison of cost and net realisable value shows that cost is still lower:

    £460 < £(800 – 270)

    and therefore no adjustment is required.

2   It is correct to include such items in stock, to avoid anticipating profit, but at cost value. Using the selling price means that the profit element has been included.

Solution to Exercise 4

The settlement discount is irrelevant here.

	Cost less 2½% trade discount £	NRV £	Valuation £
Product A	3,510.00	5,100.00	3,510.00
Product B	2,827.50	2,800.00	2,800.00
Product C	4,095.00	4,100.00	4,095.00
			10,405.00

Solution to Exercise 5

Rather than write out the ledger accounts all over again, the question may be answered as follows.

(a) The postings necessary for each transaction are:

		£	£
DEBIT	Purchases	2,000	
CREDIT	Cash		1,000
CREDIT	Creditors		1,000
DEBIT	Interest	20	
CREDIT	Cash		20
DEBIT	Electricity	25	
CREDIT	Cash		25
DEBIT	Telephone	12	
CREDIT	Cash		12
DEBIT	Cash	500	
DEBIT	Debtors	3,000	
CREDIT	Sales		3,500
DEBIT	Cash	220	
CREDIT	Debtors		220

(b) Once these have been posted and the accounts balanced off, the trial balance is:

Account	Dr £	Cr £
Cash	18,083	
Capital		9,500
Bank loan		3,000
Sales		19,300
Debtors	6,980	
Rent	2,750	
Purchases	4,100	
Creditors		2,400
Interest	370	
Electricity	425	
Telephone	192	
Drawings	1,300	
	34,200	34,200

Tutorial note. If you are not confident of your arithmetic, you may find it safer to write out and balance off all the ledger accounts individually.

PROFIT AND LOSS (LEDGER) ACCOUNT

	£		£
Rent	2,750	Sales	19,300
Purchases	4,100		
Interest	370		
Electricity	425		
Telephone	192		
Balance (net profit taken to			
balance sheet)	11,463		
	19,300		19,300

(c) A HUBBLE BALANCE SHEET AS AT 31 MARCH 19X8

	£	£
Assets		
Cash	18,083	
Debtors	6,980	
	25,063	
Current liabilities		
Creditors	(2,400)	
		22,663
Long-term liabilities		
Loan		(3,000)
		19,663
Capital		
Capital as at 1.4.19X7		9,500
Add profit for year		11,463
Less drawings		(1,300)
Capital as at 31.3.19X8		19,663

A HUBBLE
TRADING, PROFIT AND LOSS ACCOUNT
FOR THE YEAR ENDED 31 MARCH 19X8

	£	£
Sales		19,300
Less cost of sales		4,100
Gross profit		15,200
Less other expenses		
Rent	2,750	
Interest	370	
Electricity	425	
Telephone	192	
		3,737
Net profit		11,463

SOLUTIONS TO SESSION 8 PRACTICE EXERCISES

Note. Suggested solutions to Exercises 1 to 6 in this session are set out below. There are often different ways to reach a satisfactory solution to an exercise and there may be no single right answer. Having completed the exercises for yourself, compare your approach to ours and identify any errors you may have made.

Solution to Exercise 1

The ledger account will look like this.

DEBTORS CONTROL ACCOUNT

	£		£
1 January balance b/f	42,800	Bank	204,000
Sales	240,200	Discounts allowed	16,250
		31 December balance c/f	62,750
	283,000		283,000

Solution to Exercise 2

	£
Balance per list of balances	251,385
Omitted balance	(1,260)
Cash received error (£840 × 2)	(1,680)
	248,445
Balance per control account	247,533
Bad debt written off	(1,500)
Dishonoured cheque	2,412
	248,445

Solution to Exercise 3

(a) *Net pay for June 19X6*

	£	£
Gross pay		217,640
Less		
PAYE	55,720	
Employees' NIC	17,240	
Employees' savings deductions	5,080	
		78,040
Net pay		139,600

(b) The ledger accounts are as follows.

PAYE CONTROL ACCOUNT

	£		£
Bank	35,680	Balance b/f	89,944
Balance c/f	109,984	Wages and salaries control account	55,720
	145,664		145,664

NIC CONTROL ACCOUNT

	£		£
Bank	32,960	Balance b/f	58,924
Balance c/f	78,204	Wages and salaries control account	17,240
		Wages and salaries expense account	35,000
	111,164		111,164

Solutions to practice exercises

Solution to Exercise 4

	£
Creditors b/f	(1,455)
Cash paid	41,775
Creditors c/f	1,080
Credit purchases	41,400
Add cash purchases	5,850
	47,250

Solution to Exercise 5

The gross profit is £150,000 – £112,500 = £37,500.

(a) The gross profit as a percentage of cost of sales is:

$$\frac{£37,500}{£112,500} \times 100\% = 33\frac{1}{3}\%$$

(b) The gross profit as a percentage of sales is:

$$\frac{£37,500}{£150,000} \times 100\% = 25\%$$

Solution to Exercise 6

The trading account of Jennings Ltd will appear as follows.

	£	£
Sales		455,000
Less cost of sales		
Opening stock	71,300	
Purchases	282,250	
	353,550	
Closing stock (balance)	80,550	
		273,000
Gross profit (40% × £455,000)		182,000

Cost of stock destroyed = £80,550 – £1,200 = £79,350.

SOLUTIONS TO SESSION 9 PRACTICE EXERCISES

Note. Suggested solutions to Practice Exercises 1 to 9 in this session are set out below. There are often different ways to reach a satisfactory solution to an exercise and there may be no single right answer. Having completed the exercises for yourself, compare your approach to ours and identify any errors you may have made.

Solution to Exercise 1

SUBSCRIPTIONS

	£			£
Balance b/f	410	Bank:	19X4	370
			19X5	6,730
∴ I & E account	7,200		19X6	1,180
		19X4 subs written off		40
Balance c/f: 19X6 subs prepaid	1,180	Balance c/f: 19X5 subs due		470
	8,790			8,790

Solution to Exercise 2

B. The cost of an extension is capital expenditure, which would be shown as an asset in the balance sheet.

Solution to Exercise 3

C. Office wages are not a manufacturing cost; they would appear in the profit and loss account, not the manufacturing account. Factory rent and depreciation of machinery are factory overheads; they are included in factory cost of goods produced, but not in prime cost. Prime cost includes only direct materials and direct production wages.

Solution to Exercise 4

(a)

	£	£
Subscriptions received in 19X5		790
Less: amounts relating to 19X4	38	
amounts relating to 19X6	80	
		118
		672
Cash received relating to 19X5		
Add: subs paid in 19X4 relating to 19X5	72	
19X5 subs still to be paid	48	
		120
		792

Alternatively, in ledger account format:

SUBSCRIPTIONS

	£		£
Balance b/f	38	Balance b/f	72
∴ Income and expenditure a/c	792	Cash	790
Balance c/f	80	Balance c/f	48
	910		910

(b)

	£
Subscriptions received in 19X5	1,024
Less amounts relating to 19X6	58
	966
Add subs paid in 19X4 relating to 19X5	14
	980

Alternatively, in ledger account format:

SUBSCRIPTIONS

	£		£
∴ Income and expenditure a/c	980	Balance b/f	14
Balance c/f	58	Bank	1,024
	1,038		1,038

Solution to Exercise 5

(a) SUMMARY BALANCE SHEET AT 31 DECEMBER 19X5

	£
Net assets	
Tables and chairs	380
Playing cards and other accessories	102
Reference books	130
Subscriptions in arrears	27
	639
Subscriptions in advance	80
	559
Funds	
Accumulated fund	259
Life membership fund	300
	559

(b) ACCUMULATED FUND

	£
Balance at 31 December 19X5	259
Add back deficit for the year	117
	376
Less transfer from life membership fund	75
Balance at 1 January 19X5	301

Solution to Exercise 6

	£	£
Balance at 1 January		3,780
New enrolments		480
		4,260
Less release to income:		
1 × £80	80	
63 × £5	315	
4 × £6	24	
		419
Balance at 31 December		3,841

Solution to Exercise 7

MANUFACTURING ACCOUNT FOR 19X5

	£	£
Raw materials		
Opening stock	12,940	
Purchases	213,680	
Carriage inwards	3,970	
	230,590	
Closing stock	14,550	
		216,040
Direct wages		96,380
Prime cost		312,420
Factory overheads		
Wages and salaries £(12,490 + 18,330)		30,820
Other factory costs		63,310
		406,550
Work in progress		
Opening stock	42,920	
Closing stock	39,610	
		3,310
Factory cost of finished goods produced		409,860
Factory profit (£409,860 × 15/85)		72,328
Transfer price of finished goods produced		482,188

Solution to Exercise 8

(a) and (b)

The provision account looks like this.

PROVISION FOR UNREALISED PROFIT

	£		£
Balance c/f 31.12.19X6		Balance b/f 1.1.19X6	
(£5,460 × 5/105)	260	(£4,620 × 5/105)	220
		∴ Charge to P&L a/c	40
	260		260
∴ Credit to P&L a/c	80	Balance b/f 1.1.19X7	260
Balance c/f 31.12.19X7			
(£3,780 × 5/105)	180		
	260		260

Solution to Exercise 9

(a)

CREDITORS

	£		£
Bank	5,685	Bal b/f	435
Bal c/f	363	∴ Purchases	5,613
	6,048		6,048

DEBTORS

	£		£
Bal b/f	12	Bank £(6,064 + 1,040)	7,104
∴ Sales	7,100	Bal c/f	8
	7,112		7,112

The trading account shows sales of £7,100 and cost of sales £5,680 (100/125 × £7,100). Since opening stock is £390 and purchases are £5,613, closing stock is £323.

(b) Sales are £7,100, cost of sales is £5,680, and so gross profit is £1,420. From this must be deducted barman's wages of £1,040, giving £380.

SOLUTIONS TO SESSION 10 PRACTICE EXERCISES

Note. Suggested solutions to Exercises 1 to 6 in this session are set out below. There are often different ways to reach a satisfactory solution to an exercise and there may be no single right answer. Having completed the exercises for yourself, compare your approach to ours and identify any errors you may have made.

Solution to Exercise 1

The full ETB is shown on Page 79. The other details required are shown below.

Solution to Exercise 2

Journal 1

		£	£
DEBIT	Insurance	3,217.20	
	Bad debt expense	1,425.53	
	Purchases (£4,916.29 – £4,196.29)	720.00	
	Motor vehicles (£3,059.78 × 2)	6,119.56	
CREDIT	Suspense account		11,482.29

In ledger account form:

SUSPENSE ACCOUNT

	£		£
Balance b/f	11,482.29	Insurance	3,217.20
		Bad debt expense	1,425.53
		Purchases	720.00
		Motor vehicles	6,119.56
	11,482.29		11,482.29

Solution to Exercise 3

(a) UBR: prepaid 1 January to 31 March 19X5

$= \frac{3}{12} \times £21,610.18 = £5,402.55$

(b) Insurance: prepaid 1 January to 30 November 19X5

$= \frac{11}{12} \times £3,217.20 = £2,949.10$

(c) Carriage outwards: accrue 1 November to 31 December 19X4

$= \frac{2}{3} \times £772.00 = £514.67$

Solution to Exercise 4

Tutorial note. When calculating the bad debt provision in (b) you do not need to deduct the bad debts written off from the year end debtors figure. This adjustment has already been made. The suspense account balance arose because the bad debt expense entry had not been made.

Folio	Account	Trial balance Debit £	Trial balance Credit £	Ref	Adjustments Debit £	Adjustments Credit £	Accrued £	Accrued £	Prepaid £	Prepaid £	Profit and loss a/c Debit £	Profit and loss a/c Credit £	Balance sheet Debit £	Balance sheet Credit £
	Land and buildings	120,000.00											120,000.00	
	Share capital		100,000.00											100,000.00
	Sales		471,384.22									471,384.22		
	Purchases	245,897.44		1	720.00						246,617.44			
	Stock at 1.1.X4	79,533.51									79,533.51			
	Returns in	388.59									388.59			
	Returns out		1,768.62									1,768.62		
	Discounts allowed	3,978.89									3,978.89			
	Discounts received		2,115.27									2,115.27		
	Uniform Business Rate	27,450.82							5,402.55		22,048.27			
	Motor expenses	12,245.90									12,245.90			
	Salaries	103,228.19									103,228.19			
	Insurance	9,486.30		1	3,217.20				2,949.10		9,754.40			
	Trade debtors	32,381.45											32,381.45	
	Trade creditors		17,862.29											17,862.29
	Carriage in	4,197.80									4,197.80			
	Carriage out	2,557.36						514.67			3,072.03			
	Motor vehicles	65,149.25		1	6,119.56								71,268.81	
	Bank	7,826.88											7,826.88	
	Provision for dep'n: buildings		4,000.00	2		800.00								4,800.00
	Provision for dep'n: motor vehicles		21,371.42	2		14,253.76								35,625.18
	Bad debts	604.00		1/3	1,749.34						2,353.34			
	Provision for bad debts			3		323.81								323.81
	Profit and loss account 1.1.X4		107,906.85											107,906.85
	Depreciation expense			2	15,053.76						15,053.76			
	Suspense account	11,482.29		1		11,482.29								
	Stock at 31.12.X4 (P&L)			4		81,749.22						81,749.22		
	Stock at 31.12.X4 (B/S)			4	81,749.22								81,749.22	
	Prepayments/accruals						514.67			8,351.65			8,351.65	514.67
	SUB-TOTAL	726,408.67	726,408.67		108,609.08	108,609.08	514.67	514.67	8,351.65	8,351.65	502,472.12	557,017.33	321,578.01	267,032.80
	Profit for the year										54,545.21			54,545.21
	TOTAL	726,408.67	726,408.67		108,609.08	108,609.08	514.67	514.67	8,351.65	8,351.65	557,017.33	557,017.33	321,578.01	321,578.01

Solution

(a) *Depreciation*

Buildings: 2% × £40,000 = £800.00

Motor vehicles: 20% × £(65,149.25 + 6,119.56) = £14,253.76

Journal 2

		£	£
DEBIT	Depreciation expense	15,053.76	
CREDIT	Provision for depreciation		
	Buildings		800.00
	Motor vehicles		14,253.76

(b) *Bad debt provision*

Trade debtors		£32,381.45
General provision @ 1%		£323.81

Journal 3

		£	£
DEBIT	Bad debts	£323.81	
CREDIT	Provision for bad debts		£323.81

(c) *Journal 4*

		£	£
DEBIT	Closing stock (balance sheet)	£81,749.22	
CREDIT	Closing stock (P & L account)		£81,749.22

Solution to Exercise 5

See ETB on Page 79.

Solution to Exercise 6

JUSTIN & WEST LIMITED
PROFIT AND LOSS ACCOUNT
FOR THE YEAR ENDED 31 DECEMBER 19X4

	£	£
Sales (£471,384.22 – £388.59)		470,995.63
Cost of sales		
Opening stock	79,533.51	
Purchases (£246,617.44 – £1,768.62)	244,848.82	
Carriage inwards	4,197.80	
	328,580.13	
Closing stock	81,749.22	
		246,830.91
Gross profit		224,164.72
Expenses		
Carriage outwards	3,072.03	
Discounts allowed	3,978.89	
Discounts received	(2,115.27)	
UBR	22,048.27	
Motor expenses	12,245.90	
Salaries	103,228.19	
Insurance	9,754.40	
Bad debt expense	2,353.34	
Depreciation expense	15,053.76	
		169,619.51
		54,545.21

JUSTIN & WEST LIMITED
BALANCE SHEET AS AT 31 DECEMBER 19X4

	Cost £	Dep'n £	NBV £
Fixed assets			
Land and buildings	120,000.00	4,800.00	115,200.00
Motor vehicles	71,268.81	35,625.18	35,643.63
	191,268.81	40,425.18	150,843.63
Current assets			
Debtors (£32,381.45 – £323.81)		32,057.64	
Prepayments		8,351.65	
Stock		81,749.22	
Bank		7,826.88	
		129,985.39	
Current liabilities			
Creditors		17,862.29	
Accruals		514.67	
		18,376.96	
Net current assets			111,608.43
			262,452.06
Capital and reserves			
Share capital			100,000.00
Profit and loss account £(107,906.85 + 54,545.21)			162,452.06
			262,452.06

Devolved
assessments

Devolved assessment
1 Reggie Stir

Performance criteria

The following performance criteria are covered in this Devolved Assessment.

Element 4.1: Maintain records and accounts relating to capital expenditure

1   Relevant details relating to specific items of capital expenditure are correctly entered in the appropriate records

3   Any acquisition and disposal costs and revenues are correctly identified and recorded

4   Depreciation charges and other necessary entries and adjustments are correctly calculated and recorded in the appropriate ledger accounts

Notes on completing the Assessment

This Assessment is designed to test your ability to record capital transactions in the journal, the fixed assets register and the ledger.

You are provided with data (Page 86) which you must use to complete the tasks on Page 87.

You are allowed 2 hours to complete your work.

A high level of accuracy is required. Check your work carefully.

Correcting fluid should not be used. Errors should be crossed out neatly and clearly. You should write in ink and not in pencil.

A full suggested solution to this Assessment is provided on Page 115.

Do not turn to the suggested solution until you have completed all parts of the Assessment.

DEVOLVED ASSESSMENT 1: REGGIE STIR

Data

Reggie Stir Ltd is a small company producing many different kinds of jugs. Skilled craftsmen make the jugs on a potter's wheel. They are then fired in a kiln and distributed by van to various gift shops.

You are Fletcher Clink, an accounting technician and your boss is Nick McKay, the financial controller. Mr McKay is concerned that the records relating to fixed assets should be kept up to date.

The company, which operates from rented premises, does not have a large number or turnover of fixed assets, the main ones being three potter's wheels, four kilns, one pugmill (a long tube for turning the clay), three delivery vans and various items of furniture, all of which were bought some time ago and are fully depreciated.

The firm keeps a manual fixed assets register, the relevant pages of which are reproduced below.

PLANT AND EQUIPMENT

Ref	Description	Date of purchase	Cost £	Depreciation period	Accumulated depreciation 31 Dec 1994 £	Date of disposal	Net book value 31 Dec 1994 £	Sale/scrap proceeds £	Loss/ profit £
1/K	Kiln	1 Jan 1993	1200	6 years	400		800		
1/P	Pugmill	1 July 1994	300	4 years	75		225		
2/K	Kiln	1 Mar 1992	600	6 years	300		300		
3/K	Kiln	20 Aug 1991	750	6 years	500		250		
1/W	Wheel	31 Mar 1993	400	4 years	200		200		
2/W	Wheel	1 Feb 1992	400	4 years	300		100		
4/K	Kiln	1 Sep 1992	900	6 years	450		450		
3/W	Wheel	1 Mar 1994	420	4 years	105		315		
Totals			4970		2330		2640		

MOTOR VEHICLES

Ref	Description	Date of purchase	Cost £	Depreciation type	Accumulated depreciation 31 Dec 1994 £	Date of disposal	Net book value 31 Dec 1994 £	Sale/scrap proceeds £	Loss/ profit £
1/V	Van reg G249 NPO	1 Feb 1990	4000	Reducing balance 25%	3051		949		
2/V	Van reg K697 JKL	1 June 1993	6000	Reducing balance 25%	2625		3375		
3/V	Van reg M894 TMG	30 Sep 1994	8000	Reducing balance 25%	2000		6000		
Totals			18000		7676		10324		

It is the firm's policy to charge a full year's depreciation in the year of purchase and none in the year of sale. Plant and equipment are depreciated on a straight line basis over the periods shown on the register. Motor vehicles are all depreciated at a rate of 25% using the reducing balance method.

During 1995 the following transactions in fixed assets took place.

(a) On 3 August an old kiln (ref. 1/K) was traded in at Cumere Oven Ltd and a new one (ref. 5/K) purchased for £1,600 from the same supplier. A trade-in allowance of £500 was given for the old kiln, the balance to be settled at a later date. An invoice (no. 35X42) was raised by the supplier for the amount in question.

(b) On 5 September, a new potter's wheel (ref. 4/W) was purchased for £500 cash.

(c) On 10 October the oldest delivery van (ref. 1/V) was traded in for a new one (ref. 4/V), registration N583 MNO, costing £9,000. The supplier, Van Guard Ltd, gave a trade-in allowance of £1,000 on the old van and raised an invoice (no. Z/2643) for the difference.

It is now 31 December 1995 and you have been asked to help prepare the year-end accounts.

Tasks

(a) Record the above transactions and the year-end provisions for depreciation in:

    (i)   the journal;
    (ii)   the ledger accounts;
    (iii) the fixed assets register.

(b) Produce an extract from the year-end balance sheet showing the following.

    (i)   Plant and equipment (cost)
    (ii)   Motor vehicles (cost)
    (iii) Plant and equipment (provision for depreciation)
    (iv) Motor vehicles (provision for depreciation)

All workings should be to the nearest £.

The relevant ledger accounts, journal pages and fixed assets register page are attached for you to complete.

Tutorial note. In practice you would post from the journal to the ledger accounts, but in this exercise you may find it helpful to do the opposite in order to calculate any profit or loss on disposal of fixed assets.

	JOURNAL			Page 50
Date	Details	Folio Ref	£	£

JOURNAL				Page 51
Date	Details	Folio Ref	£	£

LEDGER ACCOUNTS

PLANT AND EQUIPMENT

	£		£
Date		*Date*	
1995		*1995*	
1 Jan Balance b/d	4,970		

PLANT AND EQUIPMENT: PROVISION FOR DEPRECIATION

	£		£
		Date	
		1995	
		1 Jan Balance b/d	2,330

PLANT AND EQUIPMENT: DISPOSALS

	£		£

MOTOR VEHICLES

	£		£
Date			
1995			
1 Jan Balance b/d	18,000		

MOTOR VEHICLES: PROVISION FOR DEPRECIATION

	£		£
		Date	
		1995	
		1 Jan Balance b/d	7,676

MOTOR VEHICLES: DISPOSALS

	£		£

PLANT AND EQUIPMENT

Ref	Description	Date of purchase	Cost £	Depreciation period	Accumulated depreciation 31 Dec 1995 £	Date of disposal	Net book value 31 Dec 1995 £	Sale/scrap proceeds £	Loss/ profit £
1/K	Kiln	1 Jan 1993	1200	6 years					
1/P	Pugmill	1 July 1994	300	4 years					
2/K	Kiln	1 Mar 1992	600	6 years					
3/K	Kiln	20 Aug 1991	750	6 years					
1/W	Wheel	31 Mar 1993	400	4 years					
2/W	Wheel	1 Feb 1992	400	4 years					
4/K	Kiln	1 Sep 1992	900	6 years					
3/W	Wheel	1 Mar 1994	420	4 years					
Totals									
Disposals									
Totals c/f									

MOTOR VEHICLES

Ref	Description	Date of purchase	Cost £	Depreciation type	Accumulated depreciation 31 Dec 1995 £	Date of disposal	Net book value 31 Dec 1995 £	Sale/scrap proceeds £	Loss/ profit £
1/V	Van reg G249 NPO	1 Feb 1990	4000	Reducing balance 25%					
2/V	Van reg K697 JKL	1 June 1993	6000	Reducing balance 25%					
3/V	Van reg M894 TMG	30 Sep 1994	8000	Reducing balance 25%					
Totals									
Disposals									
Totals c/f									

Devolved assessment
2 Booths

Performance criteria

The following performance criteria are covered in this Devolved Assessment.

Element 4.1: Maintain records and accounts relating to capital expenditure

1   Relevant details relating to specific items of capital expenditure are correctly entered in the appropriate records

Element 5.1: Record income and expenditure

1   Income and expenditure is correctly recorded in the appropriate ledger accounts

3   The organisation's policies, regulations, procedures and timescales are observed

4   Income and expenditure is analysed in accordance with defined requirements and appropriate information is passed to management

---

Notes on completing the Assessment

This Assessment is designed to test your ability to post transactions correctly to the ledger accounts and the trial balance.

You are provided with data (Pages 94 to 103) which you must use to complete the tasks on Page 103.

You are allowed 2 hours to complete your work.

A high level of accuracy is required. Check your work carefully.

Correcting fluid should not be used. Errors should be crossed out neatly and clearly. You should write in ink and not in pencil.

A full suggested solution to this Assessment is provided on Page 121.

Do not turn to the suggested solution until you have completed all parts of the Assessment.

DEVOLVED ASSESSMENT 2: BOOTHS

Data

You are acting as the temporary bookkeeper at Booths Ltd, a builder's merchant. The financial year end, 30 June 19X7, is approaching. During the day of 30 June 19X7, several primary documents are passed to you for posting to the ledger accounts.

All sales and all purchases are made on credit. All other expenses are paid *immediately* on receipt of a bill.

The ledger accounts appear as follows at the end of 29 June 19X7.

ADVERTISING					
19X7			19X7		
29 June Balance b/f	288	91			

ACCOUNTANCY FEES					
19X7			19X7		
29 June Balance b/f	1,500	00			

BANK ACCOUNT					
19X7			19X7		
29 June Balance b/f	19,330	65			

DOUBTFUL DEBT PROVISION

19X7			19X7		
			29 June Balance b/f	1,242	94

ELECTRICITY

19X7			19X7		
29 June Balance b/f	1,733	84			

FIXTURES AND FITTINGS

19X7			19X7		
29 June Balance b/f	11,893	55			

GAS

19X7			19X7		
29 June Balance b/f	1,161	20			

INSURANCE

19X7			19X7		
29 June Balance b/f	658	38			

INTEREST

19X7			19X7		
29 June Balance b/f	1,141	31			

MAINTENANCE					
19X7			19X7		
29 June Balance b/f	3,807	43			

MOTOR EXPENSES					
19X7			19X7		
29 June Balance b/f	606	19			

MOTOR VEHICLES					
19X7			19X7		
29 June Balance b/f	43,675	07			

PROFIT AND LOSS ACCOUNT					
19X7			19X7		
			29 June Balance b/f	27,225	92

PURCHASES					
19X7			19X7		
29 June Balance b/f	76,648	31			

PURCHASE LEDGER CONTROL A/C

19X7			19X7		
			29 June Balance b/f	9,554	93

PRINT, POSTAGE & STATIONERY

19X7			19X7		
29 June Balance b/f	117	29			

RENT

19X7			19X7		
29 June Balance b/f	9,250	00			

SHARE CAPITAL

19X7			19X7		
			29 June Balance b/f	10,000	00

ACCUMULATED DEPRECIATION

19X7			19X7		
			29 June Balance b/f	27,241	12

SALES					
19X7			19X7		
			29 June Balance b/f	180,754	17

SALES LEDGER CONTROL A/C					
19X7			19X7		
29 June Balance b/f	19,356	30			

SUNDRY EXPENSES					
19X7			19X7		
29 June Balance b/f	1,427	70			

OPENING STOCK					
19X7			19X7		
29 June Balance b/f	37,321	56			

TELEPHONE					
19X7			19X7		
29 June Balance b/f	3,879	09			

UNIFIED BUSINESS RATE					
19X7			19X7		
29 June Balance b/f	4,917	94			

VAT CONTROL A/C					
19X7			19X7		
			29 June Balance b/f	6,719	19

WAGES					
19X7			19X7		
29 June Balance b/f	21,575	63			

WATER RATES					
19X7			19X7		
29 June Balance b/f	2,447	92			

The documents which have been passed to you are as follows.

BOOTHS LTD		62 Maple St NO7 3PN Tax point 30.06.X7 VAT No. 3171156327
MP Price & Co A/C No. 01729	Q	£
Standard bricks	400	504.00
TOTAL VAT 17.5%		504.00 88.20
		£592.20

BOOTHS LTD		62 Maple St NO7 3PN Tax point 30.06.X7 VAT No. 3171156327
H Contractors A/C No. 02147	Q	£
Cement bags Trowel Spirit Level	10 1 1	67.00 5.50 17.95
TOTAL VAT 17.5%		90.45 15.83
		£106.28

BOOTHS LTD		62 Maple St NO7 3PN Tax point 30.06.X7 VAT No. 3171156327
NP Plumbers A/C No. 01227	Q	£
Piping: 1 metre length Piping: 0.5 metre length 'A' type fittings	40 40 25	210.00 102.00 30.75
TOTAL VAT 17.5%		342.75 59.98
		402.73

BOOTHS LTD		62 Maple St NO7 3PN Tax point 30.06.X7 VAT No. 3171156327
CR Harris & Co A/C No. 03994	Q	£
Standard bricks White bricks	500 50	630.00 100.00
TOTAL VAT 17.5%		730.00 127.75
		857.75

LARKIN LUMBER LTD

The Mill
Park Lane
NO4 INQ

55321194   Tax point: 30 06 X7

To Booths Ltd

£

3" Timber	1,320.00
4" Timber	1,975.00
	3,295.00
VAT 17.5%	576.63
	3,871.63

30 days net   VAT No. 371 1942 678

Tax point	Inv. no.
3006X7	X371172L

PLUMBING SUPPLIES LTD
Unit 17 Park Estate No7 1ZR

To Booths Ltd

4cm piping	20m	486.23
6cm piping	30m	1.049.82

TOTAL	1,536.05
VAT	268.81
Amount due	1,804.86

VAT No. 442 1986 883   30 days net

Post Office Counters Ltd
Tax point: 30 06 X7

To Booths Ltd

Franking services
01 March 19X7 to 31 May 19X7

869	1st	208.56
942	2nd	169.56
		378.12

HALFWAY INVESTMENTS LIMITED

To Booths Ltd

Tax point 29 June 19X7
VAT 497 3328 679

RENT

QUARTER TO
29 September 19X7   £2,312.50

WOODLEY GAZETTE

37 Half Lane
NO7 9RP

INV 21737

Tax point: 30/6/X7

VAT No. 113 4279 179

Booths Ltd Wednesday 5th June Half page ad.	33.50
VAT @ 17.5%	5.86
Total	39.36

007321

M Able & Co
Insurance Brokers
9 Green Lane
NO3 4PW

Tax point
30.06.19X7

To Booths Ltd
62 Maple St

Motor vehicle
insurance
per attatched   £1,437.50

Year to 31 May 19X8. Sorry
for the delay - you have
still been covered

Pratts Garage
114 Lark Road
NO1 1NR

S14117

Tax point: 30/6/X7

VAT No. 172 1173 499

BOOTHS LTD A/C 4173

Petrol and oil to 30 June 19X7	317.42
VAT @ 17.5%	55.55
	372.97

I134734

To: Booths Ltd
    62 Maple St
    NO7 3PN

IRT DEALERS
4 The Forecourt

VAT 147 3321 198

Tax point: 30/6/X7

Executive Car XZ3i Reg J172 BNC	12,600.00
Road Tax	100.00
Extras	542.75
	13,242.75
VAT £13,142.75 @ 17.5%	2,299.98
	15,542.73

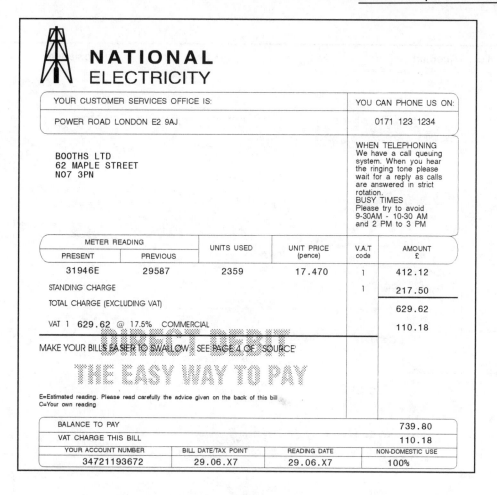

You have also received the following information.

(a) Bank interest of £67.48 has been charged on the company's bank account but has not yet been posted.

(b) The gross wages cost for June, paid on 30 June 19X7, amounted to £2,169.52.

Tasks

(a) Post the transactions shown above to the ledger accounts.

(b) Balance and close off the ledger accounts. You should balance off the revenue and accounts (as well as the asset and liability accounts), but there is no need to post the balances to the profit and loss account.

(c) Post the balances in the ledger accounts to the trial balance provided overleaf. Add up the trial balance to check that it balances. Investigate any discrepancies.

Note. For (a) to (c) ignore accruals and prepayments.

(d) Identify any accruals and prepayments which would require adjustment in the *extended* trial balance.

Folio	Account	Ref	Trial balance	
			Debit	Credit
			£	£
	TOTAL			

Devolved assessment
3 Randalls class assessment

Performance criteria

The following performance criteria are covered in this Devolved Assessment.

Element 5.1: Record income and expenditure

1   Income and expenditure is correctly recorded in the appropriate ledger accounts

2   Any accrued or prepaid income and expenditure is correctly identified and adjustments are made

4   Income and expenditure is analysed in accordance with defined requirements and appropriate information is passed to management

Element 5.2: Prepare accounts from incomplete records

1   Essential accounts and reconciliations are correctly prepared

2   Existing primary information is accurately summarised

3   Other relevant information is correctly identified and recorded

6   Discrepancies, unusual features or queries are identified and either resolved or referred to the appropriate person

Notes on completing the Assessment

This Assessment is designed to test your ability to prepare accounts from incomplete records.

You are provided with data (Page 106) which you must use to complete the tasks on Page 106.

You are allowed 3 hours to complete your work.

A high level of accuracy is required. Check your work carefully.

Correcting fluid should not be used. Errors should be crossed out neatly and clearly. You should write in ink and not in pencil.

A full suggested solution to this Assessment is included in the BPP Lecturers' Pack for these units.

DEVOLVED ASSESSMENT 3: RANDALLS CLASS ASSESSMENT

Data

Randalls Ltd runs a large furniture discount warehouse in the East End of London. On 30 September 19X2, vandals looted the warehouse, taking or destroying all the stock and stealing the till floats of £7,500. Only minor damage was done to the premises.

The company was fully insured and it is now necessary to formulate an insurance claim, which you have been called upon to assist in. The following matters were revealed by your investigation.

(a) *Net assets on 1 January 19X2*

	£	£
Fixtures and fittings		
Cost	90,000.00	
Accumulated depreciation	40,000.00	
Net book value		50,000.00
Stock		270,141.27
Debtors		42,621.92
Prepayments (uniform business rate)		2,975.00
Cash in bank		214,337.81
Cash float in till		3,000.00
Trade creditors		164,827.29
Accrued electricity		4,120.00
Share capital		350,000.00

(b) *Summary of bank statements for the nine months from 1 January*

	£
Receipts	
Cash and cheques banked	2,005,117.28
Payments	
Trade creditors	1,785,437.23
Rent (1.1.X2 - 31.12.X2)	118,685.00
Electricity	15,507.25
Insurance (theft)	15,492.32
Telephone	8,205.73
	1,943,327.53

(c) *Amounts paid in cash from the tills*

	£
Trade creditors	240,107.49
Wages (per month)	29,610.00

(d) Randalls Ltd's gross profit margin on sales has averaged 20% in recent years.

(e) The fixtures and fittings are thought to be worth only £20,000.

(f) A cheque for £5,172.40 in respect of the telephone bill for the quarter ending 29 September 19X2 is not shown on the bank statements until 3 October.

(g) The Uniform Business Rate (UBR) for the period 1 April 19X2 to 1 October 19X2 amounting to £7,520.00 has not yet been paid.

(h) Trade debtors and creditors amounted to £27,496.36 and £189,947.32 respectively on 30 September 19X2.

Tasks

(a) Prepare a trading, profit and loss account for Randalls Ltd for the nine months to 30 September 19X2.

(b) Prepare Randalls Ltd's balance sheet as at 30 September 19X2.

Devolved assessment
4 Charters class assessment

Performance criteria

The following performance criteria are covered in this Devolved Assessment.

Element 4.1: Maintain records and accounts relating to capital expenditure

4   Depreciation charges and other necessary entries and adjustments are correctly calculated and recorded in the appropriate ledger accounts

Element 5.1: Record income and expenditure

1   Income and expenditure is correctly recorded in the appropriate ledger accounts

2   Any accrued or prepaid income and expenditure is correctly identified and adjustments are made

4   Income and expenditure is analysed in accordance with defined requirements and appropriate information is passed to management

Element 5.3: Prepare the extended trial balance

1   The trial balance is accurately extended and totalled

2   Totals from the general ledger or other records are correctly entered on the extended trial balance

3   Any errors disclosed by the trial balance are traced and corrected

4   Any adjustments not dealt with in the ledger accounts are correctly entered on the extended trial balance

5   An agreed valuation of closing stock is correctly entered on the extended trial balance

Notes on completing the Assessment

This Assessment is designed to test your ability to prepare the extended trial balance.

You are provided with data (Pages 108 to 113) which you must use to complete the tasks on Page 114.

You are allowed 4 hours to complete your work.

A high level of accuracy is required. Check your work carefully.

Correcting fluid should not be used. Errors should be crossed out neatly and clearly. You should write in ink and not in pencil.

A full suggested solution to this Assessment is included in the BPP Lecturers' Pack for these units.

DEVOLVED ASSESSMENT 4: CHARTERS CLASS ASSESSMENT

Data

Charters Ltd was established in 19X1 and it trades from a leased shop. The company sells furniture to trade and retail customers. The company has traded profitably since incorporation and it is now preparing accounts for the year ended 31 December 19X8. The trial balance as at 31 December 19X8 is as follows.

Folio	Account	DR £	CR £
A1	Accountancy fees	440.00	
A2	Advertising	1,556.29	
B1	Bank account		27,488.12
B2	Bank charges	2,157.51	
B3	Bad debt expense		
C1	Credit card charges	2,212.80	
D1	Discounts allowed	5,629.31	
D2	Discounts received		4,529.69
D3	Directors' loan accounts	9,343.89	
D4	Depreciation (accumulated)		
	Fixtures and fittings		14,304.00
	Motor vehicles		22,563.10
	Leasehold		38,500.00
D5	Depreciation expense		
D6	Doubtful debt provision		
E1	Electricity	7,264.61	
F1	Fixtures and fittings	35,430.00	
G1	Gas	12,374.97	
I1	Insurance	22,298.96	
I2	Interest (bank)	1,109.11	
I3	Interest (loan)	5,000.00	
L1	Leasehold	220,000.00	
L2	Loan		50,000.00
M1	Maintenance	4,649.22	
M2	Motor expenses	1,557.10	
M3	Motor vehicles	73,482.10	
P1	Profit and loss account		160,808.95
P2	Purchases	489,227.91	
P3	Purchase ledger control account		51,444.74
P4	Petty cash	1,000.00	
P5	Purchase returns		687.08
P6	Print, post and stationery	5,885.32	
P7	PAYE and NI	91,799.27	
R1	Rent (warehouse)	18,125.00	
S1	Share capital		100,000.00
S2	Sales		1,022,734.87
S3	Sales ledger control account	105,947.07	
S4	Sales returns	2,287.03	
S5	Staff welfare	1,768.56	
S6	Sundry expenses	1,574.68	
S7	Suspense account	16,450.00	
S8	Stock 1.1.X8	48,172.29	
T1	Telephone	8,763.82	
U1	Uniform business rate	30,616.08	
V1	VAT		18,965.89
W1	Wages and salaries	276,449.27	
W2	Water rates	9,454.27	

The following transactions and adjustments must be taken into account in the preparation of the trial balance.

(a) The lease, which has a 40 year term, was purchased on 1 January 19X1. Depreciation, which is to be calculated on a straight line basis, has not yet been provided for the year ended 31 December 19X8.

(b) Depreciation has not yet been provided on the motor vehicles, which are depreciated at 25% on written down value.

(c) Depreciation is also still to be provided on fixtures and fittings at 10% of cost. A full year of depreciation is charged in the year of acquisition.

(d) An insurance bill was paid on 1 April 19X8 for £18,178.44 for the year to 31 March 19X9.

(e) The audit fee of £3,000.00 must be accrued under accountancy fees.

(f) A bank statement received at the end of January showed that bank charges of £522.18 had been incurred for the three months ended 31 January 19X9.

(g) The suspense account comprises the following items.

   (i) A new piece of fixed asset furniture was purchased during the year for £12,250.00 for cash but it was posted to the suspense account as it had not been classified.

   (ii) The company had paid £4,000 in cash for maintenance work but the bookkeeper had been unsure about whether to treat it as a capital or revenue item and it had been posted to the suspense account. The entire amount relates to revenue expenditure.

   (iii) The cash paid near the year end for the staff Christmas party of £450.00 had been debited to the suspense account.

   (iv) One of the directors put an expenses claim in for £250.00 at the end of the year and this has been posted to the suspense account rather than the director's loan account. The relevant expense accounts have already been adjusted.

(h) It has been discovered after the year end that a trade debtor owing £2,200.00 has gone into liquidation and there is no prospect of recovering any of the money. It has also been decided that, for the first time, a general provision should be made for doubtful debts. This is to be calculated as ½% of net trade debtors.

(i) An electricity bill was received dated 15 January 19X9 for £3,412.27. The last bill was dated 16 October 19X8.

(j) The last gas bill to be received was dated 30 November 19X8.

(k) The last time bank interest was charged was 31 October 19X8. The average overdrawn balance in November and December was £22,000. The prevailing average interest rate was 12% per annum.

(l) On 2 January 19X9, goods with a cost of £511.42, which had been purchased by the company before the year end on credit, were returned to suppliers. The goods had been omitted from the year-end stock valuation.

(m) On 29 December 19X8 the company paid £3,625.00 rent for the quarter to 25 March 19X9.

(n) Goods sold for £2,117.28 were returned by customers just after the year end. The stock has been included in the year end stock figure at cost, but no other adjustment has been made.

(o) The telephone bill dated 30 November 19X8 included the following charges.

	£
Rental to 28 February 19X9	142.78
Charges for 3 months to 30 November 19X8	1,667.21
	1,809.99
VAT	316.75
Total	2,126.74

(p) The Uniform Business Rate paid on 1 April 19X8 for 12 months was £24,492.88.

(q) The water rates bill paid on 1 April 19X8 for 12 months was £7,954.28.

(r) The closing stock was counted and valued at £64,565.04.

Folio	Account	Trial balance		Adjustments		Accrued	Prepaid	Profit and loss a/c		Balance sheet	
		Debit £	Credit £	Debit £	Credit £	£	£	Debit £	Credit £	Debit £	Credit £

SUB-TOTAL

Folio	Account	Trial balance		Adjustments		Accrued	Prepaid	Profit and loss a/c		Balance sheet	
		Debit £	Credit £	Debit £	Credit £	£	£	Debit £	Credit £	Debit £	Credit £
	SUB-TOTAL										
	Profit for the year										
	TOTAL										

Tasks

(a) Enter the opening trial balance on the trial balance layout provided on the previous pages.

(b) Calculate the adjustments (journals, accruals, prepayments etc) to take account of the items listed in (a) to (r) above and enter them on the trial balance.

(c) Extend the trial balance, calculate the profit and balance the ETB.

Solutions
to
devolved
assessments

SOLUTION TO DEVOLVED ASSESSMENT 1: REGGIE STIR

Tutorial note. When doing the journal entries you should not record the purchase of the potter's wheel. This is because the purchase was for *cash* and the journal only records *credit* purchases. The book of prime entry for cash purchases of fixed assets is the cash book.

Solution

(a)

	JOURNAL			Page 50
Date	Details	Folio Ref	£	£
3 August	Plant and equipment	P/E	1600	
	Plant and equipment disposals	P/D		500
	Cumere Oven Ltd	C/O		1100
	Being part exchange per agreement and invoice no 35X42			
3 August	Plant and equipment: disposals	NP/D	1200	
	Plant and equipment	P/E		1200
	Being transfer of plant (1/K) at cost to plant disposals a/c			
3 August	Plant and equipment: depreciation provision	PD/P	400	
	Plant and equipment: disposal	NP/D		400
	Being transfer of depreciation provision (1/K) to plant disposals a/c			
10 October	Motor vehicles	M/V	9000	
	Motor vehicles disposals	MV/D		1000
	Van Guard Ltd	V/G		8000
	Being part exchange per agreement and invoice no Z/2643			
10 October	Motor vehicles disposals	MV/D	4000	
	Motor vehicles	M/V		4000
	Being transfer of van 1/V at cost to disposals a/c			

Date	Details	Folio Ref	£	£
	JOURNAL			**Page 51**
10 October	Motor vehicles: depreciation provision	MV/DP	3051	
	Motor vehicles: disposals	MV/D		3051
	Being transfer of depreciation provision 1V to motor vehicles disposals a/c			
31 December	P & L a/c	P/L	300	
	Plant and equipment: disposals a/c	P/D		300
	Being loss on part exchange of kiln 1/K			
31 December	Motor vehicles: disposals	MV/D	51	
	P & L a/c	P/L		51
	Being profit on part exchange of van 1/V			
31 December	Plant and equipment: depreciation expense	P/DE	1147	
	Plant and equipment: depreciation provision	PD/P		1147
	Being year end provision for depreciation on plant			
31 December	Motor vehicles depreciation expense	MV/DE	4594	
	Motor vehicles depreciation provision	MV/DP		4594
	Being year end provision for depreciation on motor vehicles			

LEDGER ACCOUNTS

PLANT AND EQUIPMENT

Date		£	Date		£
1995			*1995*		
1 Jan	Balance b/d	4,970			
3 Aug	Creditors £(1,600 – 500)	1,100	3 Aug	Plant and equipment:	
3 Aug	Plant and equipment:			disposals	1,200
	disposals	500	31 Dec	Balance c/d	5,870
5 Sep	Bank	500			
		7,070			7,070

PLANT AND EQUIPMENT: PROVISION FOR DEPRECIATION

Date		£	Date		£
1995			*1995*		
3 Aug	Plant and equipment:		1 Jan	Balance b/d	2,330
	disposals	400	31 Dec	P & L a/c (W1)	1,147
31 Dec	Balance c/d	3,077			
		3,477			3,477

PLANT AND EQUIPMENT: DISPOSALS

Date		£	Date		£
1995			*1995*		
3 Aug	Plant and equipment	1,200	3 Aug	Depreciation	
				provision	400
			3 Aug	Plant and equipment	500
			31 Dec	P & L account	300
		1,200			1,200

MOTOR VEHICLES

Date		£	Date		£
1995			*1995*		
1 Jan	Balance b/d	18,000	10 Oct	Motor vehicles:	
10 Oct	Motor vehicles:			disposals	4,000
	disposals	1,000	31 Dec	Balance c/d	23,000
10 Oct	Creditors				
	£(9,000 – 1,000)	8,000			
		27,000			27,000

MOTOR VEHICLES: PROVISION FOR DEPRECIATION

Date		£	Date		£
1995			*1995*		
10 Oct	Motor vehicles:		1 Jan	Balance b/d	7,676
	disposals	3,051	31 Dec	P & L a/c (W2)	4,594
31 Dec	Balance c/f	9,219			
		12,270			12,270

MOTOR VEHICLES: DISPOSALS

Date		£	Date		£
1995			*1995*		
10 Oct	Motor vehicles	4,000	10 Oct	Depreciation provision	3,051
31 Dec	P & L account	51	10 Oct	Motor vehicles	1,000
		4,051			4,051

PLANT AND EQUIPMENT

Ref	Description	Date of purchase	Cost £	Depreciation period	Accumulated depreciation 31 Dec 1995 £	Date of disposal	Net book value 31 Dec 1995 £	Sale/scrap proceeds £	(Loss)/ profit £
1/K	Kiln	1 Jan 1993	1200	6 years	400	3 Aug 1995	800	500	(300)
1/P	Pugmill	1 July 1994	300	4 years	150		150		
2/K	Kiln	1 Mar 1992	600	6 years	400		200		
3/K	Kiln	20 Aug 1991	750	6 years	625		125		
1/W	Wheel	31 Mar 1993	400	4 years	300		100		
2/W	Wheel	1 Feb 1992	400	4 years	400		nil		
4/K	Kiln	1 Sep 1992	900	6 years	600		300		
3/W	Wheel	1 Mar 1994	420	4 years	210		210		
5/K	Kiln	3 Aug 1995	1600	6 years	267		1333		
4/W	Wheel	5 Sept 1995	500	4 years	125		375		
Totals			7070		3477		3593		
Disposals			1200		400		800	500	(300)
Totals c/f			5870		3077		2793		

MOTOR VEHICLES

Ref	Description	Date of purchase	Cost £	Depreciation type	Accumulated depreciation 31 Dec 1995 £	Date of disposal	Net book value 31 Dec 1995 £	Sale/scrap proceeds £	(Loss)/ profit £
1/V	Van reg D249 NPO	1 Feb 1990	4000	Reducing balance 25%	3051	10 Oct 1995	949	1000	51
2/V	Van reg K697 JKL	1 Jan 1993	6000	Reducing balance 25%	3469		2531		
3/V	Van reg J894 TMG	30 Sept 1994	8000	Reducing balance 25%	3500		4500		
4/V	Van reg N583 MNO	10 Oct 1995	9000	Reducing balance 25%	2250		6750		
Totals			27000		12270		14730		
Disposals			4000		3051		949	1000	51
Totals c/f			23000		9219		13781		

1 Depreciation charge: plant and equipment

	£
Kilns £(600 + 750 + 900 + 1,600) ÷ 6	642
Other £(300 + 400 + 400 + 420 + 500) ÷ 4	505
	1,147

Note. It should be assumed from the question that all kilns are depreciated over 6 years and all wheels over 4 years.

2 Depreciation charge: motor vehicles

	£	£
Van 2/V: NBV 1 January 1995	3,375	
Depreciation @ 25%		844
Van 3/V: NBV 1 January 1995	6,000	
Depreciation @ 25%		1,500
Van 4/V: depreciation (25% × £9,000)		2,250
Total charge to P & L		4,594

(b) REGGIE STIR LIMITED
BALANCE SHEET EXTRACT AS AT 31 DECEMBER 1995

	Cost £	Accumulated depreciation £	NBV £
Fixed assets			
Plant and equipment	5,870	3,077	2,793
Motor vehicles	23,000	9,219	13,781
	28,870	12,296	16,574

SOLUTION TO DEVOLVED ASSESSMENT 2: BOOTHS

Tutorial note. You will realise from your earlier studies that the sales and purchase invoices shown in the question would normally be posted to the sales day book and purchases day book respectively. We have bypassed the day books in the example, for the sake of simplicity and because the main emphasis of the assignment is the posting of transactions to the correct ledger accounts.

Solution

(a) and (b)

The ledger accounts will appear as follows after the postings for 30 June 19X7 and after being balanced off.

ADVERTISING					
19X7			19X7		
29 June Balance b/f	288	91			
30 June Bank	33	50	30 June P+L account	322	41
	322	41		322	41

ACCOUNTANCY FEES					
19X7			19X7		
29 June Balance b/f	1,500	00	30 June P+L account	1,500	00

BANK ACCOUNT					
19X7			19X7		
29 June Balance b/f	19,330	65			
			30 June Woodley Gazette	39	36
			Electricity	739	80
			M Able & Co	1,437	50
			Interest bank	67	48
			Pratt's Garage	372	97
			Post Office	378	12
			Halfway investments	2,312	50
			Wages	2,169	52
30 June Balance c/f	3,729	33	Motor vehicles + road tax	15,542	73
	23,059	98		23,059	98

DOUBTFUL DEBT PROVISION

19X7			19X7		
30 June Balance c/f	1,242	94	29 June Balance b/f	1,242	94

ELECTRICITY

19X7			19X7		
29 June Balance b/f	1,733	84			
30 June Bank	629	62	30 June P+L account	2,363	46
	2,363	46		2,363	46

FIXTURES AND FITTINGS

19X7			19X7		
29 June Balance b/f	11,893	55	30 June Balance c/f	11,893	55

GAS

19X7			19X7		
29 June Balance b/f	1,161	20	30 June P+L account	1,161	20

INSURANCE

19X7			19X7		
29 June Balance b/f	658	38	30 June P and L account	658	38

INTEREST

19X7			19X7		
29 June Balance b/f	1,141	31			
30 June Bank	67	48	30 June P+L account	1,208	79
	1,208	79		1,208	79

MAINTENANCE

19X7			19X7		
29 June Balance b/f	3,807	43	30 June P+L account	3,807	43

MOTOR EXPENSES

19X7			19X7		
29 June Balance b/f	606	19			
30 June Bank	317	42			
* Bank	100	00			
** Bank	1,437	50	30 June P+L account	2,461	11
	2,461	11		2,461	11

MOTOR VEHICLES

19X7			19X7		
29 June Balance b/f	43,675	07			
30 June Bank	15,442	73	30 June Balance c/f	59,117	80
	59,117	80		59,117	80

PROFIT AND LOSS ACCOUNT

19X7			19X7		
30 June Balance c/f	27,225	92	29 June Balance b/f	27,225	92

PURCHASES

19X7			19X7		
29 June Balance b/f	76,648	31			
30 June Larkin Lumber					
P/L Control a/c	3,295	00			
Plumbing supplies					
P/L Control a/c	1,536	05	30 June P+L account	81,479	36
	81,479	36		81,479	36

* A prepayment would not normally be required for such a small amount; in any case this would not be calculated until the ETB was prepared.

** This amount might have been posted to the insurance account, depending on company policy, but this is more appropriate.

PURCHASE LEDGER CONTROL A/C

19X7			19X7		
			29 June Balance b/f	9,554	93
			30 June Larkin Lumber	3,871	63
30 June Balance c/f	15,231	42	Plumbing supplies	1,804	86
	15,231	42		15,231	42

PRINT, POSTAGE & STATIONERY

19X7			19X7		
29 June Balance b/f	117	29			
30 June Bank	378	12	30 June P+L account	495	41
	495	41		495	41

RENT

19X7			19X7		
29 June Balance b/f	9,250	00			
30 June Bank	2,312	50	30 June P+L account	11,562	50
	11,562	50		11,562	50

Note. The rent invoice just paid is for rent to 30 September 19X7. This would be adjusted as a prepayment on the *extended* trial balance.

SHARE CAPITAL

19X7			19X7		
30 June Balance c/f	10,000	00	29 June Balance b/f	10,000	00

ACCUMULATED DEPRECIATION

19X7			19X7		
30 June Balance c/f	27,241	12	29 June Balance b/f	27,241	12

SALES

19X7			19X7		
			29 June Balance b/f	180,754	17
			30 June Sales Ledger		
			Control a/c		
			MP Price & Co	504	00
			H Contractors	90	45
			NP Plumbers	342	75
30 June Balance c/f	182,421	37	CR Harris & Co	730	00
	182,421	37		182,421	37

SALES LEDGER CONTROL A/C

19X7			19X7		
29 June Balance b/f	19,356	30			
30 June Sales					
MP Price & Co	592	20			
H Contractors	106	28			
NP PLumbers	402	73			
CR Harris & Co	857	75	30 June Balance c/f	21,315	26
	21,315	26		21,315	26

SUNDRY EXPENSES

19X7			19X7		
29 June Balance b/f	1,427	70	30 June P+L account	1,427	70

OPENING STOCK

19X7			19X7		
29 June Balance b/f	37,321	56	30 June Balance c/f	37,321	56

TELEPHONE					
19X7			19X7		
29 June Balance b/f	3,879	09	30 June P & L account	3,879	09

UNIFORM BUSINESS RATE					
19X7			19X7		
29 June Balance b/f	4,917	94	30 June P & L account	4,917	94

VAT CONTROL A/C					
19X7			19X7		
30 June Bank	5	86	29 June Balance b/f	6,719	19
Bank	110	18	30 June Sales ledger	88	20
Bank	55	55	Sales ledger	15	83
Purchases ledger	576	63	Sales ledger	59	98
Purchases ledger	268	81	Sales ledger	127	75
Balance c/f	5,993	92			
	7,010	95		7,010	95

WAGES					
19X7			19X7		
29 June Balance b/f	21,575	63			
30 June Bank	2,169	52	30 June P & L account	23,745	15
	23,745	15		23,745	15

WATER RATES					
19X7			19X7		
29 June Balance b/f	2,447	92	30 June P & L account	2,447	92

(c)   The balances on the ledger accounts, once extracted, will give the following trial balance.

Folio	Account	Ref	Trial balance	
			Debit	Credit
			£	£
	Advertising		322.41	
	Accountancy fees		1,500.00	
	Bank			3,729.33
	Depreciation (acumulated)			27,241.12
	Doubtful debt provision			1,242.94
	Electrcity		2,363.46	
	Fixtures and fittings		11,893.55	
	Gas		1,161.20	
	Insurance		658.38	
	Interest		1,208.79	
	Maintenance		3,807.43	
	Motor expenses		2,461.11	
	Motor vehicles		59,117.80	
	Profit and loss account			27,225.92
	Purchases		81,479.36	
	Purchase ledger control account			15,231.42
	Print, post and stationery		495.41	
	Rent		11,562.50	
	Share capital			10,000.00
	Sales			182,421.37
	Sales ledger control account		21,315.26	
	Sundry expenses		1,427.70	
	Stock at 1.1. X4		37,321.56	
	Telephone		3,879.09	
	Unified Business Rate		4,917.94	
	VAT			5,993.92
	Wages		23,745.15	
	Water rates		2,447.92	
	TOTAL		273,086.02	273,086.02

(d) The following accruals and prepayments should be identified.

Accruals

Franking services: £378.12 × 1/3 = £126.04

Prepayments

Rent: quarter to 30 September 19X7: £2,312.50

Motor insurance: £1,437.50 × 11/12 = £1,317.71

TRIAL RUN DEVOLVED ASSESSMENT

INTERMEDIATE STAGE - NVQ/SVQ3

Units 4 and 5

Recording capital transactions

and

Preparing financial accounts

The purpose of this Trial Run Devolved Assessment is to give you an idea of what a Devolved Assessment could be like. It is not intended as a definitive guide to the tasks you may be required to perform.

The suggested time allowance for this Assessment is four hours. Extra time may be permitted in a real Devolved Assessment. Breaks in assessment may be allowed, but it must normally be completed in one day.

Calculators may be used but no reference material is permitted.

DO NOT OPEN THIS PAPER UNTIL YOU ARE READY TO START
UNDER TIMED CONDITIONS

INSTRUCTIONS

This Assessment is designed to test your ability to record capital transactions and prepare financial accounts.

Background information is provided on Page 131.

The tasks you are to perform are set out on Page 132.

You are provided with data on Pages 133 to 135 which you must use to complete the tasks.

Your answers should be set out in the answer booklet on Pages 137 to 144 using the documents provided. You may require additional answer pages.

You are allowed four hours to complete your work.

A high level of accuracy is required. Check your work carefully.

Correcting fluid may not be used. Errors should be crossed out neatly and clearly. You should write in black ink, not pencil.

You are advised to read the whole of the Assessment before commencing as all of the information may be of value and is not necessarily supplied in the sequence in which you might wish to deal with it.

BACKGROUND INFORMATION

Gordon Blur Ltd manufactures and trades in high quality kitchenware for sale to trade and retail customers. The company was established in 19X2 and operates from leasehold premises in Holloway, North London.

Gordon Blur is the managing director and the chief accountant is Kit Shenett. You are the accounts clerk. You have started the job only recently: the previous accounts clerk, Karen Taddup left suddenly having made a few errors and omissions.

The firm is rather old fashioned and still uses a manual accounting system and fixed assets register.

Kit Shenett has gone on holiday leaving you with a trial balance which needs adjusting, a fixed assets register which needs updating and a memo with various pieces of information.

THE TASKS TO BE PERFORMED

In the answer booklet on Pages 137 to 144 complete the tasks outlined below for the year ended 31 December 19X6. Data for this assessment is provided on Pages 133 to 135.

(a) Enter all the information relating to fixed assets in the ledger accounts given, the journal and the fixed assets register.

(b) Show the journal entries required for items (b) and (c) in the memorandum.

(c) Enter the opening trial balance on the attached proforma after making any adjustments in connection with fixed assets, including recording the profit or loss on the sale of the van.

(d) Make any other adjustments required arising from journal entries, accruals or prepayments on the ETB.

(e) Extend the trial balance, calculate the profit and balance the ETB.

DATA

In order to complete the tasks listed on the previous page you should find attached the following items.

(a) Memorandum from Kit Shenett with some information and helpful hints.
(b) Trial balance as at 31 December 19X6.
(c) Relevant pages of fixed asset register as at 31 December 19X5 (ie last year).

MEMORANDUM

To: Accounts Clerk
From: Kit Shenett
Date: 31 December 19X6

Please find attached a trial balance as at 31 December 19X6. Before the final accounts can be prepared there are several adjustments which need to be made. You will need to do these through the journal, and the extended trial balance (proformas attached).

(a) Could you update the fixed assets register? I always like to ensure that the fixed assets register is kept up to date. Your predecessor Karen didn't do this, omitting to record the fact that on 3 August 19X6 the old van (Reg F396 HJB) was traded in for a new one (K125 ATE) costing £12,000. We were given a trade in allowance of £2,000 on the old van, the balance to be paid later in 19X7 and to be included for now in sundry creditors.

No depreciation has been provided on fixed assets. Could you make the appropriate entries in the journal and adjust the trial balance for this and for the purchase and sale of the vans?

You may find it helpful to use the attached ledger accounts to calculate the profit or loss on disposal of the van. You will need to open an account to record this in the ETB.

Don't forget - plant and equipment is depreciated on the straight line basis over the periods shown in the fixed assets register. Leasehold property is amortised over the period of the lease and motor vehicles are depreciated using the reducing balance method at 25% per annum. We charge a full year's depreciation in the year of purchase and none in the year of sale.

(b) The suspense account balance consists of £4,770 which was money spent on repairs to the equipment. Karen was not very good at understanding the difference between capital and revenue expenditure, so she did not know where to put it. I take it you know where it should go!

(c) One of our customers, a Mr D Faults, has gone into liquidation owing us £200. We also need to increase the bad debts provision to 5% of net trade debtors.

(d) As you probably know, stock at 31.12.X6 is valued at £10,412.

(e) The audit fee of £1,500 needs to be accrued under accounting fees.

(f) We have paid some wages in advance to Luke Easword, amounting to £600.

(g) Our last electricity bill was dated 31 October and was for £300, the normal quarterly charge.

GORDON BLUR LIMITED
TRIAL BALANCE AS AT 31 DECEMBER 19X6

Folio		*Dr* £	*Cr* £
P110	Plant and equipment (cost)	55,330	
P120	Plant and equipment (provision for depreciation)		39,660
P130	Plant and equipment (depreciation expense)	-	
M110	Motor vehicles (cost)	25,500	
M120	Motor vehicles (provision for depreciation)		10,788
M130	Motor vehicles (depreciation expense)	-	
L110	Leasehold premises (cost)	100,000	
L120	Leasehold premises (accumulated amortisation)		8,000
L130	Leasehold premises (amortisation expense)	-	
C300	Sundry creditors		3,500
F100	Bank	6,132	
F200	Cash in hand	505	
A100	Accountancy fee	600	
B100	Bad debts provision		150
B200	Bad debts expense		
L300	Loan		10,000
R200	Repairs and maintenance	813	
M300	Motor expenses	1,506	
S100	Sales		205,806
D100	Trade debtors	50,287	
P100	Purchases	158,142	
C100	Trade creditors		65,416
E100	Electricity	900	
P300	Printing, postage, stationery	3,717	
P200	Profit and loss account		40,956
S200	Stock at 1.1.X6	9,125	
S300	Share capital		100,000
S400	Suspense account	4,770	
S500	Sundry expenses	6,428	
W100	Wages and salaries	60,521	
		484,276	484,276

FIXED ASSET REGISTER AS AT 31 DECEMBER 19X5

PLANT AND EQUIPMENT

Ref	Description	Date of purchase	Cost £	Depreciation period	Accumulated depreciation 31.12.X5 £	Date of disposal	Net book value 31.12.X5 £	Sale/scrap proceeds £	(Loss)/ profit £
P111	Cutter	1.3.X2	24,750	5 years	19,800		4,950		
P112	Moulding machine	2.5.X3	12,300	6 years	6,150		6,150		
P113	Assembler	6.6.X3	18,280	4 years	13,710		4,570		
Totals			55,330		39,660		15,670		

MOTOR VEHICLES

Ref	Description	Date of purchase	Cost £	Depreciation type	Accumulated depreciation 31.12.X5 £	Date of disposal	Net book value 31.12.X5 £	Sale/scrap proceeds £	(Loss)/ profit £
M111	Van reg G396 HJB	22.2.X2	6,500	Reducing balance 25%	4,444		2,056		
M112	Van reg H842 GSL	17.3.X4	8,500	Reducing balance 25%	3,719		4,781		
M113	Van reg J542 KLH	12.9.X5	10,500	Reducing balance 25%	2,625		7,875		
Totals			25,500		10,788		14,712		

LEASEHOLD PREMISES

Ref	Description	Date of purchase	Cost £	Term of lease	Accumulated amortisation 31.12.X5 £	Date of disposal	Net book value 31.12.X5 £	Disposal proceeds £	(Loss)/ profit £
L110	Leasehold property	1.1.X2	100,000	50 years	8,000		92,000		

TRIAL RUN DEVOLVED ASSESSMENT

Recording Capital Transactions

and

Preparing Financial Accounts

ANSWER BOOKLET

In this answer booklet you should find attached the following documents on which to complete the tasks.

(a) Partially completed fixed asset register as at 31 December 19X6 for updating
(b) Pages of the journal
(c) Extended trial balance proformas
(d) Ledger account proformas relating to fixed assets

FIXED ASSET REGISTER AS AT 31 DECEMBER 19X6

PLANT AND EQUIPMENT									
Ref	Description	Date of purchase	Cost £	Depreciation period	Accumulated depreciation 31.12.X6 £	Date of disposal	Net book value 31.12.X6 £	Sale/scrap proceeds £	(Loss)/ profit £
P111	Cutter	1.3.X2	24,750	5 years					
P112	Moulding machine	2.5.X3	12,300	6 years					
P113	Assembler	6.6.X3	18,280	4 years					
Totals			55,330						

MOTOR VEHICLES									
Ref	Description	Date of purchase	Cost £	Depreciation type	Accumulated depreciation 31.12.X6 £	Date of disposal	Net book value 31.12.X6 £	Sale/scrap proceeds £	(Loss)/ profit £
M111	Van reg F396 HJB	22.2.X2	6,500	Reducing balance 25%					
M112	Van reg H842 GSL	17.3.X4	8,500	Reducing balance 25%					
M113	Van reg J542 KLH	12.9.X5	10,500	Reducing balance 25%					
Totals Disposals									
Totals									

LEASEHOLD PREMISES								
Ref	Description	Date of purchase	Cost £	Term of lease	Accumulated amortisation 31.12.X6 £	Net book value 31.12.X6 £	Disposal proceeds £	(Loss)/ profit £
L110	Leasehold property	1.1.X2	100,000	50 years				

	JOURNAL			Page 20
Date	Details	Folio Ref	£	£

JOURNAL

Date	Details	Folio Ref	£	£

Folio	Account	Trial balance		Adjustments		Accrued	Prepaid	Profit and loss a/c		Balance sheet	
		Debit	Credit	Debit	Credit			Debit	Credit	Debit	Credit
		£	£	£	£	£	£	£	£	£	£
	SUB-TOTAL										
	Profit for the year										
	TOTAL										

LEDGER ACCOUNTS

MOTOR VEHICLES

	£		£
Date *19X6* 1 Jan Balance b/d	25,500		

MOTOR VEHICLES: PROVISION FOR DEPRECIATION

	£		£
		Date *19X6* 1 Jan Balance b/d	10,788

MOTOR VEHICLES: DISPOSALS

	£		£

SOLUTIONS TO TRIAL RUN
DEVOLVED ASSESSMENT

DO NOT TURN THIS PAGE UNTIL YOU HAVE
COMPLETED THE TRIAL RUN DEVOLVED ASSESSMENT

PLANT AND EQUIPMENT

Ref	Description	Date of purchase	Cost £	Depreciation period	Accumulated depreciation 31.12.X6 £	Date of disposal	Net book value 31.12.X6 £	Sale/scrap proceeds £	(Loss)/ profit £
P111	Cutter	1.3.X2	24,750	5 years	24,750		- - - - -		
P112	Moulding machine	2.5.X3	12,300	6 years	8,200		4,100		
P113	Assembler	6.6.X3	18,280	4 years	18,280		- - - - -		
Totals			55,330		51,230		4,100		

MOTOR VEHICLES

Ref	Description	Date of purchase	Cost £	Depreciation type	Accumulated depreciation 31.12.X6 £	Date of disposal	Net book value 31.12.X6 £	Sale/scrap proceeds £	(Loss)/ profit £
M111	Van reg F396 HJB	22.2.X2	6,500	Reducing balance 25%	4,444	3.8.X6	2,056	2,000	56
M112	Van reg H842 GSL	17.3.X4	8,500	Reducing balance 25%	4,914		3,586		
M113	Van reg J542 KLH	12.9.X5	10,500	Reducing balance 25%	4,594		5,906		
M114	Van reg K125 ATE	3.8.X6	12,000	Reducing balance 25%	3,000		9,000		
Totals			37,500		16,952		20,548		
Disposals			6,500		4,444		2,056	2,000	56
Totals c/f			31,000		12,508		18,492		

LEASEHOLD PREMISES

Ref	Description	Date of purchase	Cost £	Term of lease	Accumulated amortisation 31.12.X6 £	Date of disposal	Net book value 31.12.X6 £	Disposal proceeds £	(Loss)/ profit £
L110	Leasehold property	1.1.X2	100,000	50 years	10,000		90,000		

LEDGER ACCOUNTS

MOTOR VEHICLES

Date 19X6		£	Date 19X6		£
1 Jan	Balance b/d	25,500	3 Aug	Motor vehicles: disposals	6,500
3 Aug	Motor vehicles: disposals	2,000	31 Dec	Balance c/d	31,000
3 Aug	Sundry creditors	10,000			
		37,500			37,500

MOTOR VEHICLES: PROVISION FOR DEPRECIATION

Date 19X6		£	Date 19X6		£
3 Aug	Motor vehicles: disposals	4,444	1 Jan	Balance b/d	10,788
31 Dec	Balance c/d	12,508	31 Dec	Motor vehicles: depreciation (W1)	6,164
		16,952			16,952

MOTOR VEHICLES: DISPOSALS

Date 19X6		£	Date 19X6		£
3 Aug	Motor vehicles	6,500	3 Aug	Motor vehicles	2,000
			3 Aug	Provision for depreciation	4,444
			31 Dec	Profit and loss	56
		6,500			6,500

JOURNAL

Page 20

Date	Details	Folio Ref	£	£
3 August	Motor vehicles	M110	12,000	
	Motor vehicles disposals	M150		2,000
	Sundry creditors	L300		10,000
	Being purchase of van K125 ATE by part exchange			
3 August	Motor vehicles disposals	M150	6,500	
	Motor vehicles	M110		6,500
	Being transfer of van F396 HJB at cost to disposals a/c			
3 August	Motor vehicles depreciation provision	M120	4,444	
	Motor vehicles disposals	M150		4,444
	Being transfer of depreciation provision to disposals a/c			
31 December	Profit and loss a/c	P200	56	
	Motor vehicles disposals a/c	M150		56
	Being loss on part exchange of van F396 HJB			
31 December	Motor vehicles depreciation	M130	6,164	
	Motor vehicles depreciation provision	M120		6,164
	Being year end provision for depreciation on motor vehicles (W1)			
31 December	Plant and equipment depreciation	P130	11,570	
	Plant and equipment depreciation provision	P120		11,570
	Being year end provision for depreciation on plant and equipment (W3)			

JOURNAL

Page 21

Date	Details	Folio Ref	£	£
	Leasehold premises amortisation	L130	2,000	
	Leasehold premises accumluated amortisation	L120		2,000
	Being year end amortisation on leasehold premises (W2)			
31 December	Repairs and maintenance	R200	4,770	
	Suspense a/c	S400		4,770
	Being elimination of suspense a/c balance and correct classification of expense			
31 December	Bad debt expense a/c	B200	200	
	Trade debtors	D100		200
	Being bad debt written off			
31 December	Bad debt expense a/c	B200	2,354	
	Bad debt provision	B100		2,354
	Being bad debt provision (W4)			

Folio	Account	Trial balance Debit £	Trial balance Credit £	Adjustments Debit £	Adjustments Credit £	Accrued £	Accrued £	Prepaid £	Prepaid £	Profit and loss a/c Debit £	Profit and loss a/c Credit £	Balance sheet Debit £	Balance sheet Credit £
P110	Plant & equipment: cost	55,330										55,330	
P120	Plant & equipment: dep'n provision		51,230										51,230
P130	Plant & equipment: dep'n expense	11,570								11,570			
M110	Motor vehicles: cost	31,000										31,000	
M120	Motor vehicles: dep'n provision		12,508										12,508
M130	Motor vehicles: dep'n expense	6,164								6,164			
L110	Leasehold premises: cost	100,000										100,000	
L120	Leasehold premises: acc amortisation		10,000										10,000
L130	Leasehold premises: amortisation exp	2,000								2,000			
C300	Sundry creditors		13,500										13,500
F100	Bank	6,132										6,132	
F200	Cash in hand	505										505	
A100	Accountancy fee	600				1,500				2,100			
B100	Bad debts provision		150		2,354								2,504
B200	Bad debt expense			2,554						2,554			
L300	Loan		10,000										10,000
R200	Repairs and maintenance	813		4,770						5,583			
M300	Motor expenses	1,506								1,506			
S100	Sales		205,806								205,806		
D100	Trade debtors	50,287			200							50,087	
P100	Purchases	158,142								158,142			
C100	Trade creditors		65,416										65,416
E100	Electricity	900				200				1,100			
P300	Printing, postage, stationery	3,717								3,717			
P200	Profit and loss account		40,956										40,956
S200	Stock at 1.1.X6	9,125								9,125			
S300	Share capital		100,000										100,000
S400	Suspense account	4,770			4,770								
S500	Sundry expenses	6,428								6,428			
W100	Wages and salaries	60,521						600		59,921			
M400	Loss on sale of van	56								56			
S200P	Stock at 31.12.X6 (P&L)			10,412							10,412		
S200B	Stock at 31.12.X6 (B/S)				10,412							10,412	
	Prepayments/accruals						1,700		600			600	1,700
	SUB-TOTAL	509,566	509,566	17,736	17,736	1,700	1,700	600	600	269,966	216,218	254,066	307,814
	Loss for the year										53,748	53,748	
	TOTAL	509,566	509,566	17,736	17,736	1,700	1,700	600	600	269,966	269,966	307,814	307,814

Workings

1 *Depreciation expense: motor vehicles*

Ref		£
M112	£4,781 × 25%	1,195
M113	£7,875 × 25%	1,969
M114	£12,000 × 25%	3,000
	Total	6,164

2 *Depreciation expense: premises*

$$\frac{£100,000}{50} = £2,000$$

3 *Depreciation expense: plant and equipment*

Ref		£
P111	£24,750 ÷ 5	4,950
P112	£12,300 ÷ 6	2,050
P113	£18,280 ÷ 4	4,570
		11,570

4 *Bad debts provision*

	£
Trade debtors per trial balance	50,287
Less bad debt written off	200
	50,087
Provision required (£50,087 × 5%)	2,504
Provision b/d	150
Increase required	2,354

Total bad debt expense £(200 + 2,354) = £2,554

Central assessments

Central assessments

The following central assessment exercises are designed as practice for the central assessment for Unit 5 *Preparing financial accounts*.

The exercises are grouped according to type. Those which are taken from past AAT assessments are indicated by dates. Solutions to the class exercises are provided in the Lecturers' Pack for Units 4 and 5.

When you have attempted the exercises you should have a go at the Trial Run Central Assessments, consisting of the June 1995, December 1995, June 1996, December 1996 and June 1997 papers.

A   Extended trial balance exercises

	Date set	Question	Solution
A Short	Sample	156	205
Country Crafts	12/93	159	207
Futon Enterprises	6/94	164	210
Kidditoys	12/94	169	212
R Senick	N/A	174	215
Class exercise: Mr Singh	N/A	177	-

B   Incomplete records exercises

	Date set	Question	Solution
Brian Hope	Sample	180	217
Kuldipa Potiwal	12/93	183	218
Fancy Flowers	6/94	184	220
Somaira Rahman	12/94	185	221
Manuel	N/A	186	223
Class exercise: Lostit	N/A	191	-

C   Short answer questions

	Date set	Question	Solution
A Short	Sample	195	227
Country Crafts	12/93	195	228
Futon Enterprises	6/94	196	229
Kidditoys	12/94	197	230
R Senick	N/A	198	231
Class exercise: Mr Singh	N/A	198	-

D   Comprehension and communication

	Date set	Question	Solution
A Short	Sample	200	233
Country Crafts	12/93	200	234
Futon Enterprises	6/94	201	236'
Kidditoys	12/94	201	237
Manuel	N/A	202	239
Class exercise: Lostit	N/A	202	-

A EXTENDED TRIAL BALANCE EXERCISES

A Short (Sample)

The suggested time allocation for this extended trial balance exercise is 1 hour 20 minutes.

In this extended trial balance exercise the tasks are based on the accounts of A Short Ltd, a small electrical wholesaling business which supplies retailers and electrical contractors in South-East London. Adam Short is the Managing Director and the employees include an accounting technician, Pat Jones (your role). Pat handles the bookkeeping and payroll to trial balance, presently using a manual system. The final annual accounts are completed by a firm of accountants.

You have been asked to complete the extended trial balance (ETB) from a list of balances and supplementary data. To condense this assessment question some of the accounts have been grouped together as 'other expenses' and 'other fixed assets'.

Data

(a) The following is a list of balances extracted from the General Ledger at the year end 31 December 1992.

	£
Opening stock	64,900
Wages and salaries	89,400
Rents received	10,700
Printing, stationery and postage	6,000
Vehicle running expenses	8,500
Other expenses	31,200
Purchases	288,200
Sales	468,400
Debtors total account	60,000
Provision for doubtful debts	1,000
Creditors total account	39,400
Petty cash	100
VAT (VAT on sales less input VAT, for last period)	2,000
PAYE/NI balance outstanding	1,000
Vehicles: cost	48,000
Vehicles: accumulated depreciation to 31 December 1991	19,200
Other fixed assets (net book value)	131,800
Share capital	150,000
Profit and loss account balance (credit)	29,400
Bank overdraft	7,600
Suspense a/c	600 (DR)

(b) Two errors have subsequently been discovered.

   (i)   A word-processing printer costing £200 had been debited to the printing, stationery and postage account.

   (ii) £300 paid for renting a copier had been entered correctly in the cash book but had been credited to the rents received account.

(c) The following matters need taking into account.

   (i)   Part of the premises is sub-let at a rent of £800 per month payable in advance. The rent for January 1993 was received in December.

   (ii) The vehicles are depreciated at 20% pa of the original cost. (*Note.* Depreciation of other fixed assets can be ignored.)

   (iii) The closing stock was valued at £62,000.

   (iv) In view of present uncertainties it has been decided to increase the provision for doubtful debts to equal 2½% of the debtors outstanding at the end of the year.

   (v)   Insurance for the vehicles of £800, covering the period October 1992 to September 1993, was paid in September 1992 (vehicle insurance is included with vehicle running expenses).

(vi)   A repair to one of the vehicles was completed in December 1992 but the invoice has not yet been received. It was estimated at £500.

Task 1

Prepare journal entries in the space below to deal with (b)(i) and (ii). (Narratives are not required.) Use the journal form below.

Task 2

Enter the balances in the first two columns of the ETB *after* allowing for the corrections in Task 1, using the blank ETB overleaf.

Task 3

Make appropriate entries in the adjustment columns of the ETB for the matters referred to in (c) adding any additional accounts which may be required. Total these columns.

Task 4

Extend the figures into the ETB columns for profit and loss account and balance sheet. Total all of these columns, transferring the balance of profit or loss as appropriate.

JOURNAL		Page 1
Details	£	£
Other Fixed Assets	200	
Printing, stationery + postage		200
Rents Received	300	
Printing, stationery + postage	300	
Suspense a/c		600

Account	Trial balance Debit £	Trial balance Credit £	Adjustments Debit £	Adjustments Credit £	Profit and loss a/c Debit £	Profit and loss a/c Credit £	Balance sheet Debit £	Balance sheet Credit £
Opening stock	64900				64900			
Wages and salaries	89400				89400			
Rents received		10400	800			9600		
Printing, stationery and postage	6100				6100			
Vehicle running expenses	8500		500	600	8400			
Other expenses	31200				31200			
Purchases	288200				288200			
Sales		468400				468400		
Debtors	60000			500			60000	
Provision for doubtful debts		1000		500				1500
Creditors		39400						39400
Petty cash	100						100	
VAT	2000	2000						2000
PAYE/NI	1000	1000						1000
Vehicles: cost	48000						48000	
Vehicles: acc dep'n		19200		9600				28800
Other fixed assets (net)	132000						132000	
Share capital		150000						150000
Profit and loss account		29400						29400
Bank balance		7600						7600
Prepayment – Bal. Sheet			9600	800	9600			800
Prov for Depn – P+L			62000					
Cl Stock = Bal Sheet – P+L				62000		62000	62000	
Prov D Debts – P+L			500		500			
Prepayment – Bal Sheet			600	500			600	
Accrual – Bal Sheet				500			500	
SUB-TOTAL	728400	728400	74000	74000	498300	540000	302700	261000
Profit for the year					41700			41700
TOTAL	728400	728400	74000	74000	540000	540000	302700	302700

Country Crafts (December 1993)

The suggested time allocation for this extended trial balance exercise is 1 hour 20 minutes.

Country Crafts Ltd is a small business started in 1989. It buys in craft items, for example, pottery, hand-made clothes and wooden toys from a large number of small craft producers, and then sells them to craft shops throughout the country.

The rented premises consist of a warehouse containing racks and bins to hold the craft products along with an adjoining office and garage. The company owns two delivery vans, used for both collections and deliveries, and two company cars.

The company was started by two friends, Sandip Patel and Abdul Mohim, who met on a small business training course in Leicester. Sandip has responsibility for buying and selling and has built up a network of small craftworkers who make stock for him. Abdul is responsible for the running of the warehouse and the office and the administration of the business.

In addition to the two owners, the business employs two drivers, a warehouseman, two accounts clerks and a secretary.

You are the senior of the two accounts clerks and you are responsible for the nominal ledger.

The company's accounts are currently operated using a manual system, but computerisation of the accounts should take place in the near future and some equipment has recently been purchased.

The sales ledger holds at present about 100 accounts; the company has no cash customers.

All purchases of craft products are on credit and the purchase ledger contains about 80 accounts.

There are very few cash transactions. Any that do occur, for example, window cleaning, office sundries and travel expenses, are dealt with by a simple petty cash system. A £50 float is maintained, expenditure is recorded in a simple petty cash book and at irregular intervals the expenditure is posted to the nominal ledger.

Depreciation policy

Rates:			
	Motor vehicles	25% pa	straight line
	Office furniture	10% pa	straight line
	Computer equipment	$33\frac{1}{3}$% pa	straight line

Depreciation is charged a full year in the year of purchase and is not charged for in the year of sale.

Zero scrap values are assumed.

Fixed asset information

Motor vehicles

Delivery vans	H247AFE	K174RFU
Date of purchase	9.8.90	12.8.92
Cost	£16,200	£19,800
Company cars	J168TFE	J169TFE
Date of purchase	11.9.91	11.9.91
Cost	£9,200	£9,200

Office furniture

All office furniture was purchased upon incorporation of the business on 1 September 1989.

Cost	£4,850

Computer equipment

Date of purchase	1 June 1993
Cost	£16,830

Mark-up policy

The company marks up all its products by 100% on cost.

Data

(a)   Listed below is the company's trial balance at 31 December 1993.

COUNTRY CRAFTS LIMITED
TRIAL BALANCE AS AT 31 DECEMBER 1993

	Dr £	Cr £
Motor vans (cost)	36,000	
Motor cars (cost)	18,400	
Office furniture (cost)	4,850	
Computer equipment (cost)	16,830	
Motor vans (provision for dep'n)		17,100
Motor cars (provision for dep'n)		9,200
Office furniture (provision for dep'n)		1,940
Computer equipment (provision for dep'n)		
Stock	24,730	
Debtors control	144,280	
Bank		610
Cash	50	
Creditors control		113,660
Sales		282,490
Purchases	152,140	
Rent	12,480	
Heat and light	1,840	
Wages and salaries	75,400	
Office expenses	7,900	
Motor expenses	14,890	
Depreciation (motor vans)		
Depreciation (office furniture)		
Depreciation (computer equipment)		
Share capital		50,000
Profit and loss		35,850
VAT		12,640
Suspense	13,700	
	523,490	523,490

(b)   Adjustments need to be made for the following.

(i)   On 2 December 1993 a new delivery van, L673NFU, was purchased for £22,600. Van H247AFE was given in part exchange, the balance of £17,600 being paid for by cheque and debited to the suspense account.   *Not yet in accounts*

(ii)   On 4 December 1993, as a cost-saving measure, company car J168TFE was sold for £3,900 and the receipt credited to the suspense account.   *CR Disp a/c*

(iii) On 20 December 1993 the company had allowed a local organisation to use its car park and adjacent field for a Car Boot Sale. For this service the company was paid £250.00. This amount had been credited to the sales account.   *CR Rent Rec*

(c)   The following additional matters need to be taken into account.

(i)   Depreciation for the year ended 31 December 1993 is to be provided for.

(ii)   On 15 December 1993 a rack full of china craft products fell in the warehouse. These products, valued at £2,300 at selling price, were so badly damaged that they had to be thrown away. The Raven Moon Insurance Company have agreed to compensate for the damage except for the first £200. A claim has been submitted, but so far no payment has been received.

(iii) The stocktake on 30 December 1993 revealed stock at cost price of £31,640.

Two batches of stock, however, were of particular note.

(1)   A batch of Baby Beatrice mugs, value at selling price £320, were judged to be saleable for only £120.

(2)   A batch of Windsor Fire Damage plates, value at selling price £620, were judged to be saleable for only £350.

(iv)   Several small customers had been going out of business recently, probably because of the recession. The company's accountant had therefore judged it prudent to create a provision for doubtful debts representing 5% of the trade debtors figure at the year end.

(v)   Petty cash transactions for December were as follows.

December 3	Window cleaning	£10.00
December 8	Tea and coffee	£4.40
December 12	Xmas decorations	£28.60
December 20	Petty cash float replenished	£50.00

These transactions, including the withdrawal from the bank, have not yet been entered into the company's books.

(vi) The electricity bill for the September, October, November quarter for £315 had been received on 16 December and entered into the purchase ledger. It is normal for the electricity bill for the December, January, February quarter to be double that for the previous quarter.

(vii) The rent of £7,488 per annum is paid annually in advance on 1 September.

Task 1

Prepare journal entries for the transactions listed in (b) above. Narratives are required. Use the journal form on Page 162.

Task 2

Enter all the account balances, including those adjusted in Task 1, in the first two columns of the extended trial balance. Use the blank ETB on Page 163.

Task 3

Make appropriate entries in the adjustment columns of the extended trial balance.

Task 4

Extend the figures into the extended trial balance columns for profit and loss account and balance sheet. Total all columns, transferring the balance of profit or loss as appropriate.

Year End Adjustments

1 Depn
Motor Vans 10600
Motor Cars 2300
Comp Equip 5610
Office Furn 485
} Dr P+L, Cr Prov for Dep

2 Cost of damaged stock 1150 - Cr Purchases
Insurance (debtor) 950 - Dr
Loss 200 - Dr P+L

3 Cost NRV
160 120 - reduce stock by 40
310 350 - no adjustment needed
∴ stock = 31600 - Dr Bal Sheet, Cr P+L

4 Prov for D. Debts = 7214 - Dr P+L, Cr Prov for D Debts

5 Petty cash - Dr office expenses, Cr petty cash £43
Dr cash, Cr Bank £43

JOURNAL

Page 20

Details	DR £	CR £
Motor Vehicles	22600	
Motor Vehicles		16200
Prov for Depn	12150	
Suspense a/c		17600
Profit + Loss		950
Being entries necessary for purchase of L 673 NFU		
Suspense a/c	3900	
Vehicles a/c		9200
Prov for Depn	4600	
Loss to P+L	700	
Being sale of J168 TFE		
Sales	250	
Rent Received		250
Being correction of error of entering rent as a sale		

Workings

Cost of Vehicle	16200	
Depn to date	12150	
	4050	
Part Exchange	5000	
Profit on sale	950	
Cost of vehicle	9200	
Depn to date	4600	
	4600	
Receipt	3900	
Loss on sale	700	

6 Dr Electricity   210   Cr Accruals   210

7 Dr Prepayments   4992   Cr Rent   4992

Account	Trial balance		Adjustments		Profit and loss a/c		Balance sheet	
	Debit	Credit	Debit	Credit	Debit	Credit	Debit	Credit
	£	£	£	£	£	£	£	£
Motor vans (cost)								
Motor cars (cost)								
Office furniture (cost)								
Computer equipment (cost)								
Motor vans (prov for depreciation)								
Motor cars (prov for depreciation)								
Office furniture (prov for depreciation)								
Computer equipment (prov for depreciation)								
Stock								
Debtors control								
Bank								
Cash								
Creditors control								
Sales								
Purchases								
Rent								
Heat and light								
Wages and salaries								
Office expenses								
Motor expenses								
Dep'n (motor vans)								
Dep'n (motor cars)								
Dep'n (office furniture)								
Dep'n (computer equipment)								
Share capital								
Profit and loss								
VAT								
SUB-TOTAL								
Profit for the year								
TOTAL								

Futon Enterprises (June 1994)

The suggested time allocation for this extended trial balance exercise is 1 hour 20 minutes.

Jason Sarmiento, trading as Futon Enterprises, is a sole trader assembling and selling futons. A futon is a Japanese-style bed, consisting of a slatted wooden frame and a mattress. Jason buys in the pre-cut timber and the mattresses and assembles the futons for sale through his retail shop in Lincoln and by mail order.

The assembly takes place in a small workshop to the rear of the shop and is carried out by a full-time assembler. The business also employs a driver, a secretary and you, the accounts clerk. Jason spends most of his time in the shop and dealing with the mail order side of the business.

The business accounts are currently operated using a manual system, though Jason is actively engaged in investigating computerised accounting systems.

A very simple sales ledger is operated and the purchase ledger contains about 20 accounts. There are few cash transactions. Any that do occur are handled through a traditional petty cash book. A £50 cash float is maintained and at weekly intervals the expenditure is posted to the nominal ledger and the float replenished.

Accounting policies

1 *Manufacturing*

Purchases of raw materials are posted to a materials account. The assembler's wages are posted to the production wages account. No separate production overheads account is maintained.

It has been agreed that finished goods stocks should be valued at a standard cost of production, calculated as follows per futon.

	£
Materials	36.00
Production wages	7.00
Overheads	5.00
	48.00

2 *Depreciation*

Rates:	Assembling machinery	10% per annum straight line
	Delivery van	30% per annum reducing balance
	Furniture and fittings	20% per annum straight line

Depreciation is charged a full year in the year of purchase and is not charged in the year of sale. Zero scrap values are assumed.

3 *Mark-up*

The company normally marks up all its products at 75% on standard production costs.

Fixed asset information

	Date of purchase	Cost	
		£	£
Assembling machinery	1.6.90		3,650
Delivery van (see note (b)(i) below)	1.8.93		12,400
Furniture and fittings			
Shop fittings	1.6.90	7,200	
Office furniture	1.6.90	2,350	
Reception (materials only)			
(see note (b)(ii) below)	1.9.93	1,240	
			10,790

Data

(a) Listed below is the company's trial balance at 31 May 1994.

FUTON ENTERPRISES
TRIAL BALANCE AS AT 31 MAY 1994

	Dr £	Cr £
Delivery vans (cost)	12,000	
Delivery vans (provision for depreciation)		7,884
Assembling machinery (cost)	3,650	
Assembling machinery (provision for depreciation)		1,095
Furniture and fittings (cost)	10,790	
Furniture and fittings (provision for depreciation)		5,730
Raw materials stock	1,320	
Finished goods stock	1,440	
Sales ledger total	1,860	
Bank		320
Cash	50	
Purchase ledger total		4,265
Sales		120,240
Materials	35,465	
Production wages	12,480	
Driver's wages	11,785	
Salaries	22,460	
Employer's national insurance	4,365	
Motor expenses	2,160	
Rent	3,930	
Sundry expenses	3,480	
VAT		1,220
Inland Revenue		1,365
Drawings	12,400	
Capital		7,516
Suspense	10,000	
	149,635	149,635

(b) Adjustments need to be made for the following.

   (i) A new delivery van was purchased for £12,400 on 1 August 1993. The old delivery van, originally purchased for £12,000 on 1 August 1990, was given in part exchange; the balance of £10,000 was paid for by cheque and debited to Suspense Account.

   (ii) The reception area was re-built in the first week of September 1993. This work was carried out by the assembler as business was rather slack at that time. He spent the whole of the first week in September on this task; his pay is £12,480 per annum.

   (iii) Jason gave two futons as Christmas presents in December 1993. An account was opened in the sales ledger to record these transactions.

(c) The following additional information needs to be taken into account.

   (i) Depreciation for the year ended 31 May 1994 is to be provided for.

   (ii) The stocktake at 31 May 1994 has revealed the following.

   Stock of timber, mattresses and sundry materials = £1,526
   23 fully completed futons were in stock

   There was no work in progress.

   (iii) The electricity bill for £180 covering the February, March, April 1994 quarter had been received on 15 May and entered into the purchase ledger. Electricity usage is relatively even throughout the year. Electricity is included within sundry expenses.

   (iv) On 12 May the delivery van was involved in an accident, suffering minor damage. The repairs, costing £164, have been carried out and the cost included in motor expenses. A letter has been received today from the Mercury Insurance Company agreeing to compensate for all but the first £50 of the repair costs.

   (v) A customer, T Young, who bought two futons at the regular price in July 1993, has disappeared without paying. It has been decided to write off the amount owing.

   (vi) The rent of £3,144 per annum is paid annually in advance on 1 September.

Task 1

Prepare journal entries for the transactions listed in (b) above. Narratives are required. Use the blank journal form on Page 167.

Task 2

Enter all the account balances, including those adjusted in Task 1 above, in the first two columns of the extended trial balance. Use the blank ETB on Page 168.

Task 3

Make appropriate entries in the adjustments columns of the extended trial balance. Create additional accounts as required.

Task 4

Extend the figures into the extended trial balance columns for profit and loss account and balance sheet. Total all columns, transferring the balance of profit or loss as appropriate.

JOURNAL		Page 20
Details	DR £	CR £
Motor Vehicles	12400	
Motor Vehicles		12000
Prov for Depn on vans	7884	
Loss on sale	1716	
suspense a/c		10000
Being entries necessary for sale of delivery van and purchase of new van on 1.8.93		
Furniture & Fittings	240	
Production wages		240
Being entries to correct error of entering improvement to premises as production cost		
Drawings	168	
Sales Ledger		168
Being entries to record giving of two futons as presents		

Account	Trial balance Debit £	Trial balance Credit £	Adjustments Debit £	Adjustments Credit £	Profit and loss a/c Debit £	Profit and loss a/c Credit £	Balance sheet Debit £	Balance sheet Credit £
Delivery vans: cost	12400						12400	
Delivery vans: prov for depreciation		-		3720				3720
Assembling machine: cost	3650						3650	
Assembling machine: prov for depreciation		1095		365				1460
Furniture and fittings: cost	11030						11030	
Furniture and fittings: prov for depreciation		5730		2206				7936
Stock: raw materials	1320				1320			
Stock: finished goods	1440				1440			
Sales ledger total	1692			168			1524	
Bank		320						320
Cash	50						50	
Purchase ledger total		4265						4265
Sales		120240				120240		
Materials	35465				35465			
Production wages	12240				12240			
Driver's wages	11785				11785			
Salaries	22460				22460			
Employer's NI	4365				4365			
Motor expenses	2160			114	2046			
Rent	3930			786	3144			
Sundry expenses	3480		60		3540			
VAT		1220						1220
Inland Revenue		1365						1365
Drawings	12568						12568	
Capital		7516						7516
Depreciation: delivery vans			3720		3720			
Depreciation: assembling machine			365		365			
Depreciation: furniture and fittings			2206		2206			
Accruals				60				60
Prepayments			786				786	
Loss on sale of van P+L	1716				1716			
closing stock P+L				2630		2630		
" Bal sheet			2630				2630	
insurance claim -debtor			114				114	
Bad debt - P+L			168		168			
SUB-TOTAL	141751	141751	10049	10049	105980	122870	44752	27862
Profit for the year					16890			16890
TOTAL					122870	122870	44752	44752

Kidditoys (December 1994)

The suggested time allocation for this extended trial balance exercise is 1 hour 20 minutes.

Kidditoys is a retail shop which specialises in the sale of unusual toys, games and other baby products. The business was started in December 1987 and is owned and run by Sophie Stewart.

About half the sales of the business are cash sales through the shop, the remainder being on mail order. Mail order customers pay cash with order.

Sophie employs one sales assistant and one packing assistant.

Her present manual system of bookkeeping comprises a purchase ledger with approximately 30 active accounts, a nominal ledger and a petty cash book. A petty cash float of £50 is maintained for sundry expenses and is replenished as required. A further cash float of £50 is maintained in the sales till. All cash receipts are banked daily.

You are an accounting technician who is helping Sophie to prepare the business's accounts up to the trial balance stage.

Fixed asset information

	Date of purchase	Cost £	Expected useful economic life (years)	
Motor van	07.08.93	12,640	5	2528
Shop fittings	10.12.87	3,240	10	324
Office equipment	08.04.91	4,250	5	850

All fixed assets are depreciated on a straight line basis using the expected useful economic lives, above, and zero-estimated residual values.

Depreciation is charged a full year in the year of purchase and is not charged for in the year of sale.

Other information

Average mark up is 100%.

The VAT rate is 17.5%.

Data

(a) The following list of balances has been extracted from the nominal ledger at the business's year end, 30 November 1994.

	£
Sales	392,182
Sales returns	1,214
Purchases	208,217
Purchase returns	643
Stock	32,165
Wages	50,000
Rent	27,300
Rates	8,460
Light and heat	2,425
Office expenses	3,162
Selling expenses	14,112
Motor expenses	14,728
Sundry expenses	6,560
Motor vans (cost)	12,640
Motor vans (provision for depreciation) at 1.12.93	2,528
Shop fittings (cost)	3,240
Shop fittings (provision for depreciation) at 1.12.93	1,944
Office equipment (cost)	4,250
Office equipment (provision for depreciation) at 1.12.93	2,550
Cash	100
Bank current account (debit balance)	4,420
Bank investment account	68,340
Interest received	3,280

	£
Purchase ledger total	27,683
Capital	22,145
VAT (credit balance)	6,420
Suspense (see note (b)(ii))	1,958

(b) After extracting the balances listed in (a), the following six errors and omissions were discovered.

    (i)   Credit purchases of £954 had been correctly posted to the purchases account, but had been debited in the supplier's account (T Ditton).

    (ii)   The shop had been entirely re-fitted during the year. The old fittings had been sold off to the local Boy Scouts for £50. This had been debited in the bank account, but had been credited in the suspense account.

        The invoice for the new shop fittings, for £9,620, had been received from Kingston Displays Ltd on 15 November. This invoice had not yet been entered into the accounts. Sophie intended to pay the invoice in January after the Christmas sales period. The new shop fittings are expected to have a useful economic life of 10 years.

    (iii)   Sophie paid herself a 'wage' of £2,000 per calendar month which she debited to wages account.

    (iv)   During the year an invoice for £843 (for zero-rated supplies) had been received from a supplier (E Molesey). When payment was made, Sophie accidentally made out the cheque for £840. Sophie noticed this error and contacted E Molesey who told her to ignore such a small sum of money. No adjustment has yet been made for this discrepancy.

    (v)   During the year Sophie gave away a number of toys from the shop as presents to relatives and friends. She kept a record of these, which came to £640 at selling price, including VAT, but has not so far entered the transactions into the accounts.

    (vi)   The company's current bank account statement arrived on 30 November 1994. This showed interest received for the month of November at £9. This has not yet been entered into the accounts.

(c) The following additional matters need to be taken into account.

    (i)   Depreciation for the year ended 30 November 1994 is to be provided for.   *962*

    (ii)   The stock in the shop at 30 November 1994 was valued at £42,120 at selling price. *21060*

    (iii)   Rent was £2,100 per month payable in advance. The rent for December 1994 had already been paid. *Prepaid 2100*

    (iv)   Business rates are paid half yearly on 1 May and 1 November. The business rates bill for the period 1 April 1994 - 31 March 1995 amounted to £6,240. *2080*

    (v)   The electricity bill for £318 covering the July, August and September quarter had been received on 15 October. This had been entered into the purchase ledger and duly paid. Electricity usage can be considered to be relatively even throughout the year. *Accrual 212*

Task 1

Prepare journal entries for the transactions listed in (b). Narratives are required. Use the journal voucher on the next two pages.

Task 2

Enter all the account balances, including those adjusted in Task 1 above, in the first two columns of the Extended Trial Balance shown on Page 173. Note that some of the balances have already been filled in for you. Create additional accounts as required.

Task 3

Make appropriate entries in the adjustments columns of the Extended Trial Balance. Create additional accounts as required.

Do not extend the figures in the extended trial balance into the profit and loss account and balance sheet columns.

Note. All final workings should be clearly shown in your finished answers.

JOURNAL			Page 20
Details	DR £	CR £	
Suspense a/c T Ditton	1908	1908	✓
Suspense a/c Shop Fittings a/c Prov for Depn Loss on sale Being sale of Fixed Asset	50 1944 1246	3240	✓ ✓ ✓
Shop Fittings a/c Displays Ltd Being Purchase of Fixed Asset	9620	9620	✓ ✓
Drawings Wages Being correction of drawings debited to wages	24000	24000	✓ ✓
E Molesley Discounts Received Being discount received now entered	3	3	
Drawings VAT Sales Being drawings from stock	640	95 545	✓ ✓ ✓
Bank Interest Received Being interest now credited	9	9	✓ ✓

JOURNAL		Page 21
Details	DR £	CR £

Account	Trial balance Debit £	Trial balance Credit £	Adjustments Debit £	Adjustments Credit £	Profit and loss a/c Debit £	Profit and loss a/c Credit £	Balance sheet Debit £	Balance sheet Credit £
Sales		392,727				392,727		
Sales returns	1214				1214			
Purchases	208202				208217			
Purchase returns		643				643		
Stock	32,165				32165			
Wages	26000				26000			
Rent	27,300			2100	25200			
Rates	8,460			2080	6380			
Light and heat	2,425		212		2637			
Office expenses	3,162				3162			
Selling expenses	14,112				14112			
Motor expenses	14,728				14728			
Sundry expenses	6,560				6560			
Motor vans (cost)	12,640						12640	
Motor vans (provision for depreciation)		2528		2528				5056
Shop fittings (cost)	9620						9620	
Shop fittings (provision for depreciation)				962				962
Office equipment (cost)	4,250						4250	
Office equipment (provision for depreciation)		2550		850				3400
Cash	100						100	
Bank current account	4429						4429	
Bank investment account	68340						68340	
Interest received		3789				5285		
Capital		22145						22145
VAT		6515						6515
Purchase ledger Control		39208						39208
Drawings	24640						24640	
Discounts Rec		3				3		
Depn J - P+L			4340		4340			
Closing stock - P+L				21060		21060		
" " B/S			21060				21060	
Prepaid rent			2100				2100	
Prepaid rates			2080				2080	
Accrual				212				212
Loss on sale	1246				1246			
SUB-TOTAL	469,608	469,608	29792	29792	345596	417222	149,259	
Profit for the year					71761			71761
TOTAL					417222		149,259	149,259

R Senick

The suggested time allocation for this extended trial balance exercise is 1 hour 20 minutes.

R Senick is a sole trader making and selling herbal remedies for chemist shops in the Bolton area. You are Tony Quine, the bookkeeper, faced with the task of producing the trial balance at the end of the year to 30 June 1996.

The following balances have been extracted from the ledgers.

	£
Sales	138,078
Purchases	82,350
Carriage	5,144
Drawings	7,800
Rent, rates and insurance	6,622
Postage and stationery	3,001
Advertising	1,330
Salaries and wages	26,420
Bad debt expense	877
Provision for bad debts	130
Debtors	12,120
Creditors	6,471
Cash in hand	177
Cash at bank	1,002
Stock as at 1 July 1995	11,927
Equipment: at cost	58,000
accumulated depreciation	19,000
Capital	53,091

Your enquiries reveal the following additional information which needs to be taken into account.

(a) Of the carriage costs, £2,211 represents carriage inwards on purchases.

(b) Rates are payable 6 months in advance. A payment of £880, made on 30 June 1996, represents rates for July to December 1996.

(c) A rent demand for £210 for the three months ended 30 June 1996 was not received until 1 July 1996.

(d) Equipment is to be depreciated at 15% per annum using the straight line method.

(e) The provision for bad debts is to be increased by £40.

(f) Stock at the close of business was valued at £13,551.

Task 1

Using the journal extract on Page 175 make the adjustment required to correct the error in (a) above.

Task 2

Assuming that the error has been corrected, complete the first two columns of the extended trial balance shown on Page 176.

Task 3

Complete the adjustments, accruals and prepayments columns.

Task 4

Extend the trial balance into the columns for profit and loss account and balance sheet. Total and complete all columns.

JOURNAL		Page 1
Details	£	£

Account	Trial balance		Adjustments		Accrued	Prepaid	Profit and loss a/c		Balance sheet	
	Debit	Credit	Debit	Credit			Debit	Credit	Debit	Credit
	£	£	£	£	£	£	£	£	£	£
Sales										
Purchases										
Carriage										
Drawings										
Rent, rates and insurance										
Postage and stationery										
Advertising										
Salaries an wages										
Bad debt expense										
Provision for bad debts										
Debtors										
Creditors										
Cash in hand										
Cash at bank										
Stock at 1 July 1995										
Equipment (cost)										
Equipment (accumulated depreciation)										
Capital										
SUB-TOTAL										
Profit for the year										
TOTAL										

Class exercise: Mr Singh

The suggested time allocation for this extended trial balance exercise is 1 hour 20 minutes.

Mr Singh owns a small manufacturing business which makes and sells toys in the Bradford area. You are Jenny Russ, responsible for the payroll and producing the trial balance.

At 31 May 1996 the following balances were extracted from the nominal ledger.

	£
Property, at cost	90,000
Equipment, at cost	57,500
Provisions for depreciation (as at 1 June 1995)	
Property	12,500
Equipment	32,500
Stock, as at 1 June 1995	27,400
Purchases	259,600
Sales	405,000
Discounts allowed	3,370
Discounts received	4,420
Wages and salaries	52,360
Bad debts	1,720
Loan interest	1,560
Carriage out	5,310
Other operating expenses	38,800
Trade debtors	46,200
Trade creditors	33,600
Provision for bad debts	280
Cash in hand	151
Bank overdraft	14,500
Drawings	28,930
13% loan	12,000
Capital	98,101

On investigation you discover the following.

(a) Stock as at the close of business was valued at £25,900.

(b) Depreciation for the year ended 31 May 1996 has yet to be provided as follows.

        Property: 1% using the straight line method.
        Equipment: 15% using the straight line method.

(c) Wages and salaries are accrued by £140.

(d) 'Other operating expenses' include certain expenses prepaid by £500. Other expenses included under this heading are accrued by £200.

(e) The provision for bad debts is to be adjusted so that it is 0.5% of trade debtors as at 31 May 1996.

(f) 'Purchases' include goods valued at £1,040 which were withdrawn by Mr Singh for his own personal use.

Task 1

Using the journal extract below, show the journal entry, if any, required to correct the error in part (f) above.

JOURNAL		Page 1
Details	£	£

Task 2

Calculate the adjustments required in respect of:

(a) depreciation;
(b) bad debts.

Task 3

Assuming that the error, if any, in part (f) has been corrected, complete the first two columns of the extended trial balance on Page 179.

Task 4

Complete the adjustments, accruals and prepayment columns.

Task 5

Extend the trial balance into the columns for profit and loss account and balance sheet. Total and complete all columns.

Account	Trial balance		Adjustments		Accrued	Prepaid	Profit and loss a/c		Balance sheet	
	Debit	Credit	Debit	Credit			Debit	Credit	Debit	Credit
	£	£	£	£	£	£	£	£	£	£
Property: cost										
Equipment: cost										
Property: depreciation provision										
Equipment: depreciation provision										
Stock as at 1 June 1995										
Purchases										
Sales										
Discounts allowed										
Discounts received										
Wages and salaries										
Bad debts										
Loan interest										
Carriage out										
Other operating expenses										
Trade debtors										
Trade creditors										
Provision for bad debts										
Cash in hand										
Bank overdraft										
Drawings										
13% loan										
Capital										
SUB-TOTAL										
Profit for the year										
TOTAL										

B INCOMPLETE RECORDS EXERCISES

Brian Hope (Sample)

The suggested time allocation for this incomplete records exercise is 1 hour.

Data

You have been asked to help in preparing the accounts of Brian Hope. Brian started in business in 1991 doing repair and servicing of electrical equipment and he works in a rented workshop. So far he has not kept proper records of his transactions. His accounts to 31 December 1991 were prepared for him on the basis of enquiries and the closing position was then shown as follows.

	£	£
Bank balance	190	
Cash in hand	10	
Van	6,000	
Stock of materials	1,210	
Trade debtors and creditors	1,420	2,220
Vehicle repair bill owing		80
Insurance prepaid	340	
Rent prepaid	400	
Capital		7,270
	9,570	9,570

You have started by summarising the bank statements for the year ended 31 December 1992 as follows.

	£	£
Opening balance		260
Cash paid in		510
Receipts from debtors		21,120
		21,890
Payments to trade creditors (see (g) below)	3,930	
New vehicle (less trade-in)	3,600	
Vehicle running expenses	1,040	
Rent	2,640	
Insurance	960	
Other expenses	1,710	
Hope's drawings	8,000	
		21,880
Closing balance		10

You discover the following information regarding Hope's 1992 transactions in the year to 31 December 1992 and the closing position.

(a) He was paid in cash for some of the work done but cannot trace how much. However, you can find sufficient evidence to show that the debtors outstanding at the end of the year totalled £1,120 though £90 of this is probably irrecoverable. Hope does keep copies of all the invoices to his customers and these total £26,720 but he remembers allowing a customer £300 after a charge was disputed.

(b) Outstanding invoices from trade creditors at the end of the year totalled £2,460. Hope says that he is usually allowed a cash discount by one of the suppliers and the total discount for the year is estimated at £200.

(c) The rent was £200 per month until the end of August but was then increased to £240. Hope usually pays two months together in advance and has already paid (in December) for January and February 1993.

(d) At the end of the year £60 is outstanding for petrol and the insurance has been prepaid by £380.

(e) Hope changed the van at the end of December buying a new one for £8,000 with a trade-in allowance for the old one of £4,400. He thinks he agreed last year to a depreciation charge of 20% per annum on book value (but this would not apply in 1992 to the new vehicle just purchased).

(f) No adequate records of cash transactions have been kept but as indicated above it is known that customers often paid their accounts in cash and that Hope frequently withdrew cash for his own personal use. He estimates that payments for vehicle running costs of £500 have been made from cash and a similar amount for other expenses. There is no closing balance of cash.

(g) At the beginning of the year there were cheques to trade creditors unpresented at the bank totalling £70 and at the end of the year the unpresented cheques to trade creditors totalled £210.

Tasks

From the above information you are asked to draw up ledger accounts for each of the following showing the balances to be carried forward at the end of the year or the amounts to be transferred to the profit and loss account. (Dates need not be shown in the accounts.)

Trade debtors
Trade creditors
Rent
Vehicles
Vehicle running expenses
Insurance
Cash
Drawings

TRADE DEBTORS			

VEHICLE RUNNING EXPENSES			

TRADE CREDITORS			

INSURANCE			

RENT			

CASH			

VEHICLES			

DRAWINGS			

Kuldipa Potiwal (December 1993)

The suggested time allocation for this incomplete records exercise is 1 hour.

A friend of yours from Leicester, Kuldipa Potiwal, runs a small computer games retail and mail order business, but she does not keep proper accounting records. She has now been approached by the Inland Revenue for the details of the profit she has earned for the last year. She has provided you with the following bank account summary for the year ended 31 October 1993.

BANK ACCOUNT SUMMARY

	£
Balance at bank (1 November 1992)	
Bank overdraft	3,250
Receipts	
Cash paid in	56,000
Cheques from debtors	46,000
Investment income	1,500
Rent received	2,500
Payments	
Payments to trade creditors	78,000
Rent and rates	6,400
Postage and packing costs	2,200
Motor expenses	5,050
Administration expenses	4,600

Additional information was provided as follows.

(a) Kuldipa intends to sell all her computer games at cost plus 50%.

(b) Before paying cash receipts into the bank, Kuldipa used some of the cash received to make a number of payments.

Wages of shop assistant and driver	£350 per week	18200
Drawings	£220 per week	11440
Administration expenses	£750 per annum	

All cash is paid into the bank daily.

(c) The investment income was interest on her private investment account.

(d) Other balances were as follows.

	31 October 1992 £	31 October 1993 £
Delivery van (valuation)	17,500	12,500
Stock of games	12,200	13,750
Trade creditors	9,000	13,400
Trade debtors	6,000	7,200
Rates paid in advance	500	200
Rent receivable	-	250
Administration expenses owing	175	215

(e) During the year a vanload of games being delivered to credit customers was stolen. The van was recovered, undamaged, but the games have not been recovered. The insurance company has agreed to pay for 50% of the stolen games, but payment has not yet been received.

Kuldipa Potiwal calculated from the copy delivery notes that the selling price value of the games stolen was £6,000.

(f) At Christmas 1992 Kuldipa Potiwal gave games as presents to her young relatives. The selling price of these games was £480.00.

Task 1

Prepare a detailed calculation of the net profit of the business for the year ended 31 October 1993.

Task 2

Calculate the balance of Kuldipa's capital account at 31 October 1993.

Fancy Flowers (June 1994)

The suggested time allocation for this incomplete records exercise is 1 hour.

You belong to a badminton club at the local leisure centre and always have a drink with one of your friends, Sarah Harvey, in the coffee shop after a game. Sarah is the owner of a small florist's business and has been trading for a year as Fancy Flowers. She has never kept proper books of account and has asked you to calculate her profit for the first year of trading which ended on 31 May 1994.

On 31 May you carried out a stocktake which revealed the following situation.

	Cost £	Mark up %
Pot plants	280	100
Roses	240	75
Tulips	160	75
Sprays	340	100
Plant food	80	50
Vases	520	100

A quarter of the pot plants were rather withered and Sarah thought she would have to throw them away. She thought a further quarter would have to be sold at cost price.

The roses were of a very high quality and Sarah thought she could probably sell them at a mark-up of 100%.

One of the sprays, costing £80, had been prepared for a customer who had never collected. This would have to be thrown away.

A box of ten vases, selling price £6 per vase, was badly damaged and would have to be thrown away.

You also elicit the following information.

(a) All sales of the business are cash sales.

(b) A summary of the bank statements revealed the following.

	£
Cash paid into the bank	31,420
Cheque payments	
To plant and sundries wholesalers	24,180
Rent	5,000
Business rates	420
Advertising	385
Insurance	390
Electricity	780
Sundry expenses	560
Interest charged by bank	84

(c) All the cash paid into the bank resulted from cash sales, except for an initial £5,000 invested by Sarah as start-up capital in the business.

(d) Before paying the cash sales into the bank, Sarah withdrew cash for the following purposes.

	£
Wages for self	14,200
Sundry expenses	345

She also retained £60 change in a cash tin after paying the remaining cash into the bank.

(e) From her file of purchase invoices, Sarah discovered that the following were unpaid.

	£
Purchase of cut flowers for May	850
Purchase of roses (28 May)	345
Electricity (quarter ended 30 April)	360
Advertising charges for May	45

(f) She pays rent of £1,000 per quarter in advance.

(g) She regularly takes home about £10 worth of flowers (at selling price) each week.

Task 1

Prepare a valuation of closing stock.

Task 2

Calculate the profit for the first year of trading for Fancy Flowers.

Task 3

Calculate the balance on capital account for Sarah at the end of the first year of trading.

Task 4

Comment briefly on the situation revealed.

Show all your workings.

Somaira Rahman (December 1994)

On 1 October 1992, a friend of yours, Somaira Rahman, started a small business selling electrical goods through the street markets of South West London and to other businesses. She has now been approached by the Inland Revenue for details of the profit she has earned through the first two years of the business.

Somaira has never kept proper accounting records and has asked you to prepare draft statements of income from the financial information she has available as follows.

Financial information

	1 October 1992 £	30 September 1993 £	30 September 1994 £
Trade debtors		2,100	5,250
Trade creditors		68,600	74,820
Overhead expenses prepaid		640	210
Overhead expenses accrued		760	190
Business premises (cost)		48,000	48,000
Motor van (at valuation)	18,000	15,000	12,000
Stock of goods (cost)	42,000	56,000	63,400
Cash		820	650
Balance at bank	16,000	41,600	29,490
Loan from T R Rahman	60,000	50,000	50,000

4000 int acc

Notes

(a) Somaira started the business on 1 October 1992 with a loan from her uncle. She provided the remainder of the start-up capital from her own resources. He uncle provided the loan free of interest for the first year, but at 8% per annum thereafter. The interest for the second year of the business has still not been paid. Somaira was able to repay £10,000 of this loan on 1 September 1993.

(b) The business premises were bought on 1 June 1993. Somaira paid 50% of the cost from her private bank account, the remainder being provided by a bank mortgage. The interest is paid monthly by direct debit.

(c) On 1 August 1994 Somaira bought a new motor car for private use for £16,400. *Drwgs*

(d) Somaira uses money from sales receipts to finance her shopping bills of £275 per week. *Dwgs*

    All the receipts during the year ended 30 September 1994 were sales receipts, except for £8,220 which represented private investment income.

(e) She analysed the payments from her bank account during the year ended 30 September 1994 as follows.

	£
Payments to trade creditors	138,400
Overhead expenses	7,440
Motor expenses (van)	12,420
Motor expenses (non-business use)	1,640
Mortgage interest payments	2,400
New motor car	16,400

Task 1

Prepare a calculation of the capital account balance at 30 September 1993.

Task 2

Prepare a calculation of the net profit or loss for the year ended 30 September 1993.

Task 3

Prepare a detailed calculation of the net profit or loss of the business for the year ended 30 September 1994.

Task 4

Prepare a calculation of the balance on Somaira's capital account at 30 September 1994.

Note. All final workings should be clearly shown.

Manuel

The suggested time allocation for this incomplete records exercise is 1 hour.

Manuel has been required to write up the June accounts for the bar of a small hotel in Torquay while the usual bookkeeper, Polly is on holiday. He finds bookkeeping very puzzling and has asked for your help. He provides you with the following information relating to transactions for the month.

(a) Bar takings (cash): £200

(b) Bar sales on credit to the Major, a valued customer: £100

(c) Wages (cash) £50

(d) Cash received from the Major for last month's bar bill: £80

(e) Cash banked: £300

(f) Wages (cheque): £40

(g) Bank charges notified by bank: £35

(h) Supplies purchased on credit from Torquay Wines: £500

(i) Payment to Torquay Wines by cheque of £300 less 5% discount for early payment

(j) Wine purchased on credit from Devon Wines, a local firm, on a sale or return basis: £175

(k) £100 worth of wine from Devon Wines sold at mark-up on cost of 20%, on credit to a Mr Twychin

(l) Wines returned to Devon Wines: £75

(m) Opening bank balance: £300, cash in till: £320

Task 1

Enter the above transactions into the following ledger accounts (shown below)

Three column cash book
Sales
Purchases
Major
Wages
Mr Twychin
Bank charges
Devon Wines
Torquay wines

Task 2

Produce a partial trial balance as far as the information allows.

Note. There will be a difference on the trial balance.

DETAIL	DISCOUNT	CASH	BANK	DISCOUNT	CASH	BANK
	£	£	£	£	£	£

CASH BOOK

SALES

PURCHASES

MAJOR

WAGES

MR TWYCHIN

BANK CHARGES

DEVON WINES

TORQUAY WINES			

PARTIAL TRIAL BALANCE AS AT 30 JUNE

	Dr £	Cr £
Bank balance		
Cash in till		
Discounts		
Sales		
Purchases		
Major		
Wages		
Mr Twychin		
Bank charges		
Devon Wines		
Torquay Wines		
Difference		

Class exercise: Lostit

The suggested time allocation for this incomplete records exercise is 1 hour.

Lostit is a baking and confectionery business based in Wigan. The bookkeeper is Miss Lade and you are her assistant, L Pinand. Unfortunately she has lost last year's balance sheet. She knows that it is possible to reconstruct the figures with the help of this year's trial balance and information relating to the year's transactions.

She has presented you with the following information.

TRIAL BALANCE 31 DECEMBER 1995

	£'000	£'000
Bank	106	
Capital		600
Land and buildings	640	
Plant and machinery: cost	400	
depreciation		160
Closing stock	200	
Sales		2,000
Cost of sales	1,200	
Operating expenses (including depreciation of 40)	280	
Bad debt written off	4	
Debtors	200	
Accruals		10
Creditors		260
	3,030	3,030

	£'000
Cash receipts (year to 31 December 1995)	
Sales	1,900
Cash payments (year to 31 December 1995)	
Purchases	1,120
Plant (1 January 1995)	180
Operating items	260
Drawings	40

The creditors figure has doubled since 1 January 1995.

Task 1

Calculate the opening balances (as at 1 January 1995) by completing the following ledger accounts.

Plant and machinery: cost
Plant and machinery: depreciation provision
Creditors
Cost of sales
Debtors
Bank
Operating expenses accrual
Capital

Task 2

Produce a summarised balance sheet using the proforma provided.

(a)

PLANT AND MACHINERY: COST			
	£'000		£'000

PLANT AND MACHINERY: DEPRECIATION PROVISION			
	£'000		£'000

CREDITORS			
	£'000		£'000

COST OF SALES			
	£'000		£'000

DEBTORS			
	£'000		£'000

BANK			
	£'000		£'000

OPERATING EXPENSES ACCRUAL			
	£'000		£'000

CAPITAL			
	£'000		£'000

(b) LOSTIT
BALANCE SHEET AS AT 1 JANUARY 1995

	£'000	£'000
Fixed assets		
Land and buildings		
Plant and machinery: cost		
depreciation	_____	
		_____
Current assets		
Stock		
Debtors	_____	
	_____	
Current liabilities		
Bank overdraft		
Creditors		
Operating expenses accrual	_____	
	_____	
Net current assets/liabilities		_____
Net assets		=====
Capital		=====

C   SHORT ANSWER QUESTIONS

A Short (Sample)

The following short answer questions are mainly based on the scenario outlined in A Short. You may have to refer back to the information in this exercise in order to answer the questions.

Your answers should be complete but as concise as possible.

The suggested time allocation for this set of short answer questions is 40 minutes.

1   In the extended trial balance exercise a word-processing printer costing £200 was debited in error to the printing, stationery and postage account.

If a set of filing trays costing £20 had been debited to the printing, stationery and postage account, would this have necessitated an adjustment similar to the one for the printer? If not, why not?

2   If the errors in part (b) of the exercise had not been made, but a credit note for £80 sent to a customer had been posted only to the appropriate personal account and control account, what then would have been the balance on the suspense account? State debit or credit and give the amount.

3   One particular stock item had been invoiced at £800, less 25% trade discount. When settlement was made, a further £30 was deducted for cash discount. Delivery had to be arranged by A Short Ltd and this cost £40. At what amount should this have been included in the end of year stock valuation?

4   Another stock item cost £1,200 several months ago with the expectation that it could be sold for £1,600. At 31 December there was little prospect of sale unless (a) a modification costing a further £300 was made and (b) the selling price was reduced to £1,300. At what amount should this then have been included in the accounts?

5   As regards the whole stock at 31 December, shown at £62,000, the potential selling price was estimated at £98,000. Why would it have been incorrect to include this figure for closing stock in the final accounts?

6   Why was it correct to include the estimated £500 for vehicle repairs in the 1992 accounts, even though the invoice had not yet been received?

7   Included in 'other fixed assets' is some packaging equipment. Apart from usage in the normal course of trade, other factors could cause this equipment to lose value as a business asset. Outline one such factor.

8   At what net book value will the vehicles be shown in the balance sheet at 31 December 1992? Does this represent an estimate of what the vehicles could be sold for at that date? If not, explain what it does represent.

9   Assume that one of the vehicles cost £10,000 in January 1990 and was sold for £5,400 in December 1991. Would the total charge against profits for that vehicle over the two years (including any profit or loss on the sale) be any different if the company had chosen to depreciate vehicles at 30% per annum using the reducing balance method instead of charging depreciation at 20% of cost on the straight line method? Say whether the total charge would have been higher, lower or no different and briefly explain.

10   At what amount will the debtors be shown in the balance sheet at 31 December 1992? Briefly explain to someone who is not an accountant what this asset is, and how it has been valued.

Country Crafts (December 1993)

The following short answer questions are mainly based on the scenario outlined in the extended trial balance exercise Country Crafts. You may have to refer back to the information in this exercise in order to answer the questions. Your answers should be complete but as concise as possible.

The suggested time allocation for this set of short answer questions is 40 minutes.

1   The company had bought a small item of computer software, cost £32.50 earlier in the year. This had been treated as office equipment. Do you agree with this treatment? Give brief reasons.

2 If the company had depreciated its motor vehicles at 50% per annum on a reducing balance basis, what would have been the profit or loss on the company car sold on 4 December 1993?

3 If the organisation which had rented the car park and field for the car boot sale had rented the field for a similar event in January 1994 and had paid £250 in advance, how would that transaction be treated in the 1993 accounts? Briefly explain the effect in the 1994 accounts.

4 (a) In manual accounts transposition errors can occur, for example, a credit purchase entered in the purchases a/c as £1,234, but entered in the supplier's account as £1,423. Can such errors occur in computerised accounting systems? Give reasons.

   (b) In manual accounts, errors of principle can occur. For example, the purchase of a piece of office machinery might be posted to the office expenses a/c. Can such errors occur in computerised accounting systems? Give reasons.

5 You have heard a rumour that one of your customers, who owes you £1,640 is about to go out of business. Should this debt be treated as a bad debt, a doubtful debt or should the rumour be ignored? Give reasons.

6 Explain fully what the balance on VAT account represents.

7 If one of the company's vans had to have its engine replaced at a cost of £1,800, would this represent capital or revenue expenditure? Give brief reasons.

8 If the company decided it needed a china coffee set to use to entertain potential customers, and it took a suitable one from the stock in the warehouse, how would you record this in the books of the company?

Futon Enterprises (June 1994)

The following short answer questions are mainly based on the scenario outlined in the extended trial balance exercise Futon Enterprises. You may have to refer back to the information in this exercise in order to answer the questions.

Your answers should be complete but as concise as possible.

The suggested time allocation for this set of short answer questions is 40 minutes.

1 Assume that two of the futons had been used as a shop window display and had faded somewhat. If it had been decided that the mattress required replacing at a cost of £18 each to make the futons saleable at a price of £50 each, how would this have affected the closing stock valuation?

Give reasons for your answer.

2 What is the net book value of the assembling machinery at 31 May 1994? Is this the amount it is estimated would be realised if the machinery were disposed of at that date?

Briefly justify your answer.

3 Give one reason why the company might have chosen reducing balance as the method for depreciating its delivery vans.

4 If the customer, T Young, whose amount owing in (c)(v) had been written off, subsequently paid later this year, how would you account for the payment?

5 Explain what the balance on Inland Revenue Account represents.

6 If the delivery van was refitted with wooden racks by the assembler in half an hour's spare time and using materials at a cost price of £24, would this be treated as capital or revenue expenditure?

Give reasons.

7 An acquaintance wishes to use the shop to display and sell framed photographs. She will pay £40 per month for this service.

   (a) How would you account for this transaction each month?

   (b) If, at the end of the year, the acquaintance owed one month's rental, how would this be treated in the accounts?

8   The business maintains a traditional petty cash book. At the end of each week, the petty cash book is balanced, the totals of the analysis columns posted to the relevant accounts and the float of £50 replenished.

   (a)   Into which account would the total of the VAT analysis column be posted and would this be a debit or credit entry?

   (b)   What would the total of the VAT column represent?

   (c)   If the petty cash expenditure in one week had been £37, what would be the double entry to replenish the float?

Kidditoys (December 1994)

The following short answer questions are mainly based on the scenario outlined in the extended trial balance exercise Kidditoys. You may have to refer back to the information in this exercise in order to answer this question.

Your answers should be complete but as concise as possible.

The suggested time allocation for this set of short answer questions is 40 minutes.

1   Give a reason why Sophie Stewart does not have any bad debts.

2   Explain in detail what the balance on her VAT a/c represents.

3   When cash sales are banked, which accounts would be debited and credited?

4   What is the net book value of the delivery van at 30 November 1994? What does this amount represent?

5   Assume that some of the shop's window display stock, comprising four dolls, had deteriorated. In their damaged state the dolls could be sold for only £5 each. Their original sales price was £16 each.

   (a)   How would this have affected the closing stock valuation at 30 November 1994?
   (b)   What would have been the effect on the company's profit?

6   Occasionally Kidditoys has to pay a special delivery charge on deliveries of toys it urgently requires. How should this delivery charge be dealt with in the accounts?

7   Sophie is considering sending a quantity of goods to John King on a sale or return basis. How should the transaction be dealt with when the goods are first delivered to John King?

   Give reasons for your answer.

8   The company is considering buying some new software for the office word processor at a cost of £85. It is expected to be in use for five years. How would you deal with this transaction in the accounts?

   Give detailed reasons for your answer.

9   If, in preparing the extended trial balance for Kidditoys, the business was found to be making a loss:

   (a)   would the loss appear in the debit or credit column of the profit and loss account balances;

   (b)   how would the loss be dealt with in the balance sheet balances columns?

10   Using your figures from the extended trial balance in Part 1, complete the profit and loss a/c and balance sheet balances columns for stock, below.

Profit and Loss A/c		*Balance Sheet Balances*	
Dr	*Cr*	*Dr*	*Cr*

R Senick

The following short answer questions are mainly based on the scenario outlined in the extended trial balance exercise R Senick. You may have to refer back to the information in this exercise in order to answer the questions.

Your answers should be complete but as concise as possible.

The suggested time allocation for this set of short answer questions is 40 minutes.

1   In the extended trial balance exercise, part of the 'carriage' costs in the profit and loss account was carriage inwards on purchases.

     Explain the treatment of carriage inward costs.

2   In the extended trial balance exercise you were asked to produce an extended trial balance. What is the point of doing this?

3   You used the journal to correct an error. Can you think of any other uses of the journal?

4   In September 1996 (in the next accounting period) R Senick returned some faulty goods. What would be the entries required to account for the goods returned?

5   What is the difference between the 'provision for bad debts' and the 'bad debt expense account'.

6   Tony Quine, the bookkeeper, produces a trial balance at the end of every month. If there is a difference on the trial balance he opens up a suspense account.

     Briefly explain what a suspense account is for.

7   During August 1996, £500 was received in settlement of a debt. This was correctly entered into the cash book, but was debited to the debtors account.

     What, if any, would be the balance on the suspense account? State the amount and whether debit or credit.

8   During September 1996 a payment of £200 for insurance was made. The cash book entry was correct but the amount was debited to 'carriage'.

     What, if any, would be the balance on the suspense account?

9   R Senick has sometimes been unable to sell all his stock because it was damaged. Give another possible reason why he might not be able to sell all his stock.

10   What accounting adjustments, if any, should be made in the case of 9 above?

Class exercise: Mr Singh

The following short answer questions are mainly based on the scenario outlined in the extended trial balance exercise Mr Singh. You may have to refer back to the information in this exercise in order to answer the questions.

Your answers should be complete but as concise as possible.

The suggested time allocation for this set of short answer questions is 40 minutes.

1   The property, recorded at £90,000 in the accounts, is now worth £120,000. Should it still be depreciated?

2   A customer whose debt had been provided for has gone bankrupt. What is the correct double entry to record this?

3   The following information is available in respect of two product lines.

	Direct costs of material and labour £	Production overheads incurred £	Expected selling price £
Product 1	2,470	2,100	5,800
Product 2	9,360	2,730	12,040

     At what amount should Product 1 be stated in the company's balance sheet?

4   At what amount should Product 2 be stated?

5   One debtor has a credit balance on his account. How might this have arisen?

6   What are the four fundamental accounting concepts identified in SSAP 2?

7   There is a figure in Mr Singh's profit and loss account for discounts received. Do you think that these will be trade discounts, settlement discounts or a mixture of both?

8   What is the correct accounting treatment for:

   (a)   trade discounts;
   (b)   settlement discounts?

9   A cheque was received for £285 from a customer, in settlement of his account of £300 from which a cash discount of £15 had been deducted. You have banked it and made all the correct entries in your books. The cheque was then returned to you by the bank marked 'refer to drawer'. Which entries would you now make in your books?

10 If an accrual is mistakenly treated as a prepayment, what is the effect on profit?

D COMPREHENSION AND COMMUNICATION

A Short (Sample)

The suggested time allocation for this exercise is 40 minutes.

The following comprehension and communication exercise is based on the scenario given in the extended trial balance exercise A Short. You are Pat Jones, the bookkeeper. Adam Short, the Managing Director has asked your advice on three matters.

Tasks

Write responses in the form of memos to each of the following questions raised by Adam Short.

(a) *Depreciation of the vehicles*

I know we have been charging depreciation on the vehicles to write them off over five years, but, in view of the fact that we have probably made a reasonable profit for 1992, and that next year might be much more difficult, I suggest that we increase the charge for 1992 to 30%. I understand that prudence is an important aspect of accounting and I guess we should be even more prudent if we did what I suggest.

(b) *Accounting standards*

I was at a Chamber of Commerce dinner last night and one of the speakers was talking about 'accounting standards'. I am unclear what these are and whether they would apply to a small business like ours anyway. Can you give me a brief idea of the main purpose of these standards? Perhaps you can also give me one example of how our accounts can be affected.

(c) *Historical cost*

I notice that each year the accountant states in the official accounts that they have been prepared on 'the historical cost basis'. What does this mean? Again, it would be helpful to have an example of how it applies to us.

Country Crafts (December 1993)

The suggested time allocation for this exercise is 40 minutes.

The following comprehension and communication exercise is based on the scenario given in the extended trial balance exercise Country Crafts. You are the senior accounts clerk.

(a) You have received the following memorandum from one of the two junior accounts clerks, James McBride.

'As you know, I am studying for my AAT qualifications at Uppingham College. Most of the work so far has been straightforward, but there are two areas where I am a little uncertain. I understand that accounting concepts are basic principles laid down in SSAP 2 and the Companies Act 1985 governing the preparation of company accounts. However, we don't always appear to adhere to these concepts. For example, I always understood that we should be objective and give the most accurate value possible to our stocks, but we know that the value of some of our stocks has risen - recent purchases of some items cost more than earlier purchases - but we must still value the stock we purchased earlier at the original cost price. On the other hand, if the value of any item falls to less than we could sell it for, as with some of our recent Royal Family souvenirs, we have to write off the loss in value of the stock even before it is sold. This also seems to go against the concept of consistency. Can you explain please?'

(b) You have received the following memorandum from the other junior accounts clerk, Sylvia Smith.

'As you know, before I joined this company I worked for a business which operated a computerised accounting system. In such systems the suspense account is used by the computer to post transactions, the nominal code for which it does not recognise. On a manual system the correct nominal ledger account should always be known; therefore, what is the purpose of the suspense account?'

(c) You have received the following memorandum from Abdul Mohim.

'I am concerned about the amount of information our accounting system gives us about our business. It shows the profit we make for our total business, but does not compare the relative profitability of the different areas of our business. I think we could divide our stock into four main categories: china, giftware, paperware and toys. It would be very informative, then, to know how profitable each line of business is. Can you let me know as soon as possible how we might go about changing our accounting system to provide us with such information?'

Task

Write memoranda in reply to the above three queries.

Futon Enterprises (June 1994)

The suggested time allocation for this exercise is 40 minutes.

The following comprehension and communication exercise is based on the scenario given in the extended trial balance exercise Futon Enterprises.

Task 1

Jason Sarmiento has been talking to two of his friends who run a mail order computer software company. Because of the recession the friends are worried about bad debts and have decided to create a provision for doubtful debts. One friend suggests a provision of 5% of the total debtors' year end balances, the other suggests a provision representing all of those debtors more than four months overdue. Jason is unclear about the difference between a bad debt and a doubtful debt and what a provision is. He also wonders whether Futon Enterprises should create a provision for doubtful debts.

Write a memorandum explaining the terms bad debt, doubtful debt and provision and recommending whether Futon Enterprises should or should not create a provision for doubtful debts.

Task 2

You were present at a meeting with Jason last week over the possible diversification of the business into the assembly and sale of sofabeds. With two distinct products Jason would be keen to access the profitability of both futons and sofabeds. He has asked you to prepare an explanation as to how the company's accounting system will have to be amended to provide this additional analysis.

Use a memorandum to explain how the company's accounting system will have to be amended.

Task 3

Jason believes that the complication of the accounting system to incorporate the additional profit analysis will result in more work for you, the accounts clerk. To help you take on this additional workload he has suggested that the accounting system be changed to a cash accounting basis. This would entail recording sales only when the customer pays and recording purchases and expenses only when payments are made. Jason also believes that depreciation can be eliminated with the cost of the asset being charged in full upon purchase.

Write a memorandum in reply to Jason's suggestions.

Kidditoys (December 1994)

The suggested time allocation for this exercise is 40 minutes.

The following comprehension and communication exercise is based on the scenario given in the extended trial balance exercise Kidditoys.

As you are a friend who is also an accounting technician, Sophie has consulted you about two aspects of her accounting system.

Task 1

Mail order customers send cash with order, and so far Sophie has always been able to fulfil the order immediately. However, she is considering branching out into some new product lines which will involve purchasing her stock from a number of different suppliers. She is a little worried, therefore, about always being able to guarantee a supply of stock for her mail order customers. She is particularly concerned about how to deal with the following two possible scenarios.

(a)   Stock will not be available for a month
(b)   Goods ordered by a customer are no longer available

Write a note, *not* a memorandum, to Sophie explaining how to deal with these two situations.

Task 2

Sophie would like to value her stock at selling price in her annual accounts to give her a better idea of the profit it is likely to generate. For example:

(a)   when the sales value of stock rises, for example, when a particular product becomes popular or when the manufacturer increases the price, Sophie would like to value the stock (both that already in stock and that which she purchases in the future) at the new selling price;

(b)   when the sales value of stock falls because it is out-of-date or slightly shop-soiled, Sophie would like to reduce the value of her stock.

Explain in a note how Sophie should deal with the valuation of her stock. Your note should refer to relevant accounting standards and concepts.

Manuel

The suggested time allocation for this exercise is 40 minutes.

The following comprehension and communication exercise is based on the scenario given in the incomplete records exercise Manuel. You are Polly, the bookkeeper. Manuel has asked you the following questions relating to accounting matters.

(a)   'Bookkeeping is very difficult to understand. I've heard there are computerised bookkeeping packages. If we bought one of those, nobody would have to learn it because the computer would do it all for you.'

(b)   'Mr Fawlty, the boss, said he was going to get Jones the builders in to extend the dining room. Perhaps we should use the depreciation provision; we have saved up plenty of money in that.'

(c)   'Why are profits and liabilities both on the same side of the balance sheet? Surely profits are a good thing, whereas liabilities are a bad thing?'

Task

Write memos to Manuel in response to each of these queries.

Class exercise: Lostit

The suggested time allocation for this exercise is 40 minutes.

The following comprehension and communication exercise is based on the scenario given in the incomplete records exercise Lostit. You are L Pinand the bookkeeper's assistant. Your friend Dunn O'Much who has recently started training as an accountant is puzzled by some of the terminology. He has written to you for an explanation.

Task

Write a reply to Dunn O'Much answering the following three queries.

(a)   What is a balance sheet and why does it balance?

(b)   Some accounting systems have a purchase ledger control account and a purchase ledger. Why do you need both? Aren't they really the same thing?

(c)   A lot of firms seem to have the word 'limited' after their name. What does this mean?

Solutions
to
central
assessments

A   SOLUTIONS TO EXTENDED TRIAL BALANCE EXERCISES

A Short

Task 1

JOURNAL		Page 1
Details	£	£
Other fixed assets	200	
Printing, stationery and postage		200
Printing, stationery and postage	300	
Rent received	300	
Suspense a/c		600

Tasks 2, 3 and 4 are dealt with in the extended trial balance overleaf.

Account	Trial balance Debit £	Trial balance Credit £	Adjustments Debit £	Adjustments Credit £	Profit and loss a/c Debit £	Profit and loss a/c Credit £	Balance sheet Debit £	Balance sheet Credit £
Opening stock	64,900				64,900			
Wages and salaries	89,400				89,400			
Rents received		10,400	800			9,600		
Printing, stationery and postage	6,100				6,100			
Vehicle running expenses	8,500		500	600	8,400			
Other expenses	31,200				31,200			
Purchases	288,200				288,200			
Sales		468,400				468,400		
Debtors	60,000						60,000	
Provision for doubtful debts		1,000		500				1,500
Creditors		39,400						39,400
Petty cash	100						100	
VAT		2,000						2,000
PAYE/NI		1,000						1,000
Vehicles: cost	48,000						48,000	
Vehicles: acc dep'n		19,200		9,600				28,800
Other fixed assets (net)	132,000						132,000	
Share capital		150,000						150,000
Profit and loss account		29,400						29,400
Bank balance		7,600						7,600
Depreciation expense			9,600		9,600			
Bad debt expense			500		500			
Closing stock (B/S)			62,000				62,000	
Closing stock (P&L)				62,000		62,000		
Prepayments			600				600	
Accruals				1,300				1,300
SUB-TOTAL	728,400	728,400	74,000	74,000	498,300	540,000	302,700	261,000
Profit for the year					41,700			41,700
TOTAL	728,400	728,400	74,000	74,000	540,000	540,000	302,700	302,700

Country Crafts

Task 1

JOURNAL		Page 20
Details	**DR £**	**CR £**
Motor vans (cost) a/c	22,600	
Motor vans (cost) a/c		16,200
Motor vans (provision for dep'n) a/c	12,150	
(£16,200 × 25% × 3)		
Suspense a/c		17,600
Profit on sale of fixed asset a/c		950
Being purchase of van L 673 NFU, transfer of provision for dep'n and sale of van H 247 AFE in part exchange		
Suspense a/c	3,900	
Motor cars (cost) a/c		9,200
Motor cars (provision for dep'n) a/c	4,600	
(£9,200 × 25% × 2)		
Profit on sale of fixed asset a/c	700	
Being disposal of motor car J 168 TFE at a loss		
Sales	250	
Sundry income		250
Being transfer of sundry income into correct account		

Solutions to Tasks 2 to 4 are shown on the extended trial balance overleaf.

Account	Trial balance Debit £	Trial balance Credit £	Adjustments Debit £	Adjustments Credit £	Profit and loss Debit £	Profit and loss Credit £	Balance sheet Debit £	Balance sheet Credit £
Motor vans (cost)	42,400						42,400	
Motor cars (cost)	9,200						9,200	
Office furniture (cost)	4,850						4,850	
Computer equipment (cost)	16,830						16,830	
Motor vans (prov for depreciation)		4,950		10,600				15,550
Motor cars (prov for depreciation)		4,600		2,300				6,900
Office furniture (prov for depreciation)		1,940		485				2,425
Computer equipment (prov for depreciation)				5,610				5,610
Stock (opening)	24,730				24,730			
Debtors control	144,280						144,280	
Bank		610	43					653
Cash	50		43				50	
Creditors control		113,660						113,660
Sales		282,240				282,240		
Purchases	152,140			1,150	150,990			
Rent	12,480			4,992	7,488			
Heat and light	1,840		210		2,050			
Wages and salaries	75,400				75,400			
Office expenses	7,900		43		7,943			
Motor expenses	14,890				14,890			
Dep'n (motor vans)			10,600		10,600			
Dep'n (motor cars)			2,300		2,300			
Dep'n (office furniture)			485		485			
Dep'n (computer equipment)			5,610		5,610			
Share capital		50,000						50,000
Profit and loss		35,850						35,850
VAT		12,640						12,640
Stock: closing (P&L)				31,600		31,600		
Stock: closing (B/S)			31,600				31,600	
Profit on sale of fixed asset		250				250		
Sundry income		250				250		
Insurance claim			950				950	
Stock loss			200		200			
Bad debt expense			7,214		7,214			
Provision for doubtful debts				7,214				7,214
Prepayments			4,992				4,992	
Accruals				210				210
SUB-TOTAL	506,990	506,990	64,247	64,247	309,900	314,340	255,152	250,712
Profit for the year					4,440			4,440
TOTAL	506,990	506,990	64,247	64,247	314,340	314,340	255,152	255,152

Workings

1 *Profit on sale of fixed asset account*

	£
Profit on van	950
Loss on car	700
Net profit	250

2 *Insurance claim*

Cost of damaged stock (mark-up 100%) = 50% × £2,300
= £1,150 (a credit to the purchases account)
Less £200 excess = £950

Note. £200 is a 'stock loss' not covered by insurance.

3 *Stock write-off*

Baby Beatrice mugs: Cost 320/2 = £160
                                  NRV = £120

NRV below cost ∴ write-off necessary

Windsor fire damage plate: Cost 620/2 = £310
                                  NRV = £350

∴ No write-off necessary, NRV above cost

Closing stock ∴ £31,640 – £(160 – 120) = £31,600.

4 *Bad debt expense/provision*

Provision required: 5% × £144,280 = £7,214

5 *Prepayments and accruals*

Rent: prepayment = 8/12 × £7,488 = £4,992

Electricity: bill for 3 months to February 1994 = 2 × £315 = £630
∴ Accrual for December = 1/3 × £630 = £210

Futon Enterprises

Details	DR £	CR £
JOURNAL		**Page 20**
(i) Delivery vans: cost	10,000	
Suspense account		10,000
Delivery vans: cost (£12,400 - £10,000)	2,400	
Van disposal account		2,400
Being correct treatment of cost of new van, clearing suspense account		
Van disposal	12,000	
Delivery van (cost)		12,000
Delivery van (provision for dep'n)	7,884	
Van disposal		7,884
Loss on sale of van	1,716*	
Van disposal		1,716
Being disposal of old van (in part exchange)		
(ii) Fixtures and fittings: cost	240	
Production wages		240
Being cost of rebuilding reception area in production wages (£12,480 ÷ 52 = £240)		
(iii) Drawings	168	
Sales ledger balances		168
Being correct treatment of two futons given as presents (£48.00 × 2 × 175%)		

	£
* Cost of van	12,000
Acc dep'n	7,884
NBV	4,116
Proceeds £(12,400 –10,000)	2,400
Loss on disposal	1,716

Account	Trial balance Debit £	Trial balance Credit £	Adjustments Debit £	Adjustments Credit £	Profit and loss Debit £	Profit and loss Credit £	Balance sheet Debit £	Balance sheet Credit £
Delivery vans: cost	12,400						12,400	
Delivery vans: prov for depreciation				3,720				3,720
Assembling machine: cost	3,650						3,650	
Assembling machine: prov for depreciation		1,095		365				1,460
Furniture and fittings: cost	11,030						11,030	
Furniture and fittings: prov for depreciation		5,730		2,206				7,936
Stock: raw materials	1,320				1,320			
Stock: finished goods	1,440				1,440			
Sales ledger total	1,692			168			1,524	
Bank		320						320
Cash	50						50	
Purchase ledger total		4,265						4,265
Sales		120,240				120,240		
Materials	35,465				35,465			
Production wages (£12840 - £240)	12,240				12,240			
Driver's wages	11,785				11,785			
Salaries	22,460				22,460			
Employer's NI	4,365				4,365			
Motor expenses	2,160			114	2,046			
Rent	3,930			786	3,144			
Sundry expenses	3,480		60		3,540			
VAT		1,220						1,220
Inland Revenue		1,365						1,365
Drawings (£12,400 + £168)	12,568						12,568	
Capital		7,516						7,516
Depreciation: delivery vans			3,720		3,720			
Depreciation: assembling machine			365		365			
Depreciation: furniture and fittings			2,206		2,206			
Accruals (£180 x 1/3)				60				60
Prepayments (£3,144 x 3/12)			786				786	
Loss on sale of van	1,716				1,716			
Closing stock (B/S): raw materials			1,526				1,526	
Closing stock (B/S): finished goods (£48 x 23)			1,104				1,104	
Closing stock (P&L): raw materials				1,526		1,526		
Closing stock (P&L): finished goods (£48 x 23)				1,104		1,104		
Insurance claim: debtor			114				114	
Bad debts (48 x 1.75 x 2)			168		168			
SUB-TOTAL	141,751	141,751	10,049	10,049	105,980	122,870	44,752	27,862
Profit for the year					16,890			16,890
TOTAL	141,751	141,751	10,049	10,049	122,870	122,870	44,752	44,752

Kidditoys

<table>
<tr><th colspan="2">JOURNAL</th><th>DR
£</th><th>CR
£</th></tr>
<tr><td colspan="2">Details</td><td></td><td></td></tr>
<tr><td>(i)</td><td>DEBIT Suspense a/c
CREDIT T. Ditton a/c (Purchase ledger)
Being correction of misposting</td><td>1,908</td><td>
1,908</td></tr>
<tr><td>(ii)</td><td>DEBIT Suspense a/c
DEBIT Provision for depreciation a/c (shop fittings)
(W1)
DEBIT Loss on sale of fixed assets a/c
CREDIT Shop fittings (cost a/c)
Being disposal of shop fittings</td><td>50
1,944

1,246</td><td>

3,240</td></tr>
<tr><td></td><td>DEBIT Shop fittings (cost) a/c
CREDIT Kingston Displays Ltd (Purchase ledger)
Being purchase of new shop fittings</td><td>9,620</td><td>
9,620</td></tr>
<tr><td>(iii)</td><td>DEBIT Drawings a/c (12 × £2,000)
CREDIT Wages a/c
Being correction of misposting</td><td>24,000</td><td>
24,000</td></tr>
<tr><td>(iv)</td><td>DEBIT E. Molesey a/c (Purchase ledger)
CREDIT Discount received a/c
Being discount received from E. Molesey after
accidental underpayment</td><td>3</td><td>
3</td></tr>
<tr><td>(v)</td><td>DEBIT Drawings a/c
CREDIT Sales a/c
CREDIT VAT a/c
Being stock withdrawn for own use</td><td>640</td><td>
545
95</td></tr>
<tr><td>(vi)</td><td>DEBIT Bank current a/c
CREDIT Interest received a/c
Being posting of bank interest received credited on
bank statement</td><td>9</td><td>
9</td></tr>
</table>

Account	Trial balance Debit £	Trial balance Credit £	Adjustments Debit £	Adjustments Credit £	Profit and loss a/c Debit £	Profit and loss a/c Credit £	Balance sheet Debit £	Balance sheet Credit £
Sales		392,727						
Sales returns	1,214							
Purchases	208,217							
Purchase returns		643						
Stock (opening)	32,165							
Wages	26,000			2,100				
Rent	27,300			2,080				
Rates	8,460							
Light and heat	2,425		212					
Office expenses	3,162							
Selling expenses	14,112							
Motor expenses	14,728							
Sundry expenses	6,560							
Motor vans (cost)	12,640							
Motor vans (provision for depreciation)		2,528		2,528				
Shop fittings (cost)	9,620							
Shop fittings (provision for depreciation)				962				
Office equipment (cost)	4,250							
Office equipment (provision for depreciation)		2,550		850				
Cash	100							
Bank current account	4,429							
Bank investment account	68,340							
Interest received		3,289						
Capital		22,145						
VAT		6,515						
Purchase ledger total		29,588						
Loss on sale of fixed assets	1,246							
Kingston Displays Limited		9,620						
Drawings	24,640							
Discount received		3						
Depreciation (motor vans)			2,528					
Depreciation (shop fittings)			962					
Depreciation (office equipment)			850					
Prepayments			4,180					
Accruals				212				
Stock (closing): P&L				21,060				
Stock (closing): B/S			21,060					
SUB-TOTAL	469,608	469,608	29,792	29,792				
Profit for the year								
TOTAL	469,608	469,608	29,792	29,792				

Workings

1   *Accumulated depreciation on shop fittings disposed of*

    £324 × 6 years = £1,944

2   *Depreciation of fixed assets*

    Motor van: annual depreciation charge $= \dfrac{£12,640}{5} = £2,528$

    ∴ Accumulated depreciation at 1.12.93 = £2,528

    Shop fittings: depreciation charge $= \dfrac{£9,620}{10} = £962$

    Office equipment: annual depreciation charge $= \dfrac{£4,250}{5} = £850$

    Accumulated depreciation as at 1.12.93 = £850 × 3 = £2,550

3   *Business rates prepayment*

    Prepayment $= £6,240 \times \dfrac{4 \text{ months}}{12 \text{ months}} = £2,080$

4   *Electricity accrual*

    Accrual $= £318 \times \dfrac{2 \text{ months}}{3 \text{ months}} = £212$

R Senick

Task 1

JOURNAL		Page 1
Details	**£**	**£**
Purchases	2,211	
Carriage		2,211

Solutions to Tasks 2 to 4 are shown on the ETB overleaf.

Account	Trial balance Debit £	Trial balance Credit £	Adjustments Debit £	Adjustments Credit £	Accrued £	Prepaid £	Profit and loss a/c Debit £	Profit and loss a/c Credit £	Balance sheet Debit £	Balance sheet Credit £
Sales		138,078						138,078		
Purchases	84,561						84,561			
Carriage	2,933						2,933			
Drawings	7,800								7,800	
Rent, rates and insurance	6,622				210	880	5,952			
Postage and stationery	3,001						3,001			
Advertising	1,330						1,330			
Salaries and wages	26,420						26,420			
Bad debt expense	877		40				917			
Provision for bad debts		130		40						170
Debtors	12,120								12,120	
Creditors		6,471								6,471
Cash in hand	177								177	
Cash at bank	1,002								1,002	
Stock at 1 July 1995	11,927						11,927			
Equipment (cost)	58,000								58,000	
Equipment (accumulated depreciation)		19,000		8,700						27,700
Capital		53,091								53,091
Closing stock (B/S)			13,551						13,551	
Closing stock (P&L)				13,551				13,551		
Depreciation expense			8,700				8,700			
Prepayments/accruals					210	880			880	210
SUB-TOTAL	216,770	216,770	22,291	22,291	210	880	145,741	151,629	93,530	87,642
Profit for the year							5,888			5,888
TOTAL	216,770	216,770	22,291	22,291	210	880	151,629	151,629	93,530	93,530

B SOLUTIONS TO INCOMPLETE RECORDS EXERCISES

Brian Hope

Tutorial note. The three most difficult accounts to complete are trade debtors, cash and drawings. It is best to put in all the figures you know and complete the 'easier' accounts first. You should then be able to calculate, as a balancing figure, the amount for debtors who pay in cash. This will slot into the 'cash account', enabling you to calculate cash drawings as a balancing figure. The suggested time allocation for this incomplete records exercise is 1 hour.

TRADE DEBTORS

Balance b/f	1,420	Bank	21,120
		Allowance	300
Sales	26,720	Bad debt	90
		Balance c/f	1,030
		£(1120-90)	
		Cash	5,600
	28,140		28,140

VEHICLE RUNNING EXPENSES

		Balance b/f	80
Cash	500		
Bank	1,040	Profit & loss	1,520
Balance c/f	60		
	1,600		1,600

TRADE CREDITORS

Balance c/f	2,460	Balance b/f	2,220
Cash discount	200	Purchases	4,510
Bank *	4,070		
	6,730		6,730

* Payments to creditors: £(3,930 - 70 + 210) = £4,070

INSURANCE

Balance b/f	340		
		Profit & loss	920
Bank	960		
		Balance c/f	380
	1,300		1,300

RENT

Balance b/f	400		
		Balance c/f	480
Bank	2,640	Profit & loss	2,560
	3,040		3,040

CASH

Balance b/f	10	Bank	510
		Vehicle running costs	500
Debtors	5,600	Other expenses	500
		Drawings (bal)	4,100
	5,610		5,610

VEHICLES

Balance b/f	6,000	Acc. dep'n	1,200
Bank	3,600	Profit & loss*	400
		Balance c/f	8,000
	9,600		9,600

* £(6,000 - 1,200 - 4,400) = £400 loss

DRAWINGS

Bank	8,000	Capital	12,100
Cash	4,100		
	12,100		12,100

Kuldipa Potiwal

Task 1

KULDIPA POTIWAL
CALCULATION OF NET PROFIT
FOR THE YEAR ENDED 31 OCTOBER 1993

	£	£
Sales (W1)		133,590
Opening stock	12,200	
Purchases (W2)	78,080	
Closing stock	(13,750)	
Cost of sales		76,530
Gross profit		57,060
Rent received (W3)		2,750
		59,810
Expenses		
Rent and rates (W3)	6,700	
Postage and packing	2,200	
Motor expenses	5,050	
Admin expenses (W3)	5,390	
Wages	18,200	
Stock loss (£6,000 × 100/150 × 50%)	2,000	
Depreciation £(17,500 − 12,500)	5,000	
		44,540
Net profit		15,270

Task 2

KULDIPA POTIWAL
CALCULATION OF CAPITAL AS AT 31 OCTOBER 1993

	£
Opening capital (W4)	23,775
Profit	15,270
	39,045
Additional capital (investment income)	1,500
	40,545
Drawings (W5)	11,760
Closing capital	28,785

This figure can be confirmed by producing a balance sheet as at 31 October 1993, although this is not required by the question.

KULDIPA POTIWAL
BALANCE SHEET AS AT 31 OCTOBER 1993

	£	£
Fixed assets		
Van		12,500
Current assets		
Stock	13,750	
Debtors	7,200	
Prepayments	200	
Insurance claim (50%)	2,000	
Rent receivable	250	
Bank	6,500	
	29,900	
Current liabilities		
Creditors	13,400	
Accruals	215	
	13,615	
Net current assets		16,285
		28,785
Closing capital		28,785

Workings

1 *Sales*

CASH BOOK

	Cash £		Bank £		Cash £		Bank £
Sales	86,390	Bankings	56,000	Bankings	56,000	Bal b/f 1.11.92	3,250
		Debtors	46,000	Wages (350 × 52)	18,200	Creditors	78,000
		Investment				Postage &	
		income	1,500	Drawings (220 × 52)	11,440	packing	2,200
		Rent	2,500	Admin exps	750	Rent & rates	6,400
						Motor exps	5,050
						Admin exps	4,600
						Bal c/f 31.10 93	6,500
	86,390		106,000		86,390		106,000

Note. As cash is banked daily, there will be no cash in hand b/fwd or c/fwd.

DEBTORS CONTROL A/C

		£			£
1.11.92	Balance b/fwd	6,000	31.10.92	Bank	46,000
	Sales (bal fig)	47,200		Balance c/fwd	7,200
		53,200			53,200

Total sales = £(86,390 + 47,200) = £133,590

2 *Purchases*

CREDITORS CONTROL A/C

		£			£
	Bank	78,000	1.11 92	Bal b/fwd	9,000
31.10.93	Bal c/fwd	13,400		Purchases (bal fig)	82,400
		91,400			91,400

	£
Purchases per CC a/c	82,400
Less stolen games £6,000 × 100/150	(4,000)
Less Christmas presents £480 × 100/150	(320)
	78,080

3 *Expenses*

Rent and rates:	£(6,400 + 500 – 200) = £6,700
Admin expenses:	£(750 + 4,600 – 175 + 215) = £5,390
Rent received:	£(2,500 + 250) = £2,750

4 *Opening capital*

	£	£
Assets		
Van	17,500	
Stock	12,200	
Debtors	6,000	
Prepayments	500	
		36,200
Liabilities		
Creditors	9,000	
Accruals	175	
Bank overdraft	3,250	
		12,425
Net assets = capital		23,775

5   *Drawings*

	£
Cash (W1)	11,440
Christmas presents* 480 × 100/150	320
	11,760

*Note.** Drawings from stock are at cost price. Selling price inclusive of VAT may also be used.

Fancy Flowers

Task 1

Closing stock valuation

	Cost	Adjust	Total
	£	£	£
Pot plants	280	(70)	210
Roses	240		240
Tulips	160		160
Sprays	340	(80)	260
Plant food	80		80
Vases	520	(30)*	490
			1,440

*£6 × 100/200 × 10 = £30

Task 2

	£	£
Sales £(31,420 – 5,000 + 14,200 + 345 + 60)		41,025
Cost of sales		
Purchases £(24,180 + 850 + 345 – (£5* × 52))	25,115	
Closing stock (see *Task 1*)	(1,440)	
		23,675
Gross profit		17,350
Expenses		
Rent £(5,000 – 1,000)	4,000	
Rates	420	
Advertising £(385 + 45)	430	
Insurance	390	
Electricity £(780 + 360) + (1/3 × £360)	1,260	
Sundry expenses £(560 + 345)	905	
Interest	84	
		7,489
Profit		9,861

*£10 × 100%/200% = £5.

Note. It is not clear whether the flowers Sarah has taken have a mark-up or 100% or 75%.

Task 3

Capital account

	£
Balance at 1 June 1993	5,000
Add profit for year (see *Task 2*)	9,861
Less drawings: cash	(14,200)
goods	(260)
Balance at 31 May 1994	401

Task 4

The business is making a reasonable profit but Sarah is taking much more in wages for herself. As well as the profit for the year, she has also withdrawn a substantial part of her initial capital investment. It is unlikely that she will be able to continue drawing at this rate, particularly if the business requires more investment in future.

The gross profit figures shows a mark-up on cost of approximately 73%, or a gross profit percentage of 42%. the net profit percentage is 24%. These figures are quite healthy, although it might be wise to reduce stock write-offs in future (charge for special orders in advance?) and reduce the more discretionary expenses, such as advertising.

Somaira Rahman

Tutorial note. Task 4 does *not* require a full balance sheet.

Task 1

CALCULATION OF CAPITAL AS AT 30 SEPTEMBER 1993

	£	£
Assets		
Trade debtors	2,100	
Overhead prepayment	640	
Business premises	48,000	
Motor van	15,000	
Stock	56,000	
Cash in hand	820	
Cash at bank	41,600	
		164,160
Liabilities		
Trade creditors	68,600	
Overhead accrued	760	
Loan	50,000	
Mortgage (50% × £48,000)	24,000	
		143,360
Net assets = capital		20,800

Task 2

CAPITAL AS AT 1 OCTOBER 1992

	£
Assets	
Motor van	18,000
Stock	42,000
Bank	16,000
	76,000
Liabilities	
Loan	(60,000)
Net assets = capital	16,000

CALCULATION OF PROFIT FOR THE YEAR TO 30 SEPTEMBER 1993

	£
Capital at 1 October 1992	16,000
Capital introduced (50% × £48,000)	24,000
	40,000
Drawings (£275 × 52)	(14,300)
	25,700
Net loss (balancing figure)	(4,900)
Closing capital	20,800

Task 3

CALCULATION OF PROFIT FOR THE YEAR ENDED 30 SEPTEMBER 1994

	£	£
Sales		175,650
Cost of sales		
Opening stock	56,000	
Purchases	144,620	
	200,620	
Closing stock	(63,400)	
		137,220
Gross profit		38,430
Expenses		
Overheads £(7,440 + 640 – 210 + 190 – 760)	7,300	
Motor	12,420	
Van depreciation £(15,000 – 12,000)	3,000	
Loan interest	4,000	
Mortgage interest	2,400	
		29,120
Net profit		9,310

Task 4

CALCULATION OF CAPITAL AS AT 30 SEPTEMBER 1994

	£	£
Capital as at 1 October 1993		20,800
Profit for the year		9,310
Capital introduced (investment income)		8,220
		38,330
Drawings		
Shopping	14,300	
Private car	16,400	
Private motor expenses	1,640	
		32,340
Capital as at 30 September 1994		5,990

Workings

1   *Sales*

CASH BOOK

	Cash £	Bank £		Cash £	Bank £
Balance b/d	820	41,600	Creditors		138,400
Investment income		8,220	Overheads		7,440
Bankings (bal fig)		158,370	Motor expenses (business)		12,420
Sales receipts (bal fig)	172,500		Motor expenses (private)		1,640
			Mortgage interest		2,400
			New car		16,400
			Drawings	14,300	
			Bankings	158,370	
			Balance c/d	650	29,490
	173,320	208,190		173,320	208,190

DEBTORS

	£		£
Balance b/d	2,100	Receipts	172,500
Shares (cash and credit) Sales	175,650	Balance c/d	5,250
	177,750		177,750

2   *Purchases*

CREDITORS

	£		£
Bank	138,400	Balance b/d	68,600
Balance c/d	74,820	Purchases	144,620
	213,220		213,220

Manuel

Task 1

CASH BOOK

DETAIL	DISCOUNT £	CASH £	BANK £	DISCOUNT £	CASH £	BANK £
Balance b/d		320	300			
Bar takings		200				
Major		80				
Bank			300		300	
Wages					50	40
Bank charges						35
Torquay Wines				15		285
Balance c/d					250	240
		600	600	15	600	600

SALES

	£		£
		Cash	200
		Major	100
		Mr Twychin	120
Balance	420		
	420		420

PURCHASES

	£		£
Devon Wines	175	Devon Wines	75
Torquay Wines	500		
		Balance	600
	675		675

MAJOR

	£		£
Balance b/d	80	Cash	80
Sales	100		
		Balance c/d	100
	180		180

WAGES

	£		£
Cash	50		
Bank	40		
		Balance	90
	90		90

MR TWYCHIN

	£		£
Sales	120	Balance c/d	120
	120		120

BANK CHARGES

	£		£
Bank	35	Balance	35
	35		35

DEVON WINES

	£		£
Purchases	75	Purchases	175
Balance c/d	100		
	175		175

TORQUAY WINES

	£		£
Bank	285	Purchases	500
Discount	15		
Balance c/d	200		
	500		500

Task 2

```
┌──────────────────────────────────────────────────────────────────┐
│                                                                    │
│              PARTIAL TRIAL BALANCE AS AT 30 JUNE                   │
│                                                                    │
│                                      Dr            Cr              │
│                                      £             £               │
│   Bank balance                      240                           │
│   Cash in till                      250                           │
│   Discounts                                        15              │
│   Sales                                            420             │
│   Purchases                         600                           │
│   Major                             100                           │
│   Wages                              90                           │
│   Mr Twychin                        120                           │
│   Bank charges                       35                           │
│   Devon Wines                                      100             │
│   Torquay Wines                                    200             │
│   Difference (Note)                                700             │
│                                    1,435          1,435            │
│                                                                    │
└──────────────────────────────────────────────────────────────────┘
```

	Dr £	Cr £
Bank balance	240	
Cash in till	250	
Discounts		15
Sales		420
Purchases	600	
Major	100	
Wages	90	
Mr Twychin	120	
Bank charges	35	
Devon Wines		100
Torquay Wines		200
Difference (Note)		700
	1,435	1,435

Note. the £700 by which debits exceed credits corresponds to the opening balances as follows.

	£
Debtor (major)	80
Opening cash balance	320
Opening bank balance	300
	700

C   SOLUTIONS TO SHORT ANSWER QUESTIONS

A Short

1   If a set of filing trays costing £20 had been debited to the printing, stationery and postage account, an adjustment would probably not be required.

Many small value assets, although purchased for continuing use in the business, will not be recorded as assets but written off directly as expenses when purchased.

The decision as to whether such items are small enough to be written off depends on whether or not the amount is material, that is whether it has a significant effect on the financial statements. It is likely that, in this case, trays costing £20 would not be considered material.

2   If a credit note had been posted to the customer's personal account and the debtors control account, a credit entry of £80 would have been made. There should also have been a debit to sales of £80. This 'missing debit' would give rise to a debit balance on the suspense account of £80.

3   The item should be valued at £640, calculated as follows.

	£
Invoiced value	800
Less 25% discount	200
	600
Plus delivery costs	40
	640

Cash discounts do not affect the stock valuation.

4   The item should be included at the lower of cost and net realisable value, calculated as follows.

	£
Required selling price	1,300
Less modification costs	300
Net realisable value	1,000

This is lower than the cost of £1,200.

5   Where alternative valuations are possible, the prudence concept requires that the one selected should be the one which gives the most cautious presentation of the business's financial position or results.

It would thus be incorrect to value the stock at the selling price of £98,000, because this would mean anticipating making a profit before the profit had been realised.

6   The treatment adopted accords with the 'accruals' or 'matching' concept, which states that, in computing profit, revenue earned must be matched against the expenditure incurred in earning it. According to SSAP 2, 'revenue and costs are accrued, that is recognised as they are earned and incurred, not as money is received or paid'.

7   As well as wearing out through use, a piece of equipment may become obsolete because of changes in technology. This is particularly true of computer equipment.

8   The vehicles will be shown at £19,200, calculated as follows.

	£
Cost	48,000
Accumulated depreciation	28,800
Net book value	19,200

This amount is not an estimate of what the vehicles could be sold for at 31 December 1992. Arriving at a resale value is not the purpose of depreciation, which aims instead to spread the cost of a fixed asset over its useful life, and so match the cost against the full period during which it earns profit for the business.

9   The total charge against profits, taking account of both depreciation and any profit or loss on disposal will be the same. This is illustrated below.

20% straight line

		£
Cost		10,000
Accumulated depreciation		
(20% × 10,000 × 2 years)		4,000
Net book value		6,000
Sale proceeds		5,400
Loss on disposal		600

Thus, the total charge against profits is 4,000 + 600 = £4,600.

30% reducing balance

	£	£
Cost		10,000
Depreciation charged in y/e 31.12.1990		
(30% × £10,000)	3,000	
Depreciation charged in y/e 31.12.1991		
(30% × £(10,000 – 3,000))	2,100	
Accumulated depreciation		5,100
Net book value		4,900
Sale proceeds		5,400
Profit on disposal		500

Total charge against profits = £(5,100 – 500) = £4,600.

10 Debtors will be shown at £58,500 which is debtors per trial balance of £60,000 less the provision for doubtful debts of £1,500.

An asset is something *owned* by a business. Debtors (amounts owed to the business) are an asset because a business has a right to the money.

Not all debtors will pay. Based on experience and judgement, we have been able to say here that about 2½% of debtors (ie £1,500 worth) will not pay, although we do not necessarily know who those debtors are.

If the business is not going to receive the money in respect of that amount it is best not to regard it as an asset. Accordingly, we deduct this amount from the total for the asset.

Country Crafts

1 The computer software has been purchased for continuing use in the business, and in that sense, could be called a fixed asset. However, many small value assets are not recorded as assets but written off directly as an expense when purchased. The decision as to how to treat the item depends on materiality, that is whether or not the item has a significant effect on the financial statements. In this particular case the expenditure on software was not material, which suggests that the item should be treated as an expense.

2

	£
Cost 1991	9,200
Depreciation 1991: 50% × £9,200	4,600
Net book value	4,600
Depreciation 1992: 50% × £4,600	2,300
Net book value	2,300
Proceeds	3,900
Profit	1,600

3 A payment in advance is *deferred income*. It would be treated as a current liability in the 1993 accounts and as income in the 1994 accounts.

4 (a) An imbalance arising from a transposition error could not occur in a computerised accounting system, because the figure is entered only once and the computer carries out the double entry.

(b) An error of principle could occur if a computerised accounting system is used. This is because the decision as to which account an item should be posted to rests with the person responsible, not with the computer.

5   It would be wrong to treat this as a bad debt since it is only a rumour, and a bad debt is a debt that has definitely gone bad. If the business is not already making a provision for doubtful debts, it should do so now, or should investigate whether the existing provision is adequate.

6   The balance on a VAT account represents the difference between output VAT (VAT collected from customers) and input VAT (VAT paid to suppliers). As the VAT account has a credit balance, the balance represents the excess of output tax over input tax.

7   The purpose of the expenditure was to maintain the existing capacity of the asset, rather than to improve it. This is therefore revenue expenditure.

8   The correct treatment would be:

DEBIT   Office expenses
CREDIT   Purchases

Futon Enterprises

1   *Stock valuation*

Cost = £48.00 × 2 = £96.00

	£
NRV	
Selling price (£50.00 × 2)	100.00
Costs to complete (£18.00 × 2)	36.00
	64.00

This stock would have been valued at £64.00, reducing the total stock value by £96.00 − £64.00 = £32.00. The stock should be valued at NRV because the prudence concept requires that losses should be recognised as soon as they are foreseen. The £32.00 is such a loss. In addition, SSAP 9 requires that stock be valued at the lower of cost and NRV.

2   The net book value of the assembling machinery at 31 May 1994 is £3,650 − £1,460 = £2,190. This does not mean that the business would obtain this amount if it sold the machinery at 31 May 1994, because the depreciation charged is not meant to reflect the market value of the asset. Rather, it is a measure of the wearing out of the asset through time and use; it is allocated to the accounting periods which are expected to benefit (ie make a profit) from the asset's use.

3   One reason for the choice of the reducing balance for vans is that motor vehicles lose a great deal of their value in the first year of use. This reflects the use made of the asset at its most efficient and it is a good example of 'matching' profits against costs.

4   The payment would have been accounted for as:

DEBIT	Bank	£168
CREDIT	Bad debt expense	£168

5   The balance on the Inland Revenue account represents the income tax owed on the profits of the business (probably just for the previous year) to the Inland Revenue, less any payments already made. Obviously, a tax charge is required for the current year and this would be accounted for as:

DEBIT   Profit and loss account
CREDIT   Inland Revenue account

6   Strictly speaking, the cost of refitting, including the assembler's wages, should be capitalised as an addition to delivery vans cost, because the refitting has added value to the van. However, the amount is immaterial to the results of the business; such small amounts are best treated as revenue expenditure in the profit and loss account.

7   (a)   The transaction should be treated on a monthly basis as:

DEBIT	Bank (or cash)	£40
CREDIT	Rental (or sundry) income	£40

(b)   The outstanding £40 would be credited to the profit and loss account and shown as a sundry debtor in the balance sheet.

8 (a) A debit entry in the VAT accounts.

   (b) This represents the VAT on petty cash payments which the business can reclaim from HM Customs & Excise.

   (c) DEBIT   Cash   £37
        CREDIT Bank   £37

Kidditoys

1 Sophie's customers either pay cash in the shop or send cash with their orders. Since, therefore, she has no debtors, Sophie will not have a problem with bad debts.

2 The credit balance on Sophie's VAT account is the amount by which VAT collected on sales exceeds VAT paid on purchases and expenses. The balance is owing to HM Customs & Excise.

3 DEBIT   Bank a/c
   CREDIT Sales a/c
   CREDIT VAT a/c

4 Net book value of van $= £12,640 \times \dfrac{3 \text{ years}}{5 \text{ years}} = £7,584$

   This figure represents the cost of the van less accumulated depreciation to date. It is not an indication of the market value of the van.

5 (a) The original sales price of each doll was £16, so the original cost must have been £8. Net realisable value at £5 is £3 lower, so the closing stock valuation will be reduced by £3 × 4 = £12.

   (b) Profit would be reduced by £12.

6 DEBIT   Purchases
   CREDIT Creditors

7 No transaction has yet taken place; the stock still belongs to Kidditoys. No entries should be made in the accounts until a sale is made by John King.

8 The accounting treatment of the £85 spent on software depends on whether the amount is regarded as material. If it is considered material it should be capitalised:

   DEBIT   Office equipment (cost)   £85
   CREDIT Bank/creditors   £85

   However if, as is more likely, the amount is not to be regarded as material, the amount would be written off to office expenses as follows.

   DEBIT   Office expenses   £85
   CREDIT Bank/creditors   £85

9 (a) It would appear in the credit column as a balancing figure because debits would exceed credits.

   (b) It would appear in the debit column as a deduction from capital.

10

	Profit and Loss A/c		Balance Sheet Balances	
Dr	Cr	Dr	Cr
32,165	21,060	21,060	

R Senick

1   'Carriage' refers to the cost of transporting purchased goods from the supplier to the premises of the business which has bought them. When the purchaser pays for these delivery costs, the cost to the purchaser is carriage inwards.

The cost of carriage inwards is usually added to the cost of purchases and is therefore included in the trading account.

2   A trial balance is a list of all the balances in the ledger accounts, made up before the preparation of the financial statements to check the accuracy of the double entry accounting. The financial statements (the profit and loss account and the balance sheet) are drawn up using the balances in the trial balance.

Usually this step of drawing up the financial statements from the trial balance involves adjusting a few of the balances in some way, for example:

(a)   correction of errors;
(b)   recognition of accruals and prepayments;
(c)   making provision for depreciation, and bad and doubtful debts; and
(d)   adding in the closing stock figure.

In order to keep track of such adjustments and set out the necessary figures neatly, an *extended trial balance* may be used.

3   Three other uses for the journal are as follows.

(a)   To transfer an amount from an account in the nominal ledger to the profit and loss account. When the trading, profit and loss account of a business is prepared, the transfers from various ledger accounts to the profit and loss account (itself ultimately a ledger account) are first of all noted in the journal.

(b)   To transfer amounts from a ledger account which has been used as a 'collecting station' for a certain item, for example, drawings, which are subsequently transferred to the capital account.

(c)   To record the double entry for the purchase or sale of fixed assets.

4   DEBIT   Creditors
     CREDIT   Purchases (or purchases returns)

5   For bad debts written off, there is a bad debts account. When it is decided that a particular debt will not be paid, the customer is taken out of outstanding debtors and becomes a bad debt.

A provision for doubtful debts (also called a provision for bad debts) is rather different. A business might know from past experience that, say, 2% of debtors' balances are unlikely to be collected. It would then be considered prudent to make a general provision of 2%. It may be that no particular balances are regarded as suspect and so it is not possible to write off any balances as bad debts. The procedure is then to leave the total debtors' balances completely untouched, but to open up a provision account by the following entries.

DEBIT   P & L account (bad debt expense account)
CREDIT   Provision for doubtful debts

6   A suspense account is a temporary account which can be opened for a number of reasons. The most common reasons are:

(a)   a trial balance is drawn up which does not balance (total debits do not equal total credits);

(b)   the bookkeeper of a business knows where to post the credit side of a transaction, but does not know where to post the debit (or vice versa). For example, a cash payment might be made and must obviously be credited to cash. But the bookkeeper may not know what the payment is for, and so will not know which account to debit.

7   The balance on the suspense account would be £1,000 (£500 + £500) debit.

8   The error would not give rise to a difference on the trial balance, and therefore there would be no balance on the suspense account.

9   Other reasons why R Senick may not be able to sell his stock include the following.

(a)   Goods might be lost or stolen.

(b)   Goods might become obsolete or out of fashion. These might have to be thrown away, or possibly sold off at a very low price in a clearance sale.

10   If, at the end of an accounting period, a business still has goods in stock which are either worthless or worth less than their original cost, the value of the stocks should be written down to:

(a)   nothing if they are worthless;
(b)   their net realisable value if this is less than their original cost.

D   SOLUTIONS TO COMPREHENSION AND COMMUNICATION TASKS

Tutorial note. These tasks are now usually combined with the short answer questions, as you will see in the trial run central assessment.

A Short

(a)

MEMORANDUM

To: Adam Short   Ref: PJI
From: Pat Jones   Date: 3 August 1993
Subject: *Depreciation of the vehicles*

An important concept in accounting is that of accruals, which states that revenue and profits dealt with in the profit and loss account of the period are *matched* with associated costs and expenses.

One way of defining depreciation is to describe it as a means of spreading the cost of a fixed asset over its useful life, thereby matching the cost against the full period during which it earns profits for the business.

Assuming that the expected life of the asset is still five years there is no justifiable reason to change the policy presently adopted. To do so would be inconsistent (there is another accounting principle called 'consistency') and would distort the level of profit reported.

(b)

MEMORANDUM

To: Adam Short   Ref: PJ2
From: Pat Jones   Date: 4 August 1993
Subject: *Accounting standards*

It is clear that different people exercising their judgement on the same facts can arrive at very different conclusions about the appropriate accounting treatment. For example, suppose that a business owns a freehold property which it purchased for £100,000.

(i)   Some people might argue that no depreciation should be charged on the building because property prices are always rising. The building would appear in the accounts permanently at £100,000.

(ii)   Others would say that this does not go far enough. If property prices are rising, not only should no depreciation be charged, but the book value of the building should be increased each year by revaluation.

(iii)   Still others might say that the £100,000 is expenditure incurred by the business and that all expenditure should at some time be charged to the profit and loss account, perhaps by equal annual depreciation charges over the building's useful life.

Working from the same data, these different groups of people would produce very different financial statements. If the exercise of judgement is completely unfettered, any comparability between the accounts of different organisations will disappear. This will be all the more significant in cases where deliberate manipulation occurs in order to present accounts in the most favourable light.

The Accounting Standards Board has developed accounting standards with the aim of narrowing the areas of difference and variety in accounting practice. They apply to all financial accounts intended to give a true and fair view, including those of small businesses such as ours. (However, in the near future small businesses may be exempt from all except the most straightforward standards.)

An example of an accounting standard is SSAP 12 *Accounting for depreciation* which recommends option (iii) above. The standard provides the answer to your earlier query (part (a)).

(c)

MEMORANDUM

To: Adam Short   Ref: PJ3
From: Pat Jones   Date: 5 August 1993
Subject: *Historical cost*

The historical cost basis (or convention) of accounting requires that transactions are normally stated in accounts at the historical amount which the business paid to acquire them. This has two implications.

(i)   Transactions are stated at their values when they occurred. This can mean that the cost of goods sold is not suddenly increased at the end of the year.

(ii)   Assets are stated at their historical cost and are written down or written off against profits on the same basis.

This basis has the advantage that there is usually objective documentary evidence to prove the purchase price of an asset or amounts paid as expenses. However, there are some problems with the principle, the main one being inflation.

Country Crafts

(a)

MEMORANDUM

To: James McBride
From: C Nearclark
Date: 3 December 1993
Subject: *Accounting concepts*

As you rightly point out, in the preparation of accounts certain accounting concepts are followed. SSAP 2 *Disclosure of accounting policies* describes four concepts as *fundamental accounting concepts*. These are going concern, prudence, accruals and consistency. These four are also identified as fundamental by the Companies Act 1985, which adds a fifth to the list (the separate valuation principle). While these concepts are very useful guidelines, there are occasions when they may seem to contradict one another, as you suggest.

Turning to the issues you raise, SSAP 9 states that stock is to be valued at *the lower of* cost and net realisable value. Thus, if stock can be sold for more than it cost, it is valued at cost, but if it will only realise less than it cost, this lower value is taken.

This may seem to you to go against the accruals concept which demands the matching of income with costs. However, in accordance with the concept of *prudence*, the most cautious treatment is adopted.

I hope this makes things clearer for you.

(b)

MEMORANDUM

To: Sylvia Smith
From: C Nearclark
Date: 3 December 1993
Subject: *Suspense account*

A suspense account is a temporary account which may be opened for a number of reasons. In a manual accounting system, the two most common reasons are as follows.

(a) The bookkeeper of a business knows where to post one 'side' of a transaction but not the other. For example, a cash payment might be made and must obviously be credited to cash. But the bookkeeper may not know what the payment is for and so will not know which account to debit.

(b) A trial balance is drawn up which does not balance (total debits do not equal total credits).

Of the two reasons, only (a) is applicable in a computerised system, the reason being that in a computerised system, the double entry is automatic. The trial balance may be wrong in other respects, but it will always balance.

The suspense account is temporary and must be cleared before the final accounts are drawn up.

(c)

MEMORANDUM

To: Abdul Mohim
From: C Nearclark
Date: 3 December 1993
Subject: *Segmentation of accounting for comparative purposes*

As you rightly point out, modification of our accounting system to give a breakdown by product line would provide very useful information on which management could base decisions. It would show us which lines are selling the most in volume terms, which are the most profitable and, if necessary, whether any lines are loss-making and should be discontinued. The following points should be borne in mind if the system is to be implemented effectively.

(a) We should set up further trading accounts, as far down as gross profit, one for each product. This means we will need four sales accounts, four purchases accounts and four stock accounts.

(b) It is probably not practical to attempt to apportion overheads to each product line. Such apportionment is often arbitrary and of limited use for decision making purposes.

(c) Each product must be clearly categorised and segregated in the warehouse. It will be necessary to set up codes for each product type.

(d) Staff must be informed about the new system as soon as possible and be given any training necessary in order to operate it.

Futon Enterprises

Task 1

MEMORANDUM

To: Jason Sarmiento
From: A Technician
Date: 8 August 1994   Ref: JS1
Subject: *Provision for doubtful debts*

You appear to be experiencing some confusion on the subject of bad debts, doubtful debts and provisions. Firstly, let me explain some of the terms.

Bad debts

When bad debts are written off, specific debts owed to the business are identified as unlikely ever to be collected. They are therefore removed from debtors and charged as an expense in the profit and loss account (a deduction from gross profit).

Doubtful debts

Because of the risks involved in selling goods on credit, it might be accepted that a certain percentage of outstanding debts at any time are unlikely to be collected. But although it might be estimated that, say 5% of debts will turn out bad, the business will not know until later which specific debts are bad. When a business expects bad debts amongst its current debtors, but does not yet know which specific debts will be bad, it can make a provision for doubtful debts.

Provisions

A 'provision' is a 'providing for' and so a provision for doubtful debts provides for future bad debts, as a prudent precaution by the business. The business will be more likely to avoid claiming profits which subsequently fail to materialise because some debts turn out to be bad.

When a provision is first made, the amount of this initial provision is charged as an expense in the profit and loss account of the business, for the period in which the provision is created. When a provision already exists, but is subsequently increased in size, the amount of the increase in provision is charged as an expense in the profit and loss account, for the period in which the *increased* provision is made. When a provision already exists, but is subsequently *reduced* in size, the amount of the decrease in provision is recorded as a decrease in bad debt expense, or as an item of 'income' in the profit and loss account, for the period in which the reduction in provision is made.

The balance sheet as well as the profit and loss account of a business must be adjusted to show a provision for doubtful debts. The value of debtors in the balance sheet must be shown after deducting the provision for doubtful debts. This is because the net realisable value of all the debtors of the business is estimated to be less than their 'sales value'. After all, this is the reason for making the provision in the first place. The net realisable value of debtors is the total value of debtors minus the provision for doubtful debts. Such a provision is an example of the *prudence concept.*

In the case of Futon Enterprises Ltd, there are two main factors to bear in mind.

(a) The envisaged 5% of total sales ledger balances would be 5% × £(1,860 − 168 − 168) = £76. This is a very small amount compared to total sales, ie it is *immaterial.*

(b) Does 5% represent your past experience of debts 'going bad'? Your friends' computer software business is probably affected by the recession much more severely than the futon business. On the other hand, the specific bad debt written off was nearly 10% of the total sales ledger balance.

Note that a provision for debts over a certain age (as suggested by one of your friends) is not a provision for doubtful debts, but rather a write off of *specific* debts.

On balance it seems unlikely that any general provision for doubtful debts would be material and therefore it would seem unnecessary to create one.

Task 2

MEMORANDUM

To: Jason Sarmiento
From: A Technician
Date: 8 August 1994   Ref: JS2
Re: *Analysis of profitability*

Last week we discussed the possibility of introducing a new product, sofabeds. If you wish to assess the profitability of each product, futons and sofabeds, then the following amendments would be required in the business's accounting system.

In general, each product would require its own set of accounts to record sales, purchases and expenses. For sales and purchases there should be few difficulties, as long as different materials are purchased for each product.

The difficulties will arise in the allocation of overheads, to produce a true gross profit for each product, (and, if necessary, the allocation of expenses to each product to give an overall net profit figure).

As far as overheads are concerned, an overhead absorption rate must be set for each product, along with an account to deal with under- and over-absorbed overheads. It is assumed that we would use an integrated system for both the cost and financial accounting information.

Task 3

MEMORANDUM

To: Jason Sarmiento
From: A Technician
Date: 8 August 1994   Ref: JS3
Re: *Cash accounting vs accruals accounting*

While I appreciate your suggestion to introduce cash accounting, which would reduce my workload, there are various problems which make such an approach impossible.

The accruals concept, which requires accruals accounting rather than cash accounting, is fundamental to the sense and usefulness of business accounts.

This concept states that, in computing profit, revenue earned must be matched against the expenditure occurred in earning it. In your accounts to 31 May 1994, you have matched the cost of producing X futons during the year with the proceeds from selling X futons. It would be incorrect to deduct the cost of the 23 futons still in stock at the year-end in computing profit because no revenue has yet been received for them. They will presumably be sold in the next accounting period and it is then that their cost will be deducted from the revenue earned from their sale.

In the same way, the net profit for a period should be calculated by charging the expenses which relate to that period. For example, in preparing the profit and loss account of a business for a period of, say, six months, it would be appropriate to charge six months' expenses for rent and rates, insurance costs and telephone costs etc.

Expenses might not be paid for during the period to which they relate. Accruals or accrued expenses are expenses which are charged against the profit for a particular period, even though they have not yet been paid for. Prepayments are payments which have been made in one accounting period, but should not be charged against profit until a later period, because they relate to that later period.

You can see that the accruals method makes much more sense: it gives meaning to the accounts from a reader's point of view: a cash method would be relatively meaningless.

As far as capital expenditure is concerned, expenditure of this nature is intended to benefit the firm for more than one accounting period and so the cost should be spread over the estimated period of benefit. This is another example of the accruals or matching concept.

Kidditoys

Task 1

---

5 December 1994

Sophie,

I believe you are concerned about a couple of issues which may arise if you start buying your stock from elsewhere. I thought I would give you some advice on the subject.

(a) If cash is received when the stock is not yet available, what we have is a *payment in advance*, the customer being a creditor. The entry would be:

DEBIT   Bank
CREDIT   Customer's personal account

When the goods are delivered, the entries would be as follows.

DEBIT   Customer's personal account
CREDIT   Sales
CREDIT   VAT

(b) If the customer's order cannot be fulfilled there are two options:

(i)   refund the payment
(ii) send the customer a credit note.

In case (i), a refund, no accounting entries are made because it is as if no transaction has taken place. In case (ii) the treatment would be:

DEBIT   Bank
CREDIT   Customer's personal account

It may be that only part of the order can be fulfilled, in which case a partial refund might be given, for which the entries would be:

DEBIT   Bank (whole payment received)
CREDIT   Bank (refund)

Task 2

---

5 December 1994

Sophie,

I understand that you would find it useful to value your stock at selling price. As far as your own management accounts are concerned, this is quite acceptable, since the format of management accounts is not governed by any regulations.

However, for the purposes of the annual accounts, by which I presume you mean the financial accounts, the treatment you suggest would not be acceptable.

Financial accounts are prepared in accordance with accounting standards and fundamental accounting concepts, which are necessary to achieve consistency and comparability between different companies. The fundamental accounting concept of prudence (as defined in SSAP 2 *Disclosure of accounting policies*) states that profits should not be anticipated but that losses should be recognised as soon as they are foreseen. SSAP 9 *Stocks and long-term contracts* applies this caution to the valuation of stocks, stating that stock must be valued at the lower of cost and net realisable value.

Thus, if the market value of stock rises, the prudent valuation of the stock would be at *cost*, otherwise profits would be anticipated. However, should the market value fall to less than cost, then this lower market value less any selling costs (*net realisable value*) should be used.

I hope this clarifies the position for you.

Manuel

MEMORANDUM

To: Manuel
From: Polly   Date: 3 July 1996
Subject: *Computerised accounting systems*

Computerised accounting systems follow exactly the same principles as manual ones; if you do not thoroughly understand manual systems you will only be able to perform the simplest and most mechanical tasks using computerised systems.

Double entry bookkeeping is the basis for all accounting practice. It is necessary to have a really clear grasp of the techniques, which can only be achieved by detailed study and plenty of practice. Even the most complex computerised accounting systems can be better understood if they can be related back to the basics.

It should be noted, furthermore, that in order to select, design or improve a given computerised application or system, you must understand exactly what you want it to do in terms of the principles of double entry bookkeeping.

MEMORANDUM

To: Manuel
From: Polly   Date: 4 July 1996
Subject: *Depreciation provision*

You appear to be labouring under the misapprehension that the creation of a provision for depreciation is a way of saving up. This is incorrect: saving up affects *cash*. In accounting terms, the creation of a savings account would involve debiting the savings account and crediting the general bank account. By contrast, the creation of a depreciation provision affects the *profit and loss account*, the entries being debit profit and loss account and credit provision.

Depreciation may be described as a means of spreading the cost of a fixed asset over its useful life and so matching the cost against the full period during which it earns profits for the business. Depreciation charges are an example of the application of the *matching concept* to calculate profits.

It could be argued that, by writing off the cost of the asset over its life, the firm is ensuring that, when it comes to replace the asset, it has the same total resources as when the asset was new. However, this is not strictly accurate because, even if total resources are maintained, those resources will not necessarily be cash. Furthermore transfers to the provision do not take account of general inflation or any increase in the price of the asset concerned.

MEMORANDUM

To: Manuel
From: Polly   Date: 5 July 1996
Subject: *Liabilities and profits*

The accounting equation states that total assets = capital plus liabilities, including profits. This becomes clearer if you consider that assets show how available *resources* have been *applied* (eg plant, buildings etc), and liabilities show where those resources *come from*, for example from capital introduced, unpaid suppliers, loans, profits etc. Thus profits and liabilities are both sources of resources and create an obligation (liability) on the part of the business, which in the case of profits is to the owner(s).

Trial run
central assessments

TRIAL RUN CENTRAL ASSESSMENT 1

INTERMEDIATE STAGE - NVQ/SVQ3

Preparing Financial Accounts

June 1995

Time allowed - 3 hours

The Central Assessment is in three sections.

Section 1   Extended trial balance exercise
                 Complete all 6 tasks

Section 2   Short answer and communication questions
                 Complete all 6 questions

Section 3   Incomplete records exercise
                 Complete the task

The purpose of this Trial Run Central Assessment is to give you an idea of what a Central Assessment looks like. It is not intended as a guide to the topics which are likely to be assessed. Time allocations, shown at the beginning of sections, will give you an idea of how long you should spend on each section, but you should not expect to be under time pressure. You may use the space on Page 257 for rough work.

**DO NOT OPEN THIS PAPER UNTIL YOU ARE READY TO START
UNDER TIMED CONDITIONS**

SECTION 1 (Suggested time allocation: 80 minutes)

Data

You have been working for some months now as an accounting technician with Highbury Discs. The business specialises in recording and distributing compact discs of choral and organ music. Recordings are made on location and artists are paid a fixed fee plus a royalty based on the number of discs sold. Royalties are calculated and paid quarterly in arrears. The owners of the recording location are paid a fee for the hire of the location.

Anthony Sedgewick, the proprietor of Highbury Discs, uses only a minimum of high quality recording equipment, believing that a wise choice of recording venue and the optimal placing of a single microphone are the dominant factors in producing a good recording. All production work is subcontracted to independent operators. This approach has resulted in a number of recordings which have been highly praised in the specialist hi-fi press. The business sells to a number of UK stores, one of which acts as an agent for overseas sales.

The business rents a unit on an industrial estate. The premises are used for administration, distribution and the storage of recording equipment and stocks of compact discs.

The financial year for the business ended on 31 May 1995.

The following alphabetical list of balances has been taken from the business ledger as at 31 May 1995.

	£
Artists' fees and royalties	41,120
Bank and cash	1,420
Capital	26,449
Drawings	14,500
Employer's national insurance	3,619
Equipment (cost)	38,200
Equipment (provision for depreciation)	19,100
Loan	10,000
Loan interest	1,350
Mastering and production costs	143,400
Motor expenses	6,330
Motor vehicles (cost)	29,800
Motor vehicles (provision for depreciation)	17,880
Recording costs	12,550
Rent	13,000
Sales	307,800
Stocks of compact discs	22,500
Sundry creditors	4,080
Sundry debtors	12,500
Sundry expenses	1,270
VAT (amount owing)	3,250
Wages and salaries	47,000

Task 1

Enter the above balances into the first two columns of the extended trial balance provided on Page 245 and total the columns. The list of balances is provided on the left of the trial balance columns to help you.

Account	Trial balance		Adjustments		Profit and loss a/c		Balance sheet	
	Debit	Credit	Debit	Credit	Debit	Credit	Debit	Credit
	£	£	£	£	£	£	£	£
Artists' fees and royalties	41,120							
Bank and cash	1,420							
Capital	26,449							
Drawings	14,500							
Employer's NI	3,619							
Equipment (cost)	38,200							
Equipment (provision for depreciation)	19,100							
Loan	10,000							
Loan interest	1,350							
Mastering and production costs	143,400							
Motor expenses	6,330							
Motor vehicles (cost)	29,800							
Motor vehicles (provision for depreciation)	17,880							
Recording costs	12,550							
Rent	13,000							
Sales	307,800							
Stocks of compact discs	22,500							
Sundry creditors	4,080							
Sundry debtors	12,500							
Sundry expenses	1,270							
VAT (amount owing)	3,250							
Wages and salaries	47,000							
SUB-TOTAL	777,118							
Profit for the year								
TOTAL								

Task 2

The policy of the business is to provide for depreciation as follows.

Motor vehicles   30% per annum, reducing balance method, full year basis
Equipment   25% per annum, straight line method, full year basis

Depreciation for the year ended 31 May 1995 has not been recorded in the accounts.

Calculate the depreciation charge for the year ended 31 May 1995 and complete the following table.

	Depreciation charge for the year ended 31 May 1995 £
Motor vehicles	
Equipment	
TOTAL	

Task 3

Stocks of compact discs are valued at cost. Cost includes a share of the recording, mastering and production costs as well as any direct overheads attributable to that recording. Stocks as at 31 May 1995 have not been recorded in the accounting system. The following is an extract of the stock sheets as at 31 May 1995 along with Anthony Sedgewick's comments.

STOCK SHEETS

Title	Number of discs in stock	Total cost £	Total price to retailers £	Total recom- mended retail price £	Comments
Total b/f from previous pages	4,500	18,000	27,600	39,800	No problems with any of these. We'll be able to make a profit on all of these discs.
Bambino choir of Prague	1,000	3,500	8,500	12,000	This batch of CDs arrived too late for the 1994 Christmas season. We're keeping them for the 1995 Christmas season. I think they will sell very well then.
The Joyful Singers sing Wesley	400	2,000	3,600 *1200*	4,800	We just cannot get rid of these. We'll have to reduce the price to retailers to £3 a disc and recommend that retailers sell them for £5.50 a disc.
Bach at St Thomas's	2,000	7,000	14,000 *8000* *less 3000 mtd* *5000*	20,000	This has not sold at all well. We're going to withdraw these discs and repackage them as 'The King of Instruments' and sell them to a chain store for £4 a disc. The repackaging will cost £1.50 per disc.
TOTAL	7,900	30,500	53,700	76,600	

Complete the following table to calculate the value of closing stock for incorporation into the accounts.

Stock sheets	Value £
Total b/f from previous pages	
Bambino choir of Prague	
The Joyful Singers sing Wesley	
Bach at St Thomas's	
VALUE OF STOCK as at 31 May 1995	

Task 4

The following additional information was discovered after the list of balances was extracted from the ledger.

(a) Royalties due to artists for the quarter ended 31 May 1995 have just been calculated at £4,500, but these have not yet been recorded in the accounts. It has also been discovered that there has been an error in the calculation of the royalties due to Arnold Willis-Brown for the quarter ended 31 December 1994. Mr Willis-Brown had been paid a £1 royalty based on sales of 28 discs. In actual fact the number of discs sold had been 280. Anthony Sedgewick has decided that the next cheque to be sent to Mr Willis-Brown should be adjusted to correct the error.

(b) A cheque for £220 received from 'The CD Shop', a credit customer, which had been correctly recorded in the accounts, has just been returned by the bank marked 'refer to drawer'. This has not yet been recorded in the accounts.

(c) Anthony Sedgewick has estimated that one third of motor expenses have been for private use.

Prepare journal entries to record the above information in the accounts. Dates are not required, but you should include narratives. Use the blank journal on Page 248.

Task 5

The following additional information is available from the business records.

(a) The loan was taken out on 1 June 1994, bears interest at 15% per annum, and is repayable in full on 31 May 1996.

(b) The rent on the business premises is fixed at £1,000 per month from 1 June 1993 to 31 May 1998.

Incorporate the following into the adjustments columns of the extended trial balance on Page 245.

(a) Any adjustments arising from the above additional information.

(b) The depreciation charge for the year and the value of closing stock you calculated as Tasks 2 and 3.

(c) Any adjustments resulting from the journal entries you prepared as Task 4.

Task 6

Extend the figures into the extended trial balance columns for the profit and loss account and the balance sheet. Total all columns, transferring the balance of profit or loss as appropriate.

JOURNAL		Page 1
Details	**£**	**£**

SECTION 2 (Suggested time allocation: 40 minutes)

Answer each of the following questions in the space provided.

These questions refer to the data given in Section 1.

1 The list of account balances on Page 244 includes an amount of £3,250 as VAT (amount owing).

    (a) **Explain fully what this balance represents.**

....

....

....

....

....

....

    (b) **To whom is the amount payable?**

....

2 Included in 'Equipment' are several high quality microphones. Apart from wear and tear through usage, there could be other factors causing these microphones to depreciate.

Identify and explain one such factor.

...........Obsolescence...

....

....

....

3 Highbury Discs uses DAT (digital to analogue) tapes to record performances. These are purchased wholesale for £8 each. They can be used over a number of years to make and archive recordings. The policy of the business is to charge the cost of the tapes as an expense in the year in which they are purchased.

Justify this treatment.

....

....

....

....

....

....

4 Suppose that the value of this year's closing stock had been mistakenly overestimated by £1,000 and that the error had not been detected.

What would the effect be:

(a)   **on this year's profit?**

....

....

(b)   **on next year's profit?**

....

....

5   Highbury Discs values its stock of compact discs at the end of each financial year so that the costs incurred in producing those discs are not charged until discs are sold.

Name the fundamental accounting concept of which this is an example.

....

6   Anthony Sedgewick has asked you to write him a memorandum explaining the rules you have used to calculate the value of closing stock in Section 1, Task 3. He would like you to refer to any relevant SSAPs and/or FRSs and illustrate the rules by demonstrating how you have calculated the value of the stocks of the three compact discs referred to in the stock sheets given for Task 3.

Prepare a suitable memorandum in reply to Anthony Sedgewick using the headed sheet on Page 251.

Task 6

MEMORANDUM

To: Ref:

From: Date:

Subject:

SECTION 3 (Suggested time allocation: 60 minutes)

You have been asked to help in preparing the accounts of Lynda Booth who has been trading as a painter and decorator for some years from a rented garage and workshop. Lynda is an excellent painter and decorator but does not have the expertise to maintain a double entry set of records. Your supervisor prepared Lynda's accounts last year and has provided you with a set of working accounts consisting of all accounts with start of year balances. The balances have been entered in the accounts.

You have already spent some time analysing the statements for Lynda's business bank account for the year ended 31 May 1995 and have the following summary.

	£	£
Opening balance		323
Payments in		
Lottery winnings (see note (a), page 253)	10,000	
Cash takings paid in	2,770	
Receipts from trade debtors	43,210	
		55,980
		56,303
Payments out		
Payments to trade creditors	30,060	
Withdrawn for personal use	12,000	
Purchase of new van	4,800	
Rent and insurance	5,330	
Motor expenses	3,400	
		55,590
		713

Your analysis of the other business documentation kept by Lynda gives you the following additional information as at 31 May 1995.

(a) Invoices for work done for customers during the year ended 31 May 1995 totalled £52,000 (of which £2,000 was unpaid as at 31 May 1995).

(b) Unpaid invoices for raw materials purchased from suppliers totalled £4,230.

(c) Insurance was prepaid by £200.

(d) Motor expenses were accrued by £209.

Your supervisor has supplied you with the following notes which were made during a meeting with Lynda Booth.

(a)   Lynda was a winner in the National Lottery earlier this year. She was not a jackpot winner and certainly did not win enough to retire. She paid some of her winnings into the business bank account to help with a temporary cash flow problem.

(b)   Lynda thinks that £480 of the amount collectable from customers as at 31 May 1995 will not be recovered because one of her customers has gone into bankruptcy.

(c)   Lynda buys all her supplies from one supplier who offers 10% discount for prompt settlement. Lynda has been able to take advantage of that discount on all payments made during the year.

(d)   Some customers paid in cash during the year but Lynda has not kept any records. We've estimated that about £600 was paid for motor expenses from these cash receipts. There was £34 in the business safe as at 31 May 1995.

(e)   Lynda bought the additional motor van on 1 February 1995 because she thought the price was particularly good. She has used both vans in the business herself but feels that this van will be particularly useful next summer when she expects she will have to employ an assistant. We have agreed that the vans should be written off equally on a month for month basis over an expected life of four years. This is what we did with the first van which was purchased on 1 June 1993.

(f)   There were materials costing £1,600 unused in the workshop at 31 May 1995.

Task 1

From the above information reconstruct the ledger accounts provided for the year ended 31 May 1995 on Pages 254 to 256, showing the balances to be carried forward at the end of the year and/or the amounts to be transferred to the profit and loss account for the year ended 31 May 1995.

Notes

(a)   Dates are not required.

(b)   The following accounts are not supplied and need not be shown.

   Capital
   Work done/sales
   Bad debts
   Discounts received/allowed

BANK

	£		£
Balance b/f	323	Creditors	30060
Lottery	10,000	Drawings	12000
Cash Takings	2770	Van	4800
Debtors	43,210	Rent + insurance	5330
		Motor Expenses	3400
		Bal c/f	713
	56303		56303
Bal b/f	713		
	56303		56303

CASH

	£		£
Balance b/f	25	Bank	2770
Cash Takings	8340	Motor expenses	600
		Drawings	4961
		Bal c/d	434
	8365		8365
Bal b/f	34		

MOTOR EXPENSES

	£		£
Bank	3400	Balance b/f	174
Cash	600	P+L a/c	4035
Bal c/d	209		
	4209		4209

MOTOR VAN(S)

	£		£
Balance b/f	7,500	Depn	2900
bank	4800	Bal c/f	9400
	12300		12300
Bal b/f	9400		

RENT AND INSURANCE

	£		£
Balance (insurance) b/f	180	Balance (rent) b/f	250
Bank	5330	P+L a/c	5060
		Bal (insurance) c/f	200
	5510		5510
Bal b/f	200		

MATERIALS USED

	£		£
Balance b/f	1,530	Bal c/f	1600
Purchases	33980	P+L a/c	33910
	35510		35510

TRADE CREDITORS			
	£		£
Bank	30,060	Balance b/f	3,650
Dis Rec.	3340	Purchases	33,980
Bal c/f	4230		
	37630		37630

TRADE DEBTORS			
	£		£
Balance b/f	1,550		
Sales	52000	Bank	43210
		Bad Debts	480
		Cash takings	8340
		Bal c/d	1520
	53550		53550

DRAWINGS			
	£		£
Bank	12000	Capital	16961
Cash	4961		
	16961		16961

ROUGH WORK

Van 1.6.93 - current value   7500   (1 yr depn)
                original value   10000
                depn   2500

Van 1.2.95 - current value   4800
             depn @ 4 months   400

TRIAL RUN CENTRAL ASSESSMENT 2

INTERMEDIATE STAGE - NVQ/SVQ3

Preparing Financial Accounts

December 1995

Time allowed - 3 hours

The Central Assessment is in three sections.

Section 1   Extended trial balance exercise
Complete all 4 tasks

Section 2   Short answer and communication questions
Complete all 8 questions

Section 3   Incomplete records exercise
Complete all 5 tasks

The purpose of this Trial Run Central Assessment is to give you an idea of what a Central Assessment looks like. It is not intended as a guide to the topics which are likely to be assessed. Time allocations, shown at the beginning of sections, will give you an idea of how long you should spend on each section, but you should not expect to be under time pressure. You may use the space on Page 272 for rough work.

**DO NOT OPEN THIS PAPER UNTIL YOU ARE READY TO START
UNDER TIMED CONDITIONS**

SECTION 1 (Suggested time allocation: 80 minutes)

Data

Jason Brown is a sole trader who operates out of a warehouse in Nottingham. He buys and sells a range of office furniture and equipment and trades under the name J B Office Supplies. Most of his sales are made on credit to businesses in the Midlands area of England, although occasionally customers will call at his premises to make purchases for cash.

You are employed by Jason to assist with the bookkeeping. This is currently a manual system and consists of a general ledger, where double entry takes place, a sales ledger and a purchases ledger. The individual accounts of debtors and creditors are therefore regarded as memoranda accounts. Day books are used and totals from the columns of these are transferred periodically into the general ledger.

The following balances were extracted from the general ledger at the end of the financial year on 31 October 1995.

	£
Purchases	170,240
Sales	246,412
Purchases returns	480
Sales returns	670
Stock at 1 November 1994	54,200
Salaries	30,120
Rent	2,200
Insurance	360
Delivery vans at cost	12,800
Provision for depreciation - delivery vans	3,520
Equipment at cost	22,800
Provision for depreciation - equipment	5,760
Bad debts	2,700
Provision for doubtful debts	1,980
Debtors control account	41,600
Creditors control account	33,643
Drawings	10,522
Capital	83,171
Bank overdraft	348
Cash	568
VAT (credit balance)	2,246
Bank interest received	1,200
Bank deposit account	30,000
Suspense account	?

Task 1

Enter the above balances into the first two columns of the extended trial balance provided on Page 261. Total the two columns whilst at the same time entering an appropriate balance for the suspense account to ensure that the two totals agree.

Account	Trial balance		Adjustments		Profit and loss a/c		Balance sheet	
	Debit	Credit	Debit	Credit	Debit	Credit	Debit	Credit
	£	£	£	£	£	£	£	£
Purchases								
Sales								
Purchases returns								
Sales returns								
Opening stock								
Salaries								
Rent								
Insurance								
Delivery vans								
Provision for depreciation: delivery vans								
Equipment								
Provision for depreciation: equipment								
Bad debts								
Provision for bad debts								
Debtors control account								
Creditors control account								
Drawings								
Capital								
Bank overdraft								
Cash								
VAT								
Bank interest received								
Bank deposit account								
Suspense account								
Accruals								
Prepayments								
Depreciation								
Bank interest owing								
Closing stock (P&L)								
Closing stock (B/S)								
Provision for bad debts (adjustment)								
SUB-TOTAL								
Profit for the year								
TOTAL								

Task 2

Unfortunately the errors causing the need for the suspense account cannot immediately be found and Jason is anxious that a draft extended trial balance should be produced as quickly as possible.

Make appropriate entries in the adjustment columns of the extended trial balance to take account of the following.

(a) Depreciation is to be provided as follows.

Delivery vans: 20% per annum reducing balance method
Equipment: 10% per annum straight line method

(b) The £30,000 in the bank deposit account was invested on 1 November 1994 at a fixed rate of interest of 6% per annum. A cheque for £300 interest was received by J B Office Supplies on 2 January 1995 and a further cheque for £900 on 3 July 1995.

(c) It is thought highly unlikely that £2,460 owed by M C Miller will be recovered and towards the end of October the decision was made for the debt to be written off. To date no entries have been passed. The provision on remaining debtors should be adjusted to a figure of 5%.

(d) Closing stock has been valued at cost at £58,394. However, this figure includes four office chairs, cost price £230 each, which have been damaged in storage. It has been estimated that if a total of £40 was spent on repairing the worst of the damage then they could be sold for £190 each.

(e) J B Office Supplies had sent a cheque for £1,260 to Metalux Imports, a supplier on 15 October 1995. Unfortunately the cheque had not been signed and was returned in the post on 30 October. No entries have been passed.

(f) Insurance is paid annually in advance on 1 April. The premium for the period 1 May 1995 to 30 April 1996 was £260.

(g) The rent on the property used by J B Office Supplies was set on 1 January 1994 at £200 per month payable in arrears. The next rent review has been scheduled to take place on 1 January 1996.

Task 3

Extend the figures into the extended trial balance columns for profit and loss and balance sheet. Total all of these columns, transferring the balance of the profit or loss as appropriate.

Task 4

Subsequent to the completion of the extended trial balance a further search for the errors which necessitated the opening of the suspense account takes place. The following are found.

(a) A cheque for £60 received from Pauline Ransome, a credit customer, had been entered in the bank account but not in the appropriate control account.

(b) Discounts allowed totalling £125 had been credited to discounts received.

(c) Credit purchases totalling £15,840 had been transferred from the day book into the purchases account at £15,480.

(d) In totalling the columns of the sales day book, the 'net' column had been undercast by £570.

Prepare journal entries to record the correction of these errors. Dates and narratives are not required. Use the blank journal on Page 263.

JOURNAL

Page 1

Details	£	£

SECTION 2 (Suggested time allocation: 45 minutes)

Answer each of the following questions in the space provided as clearly and concisely as you can.

These questions refer to the data given in Section 1.

1   The delivery vans figures of £12,800 shown in the trial balance is made up from two vehicles, one costing £6,000 bought on 1 November 1993 and one costing £6,800 bought on 1 November 1994. If the first van was now to be sold on 1 May 1996 for £3,200, then assuming that depreciation is calculated on a monthly basis:

   (a)   **What would be the book value of the van at the date of sale?**

   ....

   ....

   ....

   ....

   ....

   ....

   ....

   ....

   ....

   (b)   **Show the disposals account as it would appear in the ledger on 31 October 1996.**

MOTOR VANS DISPOSAL ACCOUNT			
	£		£

2   Jason Brown intends to launch a new computer consultancy service during 1997. He is confident that this will bring about a substantial increase in business for his financial year ended 31 October 1997. A major advertising campaign has been planned for September and October 1996.

What is the argument for including the cost of the campaign in the calculation of profit for the year end 31 October 1997? Make reference in your answer to the accounting concept or concepts that relate to this matter.

....

....

....

....

....

....

....

....

3   In Task 4 of Section 1 the following errors, amongst others, were identified.

(a)   Discounts allowed totalling £125 had been credited to discounts received.

(b)   Credit purchases totalling £15,840 had been transferred from the day book into the purchases account as £15,480.

In correcting each error, would the reported profit be increased or decreased and by what amount?

(a)   Increased / Decreased £.................

(b)   Increased / Decreased £.................

4   Included in Jason Brown's stock are some standard office swivel chairs. At the beginning of October ten chairs each costing £30 were in stock. Stock movements during the month were as follows.

Stock at	1/10/95	10 at £30
Purchases	10/10/95	12 at £32
Sales	13/10/95	2
Sales	18/10/95	4
Purchases	23/10/95	10 at £31
Sales	30/10/95	6

Chairs are sold at £50 each.
Stock is valued on a FIFO basis.

Calculate the value of the following.

(a)   **Sales for October.**

....

(b)   **Cost of goods sold for October.**

....

(c)   **Closing stock at the end of October.**

....

5   'Capital expenditure is expenditure on fixed assets which appear in the balance sheet. The cost of a fixed asset does not therefore affect the calculation of profit.'

State whether or not you agree with the above statement and briefly explain the reason for your answer.

....

.........P.+.L...affected...by...depn..

....

....

....

....

....

6   The total sales figure to be used in the calculation of profit is £246,412.

(a)   **Does this figure include or exclude VAT?**

....

(b)   **Briefly explain the reason for your answer.**

....

....

7   You have received the following note from Jason Brown.

'Thank you for producing the extended trial balance showing key figures for the year. I am concerned about the profitability of the business for next year and I am considering the following changes to improve the profit figure.

(a)   Running down the stock levels at the end of the financial year. This can be achieved by reducing purchases and a smaller purchases figure will increase profit.

(b)   Writing off M C Millar's debt this year significantly reduce the profit. If towards the end of next year any large bad debts are identified we should delay writing them off until the following year.

(c)   We should calculate depreciation on all fixed assets using both the straight line and reducing balance methods. Each year we can then use the method which gives us the highest profit.'

Prepare a memorandum to Jason Brown covering each of the points he has raised. Use the headed paper on Page 267 for your answer.

8   Some days after preparing the extended trial balance it was discovered that a credit sale for £96.20 had, in error, not been entered into the account of John Pearce Furniture in the sales ledger. Jason Brown is concerned about the control of errors and had contacted you for an explanation.

Write a note to Jason in the form of a memorandum, explaining why the error would not have been detected by drawing up a trial balance and how the existence of such an error would normally be detected by checking the total of the balances in the sales ledger. Use the headed paper on Page 268.

Task 7

MEMORANDUM

To: Ref:

From: Date:

Subject:

Task 8

MEMORANDUM

To: Ref:

From: Date:

Subject:

SECTION 3 (Suggested time allocation: 55 minutes)

Jason's younger sister Natasha had originally intended joining him in the business as his assistant. However, when she inherited some money an opportunity arose to set up on her own buying and selling stationery and eventually she decided to go ahead with this venture. During October 1995 she purchased premises costing £74,400, fixtures and fittings at £28,800 and stock at £15,613. The stock was partly bought with her own funds and partly on credit. Her supplier, Carlton Office Supplies Ltd, offered her £10,000 credit and at this point she made full use of the facility. At the end of the month she borrowed £48,000 by way of a loan from the bank at an interest rate of 10% per annum. After these transactions had taken place she had £1,220 of surplus funds remaining and on 1 November, the date the business opened, this sum was paid into a business bank account.

All of Natasha's sales were for cash and all were at a mark up of 25% on cost. Unfortunately Natasha did not appreciate the importance of recording sales despite the fact that she had bought a computer on 1 November with the intention of using it to record business transactions. It is estimated that the computer will be used for three years after which time it will have a residual value of £250. Depreciation should be calculated on a monthly basis for the computer and for other fixed assets. (Any depreciation for October should, however, be ignored.)

During November, Natasha took out from the takings any money she needed for her own use but, again, without recording the sums involved. The following amounts were also paid out of the cash and the remainder of the takings were then deposited in the bank.

Postages   £43
Cash purchases   £187
Sundry expenses   £52

Apart from the cash purchases, all other purchases of stock during November were made on credit from Carlton Office Supplies Ltd. Natasha's summarised business bank account for the period appeared as follows.

	Discount £	Bank £		Discount £	Bank £
Balance b/d		1,220	Purchase of the computer		1,402
Takings		30,408	Carlton Office Supplies	200	9,800
			Sundry expenses		61
			Insurance		384
			Carlton Office Supplies	250	12,250
			Balance c/d		7,731
		31,628		450	31,628

The insurance payment covered the period 1 November 1995 to 31 October 1996. On 30 November an invoice received from Carlton Office Supplies Ltd for £8,600 was still *-cl creds.* outstanding and this sum was therefore owed to the company. On the same date Natasha's stock was valued at £11,475. This, however, included £275 for a new electronic diary supplied *- deduct* for trial purposes on a sale or return basis. The £275 had not been included in any of the invoices received.

Depreciation is to be calculated at 2% per annum on cost for the premises and at 10% per annum on cost for the fixtures and fittings.

Jason has asked you to help his sister by producing some figures for her business.

Task 1

Calculate Natasha's original capital sum introduced into the business.

Premises	74400	
F+F	28800	
Stock	15 613	
Bank	1 220	120 033
Creditors	10,000	
Loan	48,000	62 033
∴ Capital =		62 033

Task 2

Draw up the account for Carlton Office Supplies Ltd showing clearly the total purchases made on credit from the company during October and November.

Creditors Control a/c

Bank	9800	Purchases	10,000
Dis. Rec	200	Purchases	12 500
Bank	12250	Purchases	8 600
Dis. Rec	250		
Bal c/d	8 600		
	31100		31100
		Bal b/d	8,600

Task 3

Calculate the value of the total purchases made up to the end of November, including the purchase of the initial stock.

```
            Purchases                   31,100
            Cash Purchases      5613
                                 187    5800
                                       36,900
```

Task 4

Prepare a draft statement calculating the net profit for the month ended 30 November 1995 and clearly showing the total sales for the period.

```
            Trading + P+L a/c  for month ended 30 Nov
    Sales                                   32.125
    Opening Stock              -
    Purchases              36900
                           36,900
    Less cl Stock          11 200
    Cost of Sales                           25700
    Profit                                   6425    - 25% on
    Discount Rec                              450          cost
                                             6 875
    Postage                43
    Insurance              32
    Loan Interest         400
    Sundry expenses       113
    Depn - premises       124
            f+f           240
            computer       32              984
    Net Profit                            5891
```

Task 5

Prepare the cash account for November showing clearly the total drawings made by Natasha during the month.

Cash a/c			
Sales	32125	Postage	43
		Sundries	52
		Purchases	187
		Bank	30,408
		Drawings	1,435
	32125		32,125

ROUGH WORK

TRIAL RUN CENTRAL ASSESSMENT 3

INTERMEDIATE STAGE - NVQ/SVQ3

Preparing Financial Accounts

June 1996

Time allowed - 3 hours

The Central Assessment is in three sections.

Section 1   Extended trial balance exercise
                 Complete all 4 tasks

Section 2   Short answer and communication questions
                 Complete all 7 questions

Section 3   Incomplete records exercise
                 Complete all 6 tasks

The purpose of this Trial Run Central Assessment is to give you an idea of what a Central Assessment looks like. It is not intended as a guide to the topics which are likely to be assessed. Time allocations, shown at the beginning of sections, will give you an idea of how long you should spend on each section, but you should not expect to be under time pressure. You may use the space on Page 285 for rough work.

**DO NOT OPEN THIS PAPER UNTIL YOU ARE READY TO START
UNDER TIMED CONDITIONS**

SECTION 1 (Suggested time allocation: 85 minutes)

Data

Melanie Lancton trades under the name of Explosives and operates out of a store and warehouse. She is a sole trader and has been in the clothes business for approximately ten years. Explosives deals mainly in jeans and speciality T shirts. All of the sales out of the store are for cash but the warehouse is used to supply other clothing retailers throughout the UK on a credit basis. Occasionally, orders are received on a limited scale from shops in northern France.

You are employed by Melanie to assist with the book-keeping. This is currently a manual system and consists of a general ledger, where double entry takes place, a sales ledger and a purchases ledger. The individual accounts of debtors and creditors are therefore regarded as memoranda accounts. Day books are used and totals from their various columns are transferred periodically into the general ledger.

The following balances were extracted from the general ledger at the end of the financial year on 31 May 1996.

	£	£
Stock at 1 June 1995	180,420	
Purchases	610,080	
Sales		840,560
Purchases returns		2,390
Sales returns	2,650	
Motor expenses	5,430	
Bank	20,415	
Cash	3,420	
Rent	11,000	
Lighting and heating	4,180	
Stationery and advertising	6,120	
Provision for bad debts		5,620
Debtors control account	120,860	
Creditors control account		102,860
Salaries	96,200	
Bad debts	7,200	
Drawings	31,600	
Discounts allowed	20,520	
Discounts received		18,400
Motor vehicles: at cost	60,480	
provision for depreciation		12,590
Office furniture and equipment: at cost	26,750	
provision for depreciation		3,170
VAT		10,260
Capital account at 1 June 1995		211,475
	1,207,325	1,207,325

Having extracted the above figures, the following errors were found in the books.

(a) The purchases day book totals for the month of March were as follows.

	£
Total	50,160
VAT	7,471
Net	42,689
Goods for resale	40,463
Other items	2,226

(i) An invoice for £200 plus £35 VAT received from Just Jeans Ltd had been entered as £2,000 plus £35 VAT thus causing errors in both the net and total columns.

(ii) The total of the net column was debited to the purchases account. An analysis of 'other items' showed £1,201 for lighting and heating and £1,025 for stationery and advertising. No entries had been passed in these accounts.

(b) A credit note received from Astra Clothing for £40 plus £7 VAT had, in error, been left out altogether from the returns outwards day book.

(c) Cash sales of £1,645 (inclusive of £245 VAT) had been entered as follows.

Dr Cash book   £1,645
Cr Sales   £1,645

(d) An invoice had been received and correctly entered in the books from Kay Imports Ltd for £1,080 plus £180 VAT, total £1,260. A payment by cheque was made for £1,206 but the discount had been omitted from the discount column of the cash book.

The following adjustments also need to be taken into account.

(1) Depreciation is to be provided as follows.

Motor vehicles - 20% per annum on cost
Office furniture and equipment - 10% per annum reducing balance method

It should be noted that no depreciation is charged on assets in their year of purchase or in their year of sale. On 10 January 1996 a new vehicle had been purchased for £9,800.

(2) Rent payable on the store and warehouse is £1,000 per month.

(3) The stationery and advertising figure includes the sum of £1,560 paid to the Wise Advertising Agency for a series of newspaper advertisements covering all of Explosives' products and due to appear during the period October to December 1996.

(4) Stock has been valued on 31 May 1996 at £208,540. This figure excludes £2,300 of jeans (cost price) which had been damaged by a leak in the roof of the warehouse. The jeans were considered worthless and were thrown out. The Regal Insurance Company has agreed to pay a claim for the full cost of the jeans although as yet no payment has been received.

(5) The provision for bad debts is to be adjusted to a figure representing 5% of debtors.

Task 1

Prepare journal entries to correct the errors (a) to (d) shown on Pages 274 and 275. Dates and narratives are not required.

Use the blank journal on Page 276 for your answer.

Task 2

Enter the corrected balances into the first two columns of the extended trial balance provided on Page 277.

Note. It is the *corrected* balances that should be used, thus taking into account the journal entries prepared for Task 1. Total the two columns ensuring that the two totals agree.

Task 3

Make appropriate entries in the adjustment columns of the extended trial balance to take account of the adjustments (1) to (5) above.

Task 4

Extend the figures into the extended trial balance columns for profit and loss and balance sheet. Total all of these columns, transferring the balance of the profit or loss as appropriate.

JOURNAL		Page 1
Details	£	£

Account	Trial balance		Adjustments		Profit and loss a/c		Balance sheet	
	Debit	Credit	Debit	Credit	Debit	Credit	Debit	Credit
	£	£	£	£	£	£	£	£
Opening stock								
Purchases								
Sales								
Purchases returns								
Sales returns								
Motor expenses								
Bank								
Cash								
Rent								
Lighting and heating								
Stationery and advertising								
Provision for bad debts								
Debtors control account								
Creditors control account								
Salaries								
Bad debts								
Drawings								
Discounts allowed								
Discounts received								
Motor vehicles								
Provision for depreceiation: motor vehicles								
Office furniture and equipment								
Provision for depreciation: office furniture and equipment								
VAT								
Capital								
Accruals								
Prepayments								
Depreciation								
Royal Insurance Company								
Closing stock (P&L)								
Closing stock (B/S)								
Provision for bad debts (adjustment)								
SUB-TOTAL								
Profit for the year								
TOTAL								

SECTION 2 (Suggested time allocation: 40 minutes)

1   **Indicate with a circle the effect on the calculation of profit and on the assets in the balance sheet if capital expenditure is treated as revenue expenditure.**

    (a)   Profit would be:

        Overstated/Understated

    (b)   The value of the assets would be:

        Overstated/Understated

2   Explosives makes a credit sale to Dillon Clothes for £600 plus VAT £105. (*Note.* State clearly for each entry the name of the account, the amount and whether debit or credit.)

    (a)   What double entry is made in the general ledger to record the sale?

    ....

    ....

    ....

    (b)   What double entry is made in the general ledger to record the debtor clearing the debt by cheque?

    ....

    ....

    ....

3   Expenditure on applied research may be capitalised should a company so wish.

    (a)   State whether or not you agree with the above statement. (Assume the expenditure is not on fixed assets.)

    Agree/Disagree

    (b)   Explain *briefly* the reason for your answer to (a), referring to the relevant statement of standard accounting practice.

    ....

    ....

4   Julie Owens is a credit customer of Explosives and currently owes approximately £5,000. She has recently become very slow in paying for purchases and has been sent numerous reminders for most of the larger invoices issued to her. A cheque for £2,500 sent to Explosives has now been returned by Julie Owens' bankers marked 'refer to drawer'.

    Which accounting concept would suggest that a provision for doubtful debts should be created to cover the debt of Julie Owens?

    ....

5   It is found that cash sales have, in error, been credited to purchases instead of sales.

    In correcting this error and adjusting the profit, would profit be increased, reduced or stay the same?

    Increased/Reduced/Stay the same

6   At the end of a previous accounting period, a suspense account with a £200 credit balance had been opened to agree the trial balance. It was subsequently found that only one error had been made, which related to cash drawings. Two debit entries had been made for the same amount instead of a debit and a credit.

    What entries should be passed to correct the error? (*Note.* State clearly for each entry the name of the account, the amount and whether debit or credit.)

    ....

    ....

7   You have receive the following note from Melanie Lancton.

'I have been looking at the draft final accounts you have produced. In the valuation of the closing stock you have included some of the jeans at less than cost price. The figure you used is net realisable value and this has effectively reduced the profit for the period. The closing stock will be sold in the next financial period and my understanding of the accruals concept is that the revenue from selling the stock should be matched against the cost of that stock. This is not now possible since part of the cost of the stock has been written off in reducing the closing stock valuation from cost price to net realisable value.'

Write a suitable response to Melanie Lancton in the form of a memorandum. Your answer should include references to relevant accounting concepts and to SSAP 9. Use the headed paper on Page 280 for your answer.

Task 7

MEMORANDUM

To: Ref:

From: Date:

Subject:

SECTION 3 (Suggested time allocation: 55 minutes)

Melanie Lancton is considering taking over a small clothing wholesalers which belongs to Rahul Gupta. You have been asked to prepare some figures for Melanie from the records kept for the business.

You are presented with the following.

Rahul Gupta assets and liabilities at 31 May 1995

	£
Freehold buildings at cost	80,000
Less depreciation to date	16,000
	64,000
Fixtures and fittings at cost	17,500
Less depreciation to date	12,000
	5,500
Stock	33,200
Debtors	39,470
Prepaid general expenses	550
Cash	900
	74,120
Creditors	35,960
Bank overdraft	17,390
	53,350

Summary of the business bank account for the year ended 31 May 1996

	£		£
Cash sales	147,890	Balance b/d	17,390
From debtors	863,740	To creditors	607,650
Sale proceeds fixtures and fittings	1,360	General expenses	6,240
		Salaries	94,170
		Security devices	5,100
		Drawings	28,310
		Balance c/d	254,130
	1,012,990		1,012,990

Other information

(a) The profit margin achieved on all sales is 40%. At the end of the year on 31 May 1996 the stock was valued at £38,700. However, Rahul Gupta is convinced that various items have been stolen during the year. To prevent further theft the premises were fitted out with various security devices on 31 May 1996.

(b) Depreciation is calculated on a *monthly* basis as follows.

Premises	2% on cost
Fixtures and fittings	10% on cost

Fixtures and fittings purchased on 1 June 1990 for £4,000 were sold on 30 November 1995, the purchaser paying by cheque.

(c) The proceeds of cash sales are held in tills and paid into the bank at the end of the day, apart from a float which is retained on the premises to be used at the start of the following day. During May 1996 a decision was made to increase the size of the float from the £900 held at the beginning of the year to £1,000.

(d) On 31 May 1996 creditors amounted to £49,310, debtors £45,400 and £170 was owing for general expenses. During the year bad debts of £2,340 have been written off.

Task 1

Draw up a total debtors account (debtors control account) showing clearly the total value of the credit sales for the year ended 31 May 1996.

Debtors Control a/c

Balance b/d	39470	Receipts	863740
Sales	872010	Bad Debts	2340
		Balance c/d	45400
	911480		911480
Balance b/d	45400		

Task 2

Calculate the total sales for the year ended 31 May 1996.

Credit Sales	872,010
Cash Sales	147,890
Increase in Float	100
	1,020,000

Task 3

Draw up a total creditors account (creditors control account) showing clearly the total purchases for the year ended 31 May 1996.

Creditors Control a/c

Bank	607,650	balance b/d	35,960
Balance c/d	49,310	Purchases	621,000
	656,960		656,960
		Balance b/d	49,310

Task 4

Calculate the value of the stock stolen during the year.

Trading a/c

Sales		1,020,000
Opening Stock	33,200	
Purchases	621,000	
	654,200	
Less Closing Stock	42,200	
Cost of Sales		612,000
Gross Profit		408,000 — 40% Margin

Per 40% margin, stock = 42,200
Actual stock 38,700
∴ stolen stock must be 3500

Task 5

Calculate the profit or loss made from the sale of fixtures and fittings on 30 November 1995.

```
        Cost of F+F                    4,000
        less Depn to date              2200
        NBV                            1800
        Proceeds from sale             1360
        Loss on sale                    440
```

Task 6

Calculate the figure for general expenses which would be included in the calculation of profit for the year ended 31 May 1996.

```
                    General Expenses a/c
Balance b/d          550      P + L a/c           6960
Bank                6240
Balance c/d          170
                    ────                          ────
                    6960                          6960

                             Balance b/d           170
```

ROUGH WORK

TRIAL RUN CENTRAL ASSESSMENT 4

INTERMEDIATE STAGE - NVQ/SVQ3

Preparing Financial Accounts

December 1996

Time allowed - 3 hours

The Central Assessment is in three sections.

Section 1   Extended trial balance exercise
                 Complete both tasks

Section 2   Short answer and communication questions
                 Complete all 8 questions

Section 3   Incomplete records exercise
                 Complete all 4 tasks

The purpose of this Trial Run Central Assessment is to give you an idea of what a Central Assessment looks like. It is not intended as a guide to the topics which are likely to be assessed. Time allocations, shown at the beginning of sections, will give you an idea of how long you should spend on each section, but you should not expect to be under time pressure. You may use the space on Page 297 for rough work.

**DO NOT OPEN THIS PAPER UNTIL YOU ARE READY TO START
UNDER TIMED CONDITIONS**

SECTION 1 (Suggested time allocation: 80 minutes)

Data

Andrew Hallgrove is the proprietor of Castle Alarms, which specialises in supplying domestic and commercial burglar alarm systems. Although the business operates throughout the UK, the offices and warehouse are located in the north of England.

You are employed within the business to assist with the bookkeeping. This is currently a manual system and consists of a general ledger, where double entry takes place, a sales ledger and a purchases ledger. The individual accounts of debtors and creditors are therefore regarded as memoranda accounts. Day books are used and totals from the various columns of these are transferred periodically into the general ledger.

At the end of the financial year of 31 October 1996, the balances were extracted from the general ledger and entered into an extended trial balance as shown on Page 289.

Task 1

Make appropriate entries in the adjustment columns of the extended trial balance to take account of the following.

(a) Depreciation is to be provided as follows.

Motor vehicles: 20% per annum straight line method
Equipment: 10% per annum reducing balance method

(b) The bank loan of £50,000 was taken out on 31 January 1996. The interest rate charged on the loan is fixed at 10% per annum.

(c) In August a system invoiced at £3,400 was installed at a local restaurant. Unfortunately no money was received in payment, the restaurant closed and the owner disappeared. A decision has now been made to write off the debt.

(d) Having written off all bad debts, the provision for bad debts is to be adjusted to 6% of remaining debtors.

(e) At the stocktake on 31 October 1996 the stock was valued at £289,400 cost price. However, this figures includes the following.

(i) Five system costing £1,200 each which have now been replaced by improved models. It is thought that in order to sell them the price of each system will have to be reduced to £1,000.

(ii) A system costing £2,000 was damaged in the warehouse. Repairs will cost £200 before it can be used in an installation.

(f) The business took advantage of an offer to advertise on local radio during October 1996 at a cost of £2,250. Although the invoice has now been received no entries have been made.

(g) Rent for the business property is £2,100 payable monthly in advance. This has been the figure payable over the last 12 months and a rent review is not due at the present time.

(h) On 30 October 1996 £45,000 cash was withdrawn from the bank for use within the business. To date no entries have been made to reflect this transaction.

(i) A credit note received from Ashito Electronics and relating to goods returned has just been found in a pile of correspondence. The credit note, dated 20 October 1996, is for £2,900 and has not been entered in any of the books of the business.

Task 2

Extend the figures into the extended trial balance columns for profit and loss and balance sheet. Total all of these columns, transferring the balance of the profit or loss as appropriate.

Account	Trial balance		Adjustments		Profit and loss a/c		Balance sheet	
	Debit £	Credit £	Debit £	Credit £	Debit £	Credit £	Debit £	Credit £
Sales		1,200,000						
Purchases	667,820							
Sales returns	96,570							
Purchases returns		52,790						
Opening stock	301,840							
Debtors control account	189,600							
Cash	1,200							
Bank	25,300							
Creditors control account		95,000						
Provision for bad debts		12,000						
Bad debts	10,100							
Discounts allowed	6,320							
Salaries	103,030							
Drawings	26,170							
Rent	27,300							
General expenses	14,310							
Capital		121,860						
VAT		22,600						
Bank loan		50,000						
Interest on bank loan	2,500							
Advertising	11,450							
Motor vehicles	32,600							
Provision for depreciation: motor vehicles		4,100						
Equipment	48,860							
Provision for depreciation: equipment		6,620						
Prepayments								
Depreciation								
Loan interest owing								
Other accruals								
Closing stock (P&L)								
Closing stock (B/S)								
Provision for bad debts (adjustment)								
SUB-TOTAL	1,564,970	1,564,970						
Profit for the year								
TOTAL	1,564,970	1,564,970						

Trial run central assessments

SECTION 2 (Suggested time allocation: 30 minutes)

Answer each of the following questions by writing in the space provided, as clearly and concisely as you can. Circle the correct answer where appropriate.

1 Andrew Hallgrove bought a calculator costing £10 for use in the office.

    Referring to the relevant accounting concept, briefly explain why the purchase would normally be treated as revenue rather than as capital expenditure, despite the fact that the calculator will probably be used for several years.

    ....

    ....

    ....

    ....

    ....

2 At the end of a particular quarter, Castle Alarms' VAT account showed a balance of £2,100 debit.

    Explain briefly what the balance represents.

    ....

    ....

3 Andrew Hallgrove is considering leasing a car for use by one of his stales staff. He understands that leases are classified as operating leases or finance leases and the two types affect the books of a business in different ways.

    Which type of lease would have to be capitalised in the books of Castle Alarms?

    Finance lease / Operating lease / Both finance and operating lease / Neither finance nor operating lease

4 Castle Alarms makes a credit sale to Turnbull Haircare for £200 plus £35 VAT. Unfortunately, in error, the sale invoice is not entered in the sales day book.

    (a) **Would the error be detected by drawing up a trial balance?**

        Yes / No

    (b) **Briefly explain the reason for your answer to (a)**

        ....

        ...... Error of emission ....

        ....

        ....

        ....

        ....

        ....

5 A motor vehicle which has been purchased by Castle Alarms for £10,450 was eventually sold for £3,000, when it had a net book value of £4,100.

    What is the total charge to the profits of Castle Alarms with respect to the capital cost of the vehicle, during the life of the asset?

    £................................

6   Castle Alarms purchases an alarm from Ace Electronics. Ace Electronics normally sells the alarm at a price of £2,400, but Castle Alarms is given a 20% trade discount. Ace Electronics charges £10 for delivery to Castle Alarms' premises. Castle Alarms puts a price on the alarm of £2,425.

   What value would be placed on this particular item by Castle Alarms in valuing the stock of the business?

   £.....................................

7   Castle Alarms purchases 20 alarm sirens from Northern Imports Ltd. The price charged for each siren is £40 plus VAT calculated at 17.5%. A 10% cash discount is offered by Northern Imports Ltd provided that payment is made within 14 days. (*Note.* State clearly for each entry the name of the account, the amount and whether it is debit or credit.)

   (a)   **What double entry is made in the general ledger to record the purchase (the date of payment has not yet been determined)?**

   ....

   ....

   ....

   (b)   **What double entry is made in the general ledger to record Castle Alarms' clearing the debt by cheque whilst at the same time taking advantage of the discount offered?**

   ....Dr Cred Cont a/c............................926............

   ....Cr Bank............................846............

   ....Cr Dis Rec............................80............

8   Although Andrew Hallgrove has proved to be a good businessman, his knowledge of accounting is rather limited. In particular he does not understand how it is possible for a business to make a profit whilst at the same time the bank balance can remain static or even decrease. He has asked you to provide some guidance.

   Draft a memorandum to him clearly stating how profit is measured and giving examples of why the movement of the bank balance does not necessarily reflect the profits made. Use the headed paper on Page 292 for your answer.

MEMORANDUM

To: Ref:

From: Date:

Subject:

SECTION 3 (Suggested time allocation: 80 minutes)

Data

(a) Andrew Hallgrove decided to open a shop selling cheap alarm systems and security equipment direct to the public. Trading was to start at the beginning of October 1996. He decided to call the shop and business 'Total Security'.

(b) On 1 September he opened a new bank account and paid in £50,000 of his own money as his investment in the business.

(c) During September he purchased shop fixtures and fittings at £22,500 and stock at £47,300. He paid £9,000 for 6 months' rent covering the period 1 September 1996 to 28 February 1997. Insurance of £480 covering the 12 months from 1 September 1996 was also paid, as were various items of general expenditure totalling £220.

(d) Since it was convenient to make some of the payments in cash he withdrew a lump sum from the bank.

(e) Unfortunately, is £50,000 investment was insufficient to cover all of the expenditure. However, he managed to negotiate a bank loan and all the monies from this were paid into the business's bank account.

(f) The interest rate for the bank loan was fixed at 12% per annum.

(g) At the end of September he had a £10,000 balance remaining in the bank account and £500 in cash.

(h) A summary of the business bank account for October 1996 is shown below.

	£		£
Balance b/d	10,000	To creditors	20,250
Cash banked	22,000	Drawings	3,500
		General expenses	500
		Stationery	320
		Customer refund	2,000
		Balance c/d	5,430
	32,000		32,000

(i) The cash banked all came from sales to customers. However, before banking the takings, £2,400 had been paid out as wages. the cash float at the end of October remained at £500.

(j) In paying his creditors he had been able to take advantage of discounts totalling £1,250. At the end of the month not all creditors had been paid, however, and he calculated that the total of the unpaid invoices amounted to £3,400.

(k) Depreciation is calculated on the fixtures and fittings at 20% per annum on cost.

(l) On 31 October 1996 a customer returned an alarm system which he had decided was not appropriate for his premises. He was given a refund by cheque.

(m) Unsold stock on 31 October was valued at £55,000, but this did not include the returned system. The profit margin on this type of system is 30%.

Task 1

Calculate the amount of the bank loan taken out in September, clearly showing your workings.

....

....

....

....

....

....

....

....

....

....

....

....

....

Task 2

List the business assets as at 30 September 1996 together with their value. (Depreciation for September should be ignored.)

....

....

....

....

....

....

....

....

....

....

....

Task 3

Calculate the value of the purchases made during October 1996

....BPP Publishing...............

....

....

....

....

....

....

....

....

....

....

Task 4

Prepare a draft statement calculating the net profit for the month ended 31 October 1996.

....

....

....

....

....

....

....

....

....

....

....

....

....

....

....

....

....

....

....

....

....

....

....

....

....

....

ROUGH WORK

TRIAL RUN CENTRAL ASSESSMENT 5

INTERMEDIATE STAGE - NVQ/SVQ3

Preparing Financial Accounts

June 1997

Time allowed - 3 hours

The Central Assessment is in three sections.

Section 1   Extended trial balance exercise
             Complete all 3 tasks

Section 2   Short answer and communication questions
             Complete all 5 questions

Section 3   Incomplete records exercise
             Complete all 8 tasks

The purpose of this Trial Run Central Assessment is to give you an idea of what a Central Assessment looks like. It is not intended as a guide to the topics which are likely to be assessed. Time allocations, shown at the beginning of sections, will give you an idea of how long you should spend on each section, but you should not expect to be under time pressure. You may use the space on Page 310 for rough work.

**DO NOT OPEN THIS PAPER UNTIL YOU ARE READY TO START
UNDER TIMED CONDITIONS**

SECTION 1 (Suggested time allocation: 75 minutes)

Data

The company Electronics World Ltd operates out of offices and a warehouse located in Wales. The company purchases hi-fi systems, televisions and other electronic goods from manufacturers world-wide. Customers are mainly UK based shops specialising in electronic items.

- You are employed by Electronics World Ltd to assist with the bookkeeping.

- The company is relatively new and is still considering an appropriate computerised accounting system.

- The manual system currently in use consists of a general ledger, a sales ledger and a purchases ledger.

- Double entry takes place in the general ledger and the individual accounts of debtors and creditors are therefore regarded as memoranda accounts.

- Day books consisting of a purchases day book, a sales day book, a purchases returns day book and a sales returns day book are used. Totals from the various columns of the day books are transferred periodically into the general ledger.

The following balances were extracted by a colleague from the general ledger on 24 May 1997, one week before the end of the financial year, which is on 31 May 1997.

	£
Share capital	600,000
Premises	360,000
Fixtures and fittings (F and F) at cost	140,000
Provision for depreciation (F and F)	65,000
Purchases	972,140
Sales	1,530,630
Salaries	206,420
Sales returns	23,200
Purchases returns	17,350
General expenses	74,322
Insurance	16,390
Bad debts	7,506
Provision for bad debts	6,000
Debtors control account	237,855
Creditors control account	121,433
Stock at 1 June 1996	188,960
Bank	65,200
Bank deposit account	150,000
Bank interest received	3,750
Motor vehicles (MV) at cost	22,400
Provision for depreciation (MV)	3,800
VAT (credit balance)	24,720
Profit and loss	91,710

During the last week of the financial year a number of transactions took place and these are summarised below.

Purchases day book	Total	VAT	Net
	£	£	£
	23,970	3,570	20,400

Sales day book	Total	VAT	Net
	£	£	£
	35,955	5,355	30,600

Sales returns day book	Total	VAT	Net
	£	£	£
	1,410	210	1,200

Cheques issued	£
Payable to various creditors in settlement of debts	5,000

Task 1

Complete the table below to show the double entry which would have to be carried out in order to update the balances extracted on 24 May 1997, to take account of the summarised transactions shown above.

DOUBLE ENTRY TO UPDATE BALANCES EXTRACTED ON 24 MAY 1997		
Names of accounts	Dr £	Cr £
Entries from purchases day book		
Purchases	20,400	
VAT a/c	3570	
Creditors Control a/c		23,970
Entries from sales day book		
Debtors Control a/c	35,955	
Sales		30,600
VAT a/c		5,355
Entries from sales returns day book		
Sales Returns	1200	
VAT a/c	210	
Debtors Control a/c		1410
Entries from cheques issued		
Creditors Control a/c	5000	
Bank book		5000

Task 2

Enter the updated balances into the first two columns of the extended trial balance provided on Page 303. Total the two columns ensuring that the two totals agree.

Note. It is the *updated* balances that should be used taking into account the effects of the entries prepared for Task 1.

Task 3

Make appropriate entries in the adjustment columns of the extended trial balance to take account of the following.

(a) Depreciation is to be provided as follows.

Motor vehicles: 20% per annum on cost
Fixtures and fittings: 10% per annum reducing balance method

No depreciation is charged on assets in their year of purchase or in their year of sale. On 12 November 1996 new fixture and fittings costing £6,000 had been purchased.

(b) The £150,000 was invested in the bank deposit account on 30 November 1996 at a fixed rate of interest of 6% per annum.

(c) The general expenses figure includes the sum of £2,400 paid to a company to clean the offices of Electronics World Ltd during the period 1 April 1997 to 30 September 1997.

(d) Stock has been valued on 31 May 1997 at £198,650. This figure excludes a television which was damaged beyond repair and had to be scrapped (no sale proceeds). Regis Insurance has agreed to cover the loss incurred in writing off the television.

Cost price of television: £420
Sales price of television: £630

(e) A cheque for £60 was issued at the beginning of May 1997 to pay for insurance cover which expired on 31 May 1997. A bank statement showed that the cheque was paid on 20 May. As yet no entries have been made in the books of Electronics World Ltd.

(f) The provision for bad debts is to be adjusted to a figure representing 5% of debtors.

Account	Trial balance		Adjustments	
	Debit	Credit	Debit	Credit
	£	£	£	£
Share capital		600,000		
Premises	360,000			
Fixtures and fittings (F and F) at cost	140,000			
Provision for depreciation (F and F)		65,000		6900
Purchases	992,540		420	420
Sales		1561,230		
Salaries	206,420			
Sales returns	24,400			
Purchases returns		17,350		
General expenses	74322			1600
Insurance	16390		60	
Bad debts	7506			
Provision for bad debts		6000		7620
Debtors control account	272,400			
Creditors control account		140,403		
Stock at 1 June 1996	188,960			60
Bank	60,200			
Bank deposit account	150,000		750	
Bank interest received		3750		750
Motor vehicles (MV) at cost	22400			
Provision for depreciation (MV)		3800		4480
VAT: credit balance		26295		
Profit and loss		91710		
Prepayments			1600	
Depreciation - P+L			11380	
Regis Insurance			420	1600
Closing stock (P&L)				198,650
Closing stock (B/S)			198,650	
Provision for bad debts (adjustment)			7,620	
Bank interest owing			750	
TOTAL	2,515,538	2,515,538	220,480	220,480

SECTION 2 (Suggested time allocation: 50 minutes)

Answer each of the following questions in the space provided, as clearly and concisely as you can or, where appropriate, circle the correct answer.

1   On 31 May 1997, the balances of the accounts in the sales ledger were listed, totalled then compared with the balance of the debtors control account. The total of the list of balances amounted to £274,189. Investigations were carried out and the following errors discovered.

    (a)   A customer balance of £484 had been listed as £448.

    (b)   A customer balance of £1,490 had been listed twice.

    (c)   A discount of £100 allowed to a customer had been debited to the account in the sales ledger.

    (d)   Although goods of £135 (inclusive of VAT) had been returned by a customer, no entry had been made in the sales ledger.

Enter the appropriate adjustments in the table shown below. For each adjustment show clearly the amount involved and whether that amount is to be added or subtracted.

		£
Total from listing of balances		274,189
Adjustment for (a)	add/~~subtract~~	36
Adjustment for (b)	~~add~~/subtract	(1490)
Adjustment for (c)	~~add~~/subtract	(200)
Adjustment for (d)	add/subtract	(135)
Revised total to agree with debtors control account		272,400

2   Stock has always been valued by Electronics World Ltd on a FIFO basis and this includes the closing stock figure of £198,650 as at 31 May 1997. It has been suggested that the closing stock figure should now be recalculated on a LIFO basis.

    (a)   Assuming that the prices of electronic goods have been gradually rising throughout the year would the change suggested increase profit for the year ended 31 May 1997, decrease profit or would profit remain the same?

    Increase/**Decrease**/Remain the same

    (b)   Which accounting concept states that the company should not normally change its basis for valuing stock unless it has very good reasons for doing so?

    SSAP 2 – Consistency

3   Electronics World Ltd recently arranged for a local builder to design and build an extension to the company offices. An invoice is received from the builder on completion of the work showing two main categories of expenditure: materials (bricks, doors, windows, frames etc) and labour. It has been suggested that:

'Since salaries and wages are normally shown in the profit and loss account the labour cost in the invoice should be written off as an expense whilst the cost of the materials should be debited to the premises account.'

    (a)   Do you agree with the above statement?

    Yes/**No**

    (b)   Briefly explain the reason for your answer.

    Any work involved in improving the building should be capitalised – the whole invoice should be debited to premises

4   You are reviewing some accounting records on 10 June 1997 and discover an error in the sales day book. Although the VAT and net columns have been correctly totalled, the total column itself has been miscast. The appropriate figures have then been transferred from the day book into the ledgers.

Preparation of which of the following, if any, would be likely to detect the error?

Bank reconciliation statement/Trial balance/VAT return/None of these

5   For some months Electronic World Ltd has been purchasing a range of CD racks from Arun Divan, a small local supplier, who deals exclusively with the company. Initially invoices received from this business did not include VAT but the last invoice did have VAT, calculated at 17.5%, added to the cost of the racks. Jackie Brown, a colleague, is confused about the regulations regarding VAT and the implications of the change. A note is left for you by Jackie raising the following specific points.

(a)   If Electronics World Ltd is now having to pay more money for the CD racks then this must affect the profits of the company.

(b)   Arun Divan has now registered for VAT. Since the increased money he receives from Electronics World Ltd is payable to HM Customs and Excise then his profitability must remain unchanged.

Prepare a memo to Jackie Brown covering both of the points raised. Use the headed paper on Page 306 for your answer.

MEMORANDUM

To: Jackie Brown

Ref:

From:

Date:

Since Electronics World is registered for VAT, we can claim the VAT as shown on the invoice from Arun Divan, back from C+E, therefore there will be no adverse effect on our profits.

Now that Arun Divan has been registered for VAT, he can net off the VAT he charges his customers, with the VAT he pays his suppliers. This should improve his profitability since he could not reclaim any VAT he paid when he was not registered.

SECTION 3 (Suggested time allocation: 55 minutes)

Note. Clearly show your workings for all tasks.

Lucy Barber previously worked full-time for a furniture manufacturing company. Approximately two years ago, however, she decided to set up a part-time business making and selling speaker stands for hi-fi systems. She now has an arrangement to sell exclusively to Electronics World Ltd and you have been asked to assist her in preparing her accounts for the year ended 30 April 1997.

The following information is available.

(a) Tools and equipment costing £3,000 were purchased for the business on 31 July 1995.

(b) A van costing £4,800 was purchased on 31 October 1995, again for use in the business.

(c) Lucy Barber rents a small workshop on a light industrial estate. The rent payable was £100 a month until 31 October 1996 but then it was increased to £120 a month and this remains as the current rate. On 30 April 1996 one month's rent was owing to the landlord.

(d) During Lucy Barber's first period of trading, which ended on 30 April 1996, all of the transactions were for cash. On 30 April 1996 the cash balance of the business was £4,250. On 1 May 1996 she opened a business bank account and a private bank account. The £4,250 was paid into the business account but no funds were paid at that time into the private account. From 1 May 1996 all business transactions passed through the business bank account with the exception of some cheques from Electronics World Ltd (see below).

(e) From 1 May 1996 sales to Electronics World Ltd were on credit as were purchases from her supplier, Johnson Materials Ltd. Cheques received from Electronics World were all paid into the business bank account apart from three which Lucy Barber paid directly into her private account.

(f) Throughout the year ended 30 April 1997 Lucy Barber withdrew £200 a month cash from her private account for personal spending. No other transactions passed through the account other than the three cheques paid in from Electronics World Ltd. On the 30 April 1997 the balance of the account was £600.

(g) During the year ended 30 April 1997 she made and sold 500 pairs of speaker stands. In determining the price charged for each pair she calculated the cost of materials used for the pair then doubled this figure.

(h) On 30 April 1997:
     (i)   £4,400 was owed to the business by Electronics World Ltd;
     (ii)   £1,500 was owed by the business to Johnson Materials Ltd;
     (iii) materials were in stock to make 120 pairs of speaker stands.

(i) Lucy Barber does not have a record of the materials that were in stock on 30 April 1996.

(j) The van is to be depreciated at 10% per annum on cost. The tools and equipment are to be depreciated at 20% per annum on cost.

(k) The following is a summary made by Lucy Barber of the entries which passed through the business bank account during the year ended 30 April 1997.

	£
Money received	
Electronics World Ltd	17,600
Money paid out	
Rent	1,300
Johnson Materials Ltd	12,000
Tools and equipment	250
Electricity	640
Telephone	560

Task 1

Calculate the total sales made by Lucy Barber during the year ended 30 April 1997.

```
Receipts from Debtors      17600
Owed                        4400
                           22000
Dwgs 200×12                 2400
Bal on private a/c           600
Sales                      25000
```

Task 2

Calculate the selling price for one pair of speaker stands.

```
Sold   500
Sales  25000  =  £50 each
       ─────
        500
```

Task 3

Calculate the cost of materials used in making one pair of speaker stands.

```
Selling price  =  50
Cost price     =  50  =  £25
                  ──
                   2
```

Task 4

Calculate the total cost of goods sold during the year ended 30 April 1997 (ie the cost of materials used in making the sales calculated in Task 1).

```
Total cost =  500 × £25  =  £12500
```

Task 5

Calculate the cost of materials purchased by Lucy Barber during the year ended 30 April 1997.

```
Materials     12000
Owing          1500
              13500
```

Task 6

Calculate the stock of materials held by Lucy Barber on 30 April 1996

Opening stock	2000
Purchases	13500
	15500
Less Closing stock $^{120 \times 25}$	3000
Cost of sales	12500

Task 7

Calculate the capital invested in the business by Lucy Barber on 30 April 1996.

Bank		4250
Stock		2000
Tools	3000	
Less	450	2550
Van	4800	
Less	240	4560
		13360
Less accrual		100
CAPITAL		13260

Task 8

Calculate the figure for rent which would be included in the calculation of profit for the year ended 30 April 1997.

			or	Rent paid	1300
6 x 100	=	600		Owing last yr	100
6 x 120	=	720			1200
		1320		Owing this yr	120
					1320

ROUGH WORK

Solutions
to
trial run central
assessments

SOLUTION TO TRIAL RUN
CENTRAL ASSESSMENT 1

DO NOT TURN THIS PAGE UNTIL YOU HAVE
COMPLETED TRIAL RUN CENTRAL ASSESSMENT 1

SECTION 1

Task 1

See extended trial balance on Page 315.

Task 2

	Depreciation charge for the year ended 31 May 1995
	£
Motor vehicles	3,576
Equipment	9,550
Total	13,126

Task 3

Stock sheets	Value
	£
Total b/f from previous pages	18,000
Bambino choir of Prague	3,500
The Joyful Singers sing Wesley	1,200
Bach at St Thomas's	5,000
Value of stock as at 31 May 1995	27,700

Task 4

JOURNAL		Page 1
Details	**£**	**£**
(a) DEBIT Artists' fees and royalties	4,500	
CREDIT Sundry creditors		4,500
Being royalties due to artists for the quarter ended 31 May 1995.		
DEBIT Artists' fees and royalties	252	
CREDIT Sundry creditors		252
Being correction of under-calculation of royalties due to Mr Willis-Brown for quarter ended 31 December 1994		
(b) DEBIT Debtors	220	
CREDIT Bank		220
Being dishonoured cheque		
(c) DEBIT Drawings	2,110	
CREDIT Motor expenses		2,110
Being correct posting of private motoring expenses		

Tasks 5 and 6

See extended trial balance on Page 315.

Account	Trial balance Debit £	Trial balance Credit £	Adjustments Debit £	Adjustments Credit £	Profit and loss a/c Debit £	Profit and loss a/c Credit £	Balance sheet Debit £	Balance sheet Credit £
Artists' fees and royalties	41,120		4,752		45,872			
Bank and cash	1,420			220			1,200	
Capital		26,449						26,449
Drawings	14,500		2,110				16,610	
Employer's NI	3,619				3,619			
Equipment (cost)	38,200						38,200	
Equipment (provision for depreciation)		19,100		9,550				28,650
Loan		10,000						10,000
Loan interest	1,350		150		1,500			
Mastering and production costs	143,400				143,400			
Motor expenses	6,330			2,110	4,220			
Motor vehicles (cost)	29,800						29,800	
Motor vehicles (provision for depreciation)		17,880		3,576				21,456
Recording costs	12,550				12,550			
Rent	13,000			1,000	12,000			
Sales		307,800				307,800		
Stocks of compact discs	22,500				22,500			
Sundry creditors		4,080						4,080
Sundry debtors	12,500		220				12,720	
Sundry expenses	1,270				1,270			
VAT (amount owing)		3,250						3,250
Wages and salaries	47,000				47,000			
Depreciation			13,126		13,126			
Closing stock (B/S)			27,700				27,700	
Closing stock (P&L)				27,700		27,700		
Accrued expenses				4,902				4,902
Prepaid expenses			1,000				1,000	
SUB-TOTAL	388,559	388,559	49,058	49,058	307,057	335,500	98,787	127,230
Profit for the year					28,443			28,443
TOTAL	388,559	388,559	49,058	49,058	335,500	335,500	127,230	127,230

SECTION 2

1   (a)   The credit balance on the VAT account represents the excess of VAT collected on sales (output tax) over VAT paid on purchases or expenses (input tax).

    (b)   This amount is owed to HM Customs & Excise.

2   The microphones could become obsolete as a newer, better model comes onto the market.

3   A case could be made for capitalising the cost of the tapes, on the grounds that they are for use over a number of accounting periods. Highbury Discs has not, however, adopted this treatment because, at only £8 each, the cost of the tapes is not material. They have therefore been expensed in the year of purchase.

    It should be emphasised that this type of decision is not always clear cut. In particular, what is material to a small business may not be to a large one.

4   (a)   This year's profit would be overstated since closing stock is a deduction from cost of sales.

    (b)   Next year's profit would be understated since opening stock is an addition to cost of sales.

5   The accruals or matching concept.

6

MEMORANDUM

To: Anthony Sedgewick   Ref:
From: Accounting Technician   Date: 6 June 1995
Subject: *Rules for stock valuation*

The fundamental accounting concept of prudence dictates that profits are not anticipated but losses are taken into account as soon as they are foreseen.

This cautious approach is adopted in SSAP 9 *Stocks and long-term contracts* which states that stock should be valued at the lower of cost and net realisable value (NRV). Cost, here, is the cost of producing the discs, together with a share of manufacturing overheads. Net realisable value is the estimated selling price less any further costs required to sell the product or get the product into saleable form.

It should be noted further that the comparison of cost and NRV should be carried out for each item separately. It is not sufficient to compare the total cost of all stock items with their total NRV.

When net realisable value is lower than cost, net realisable value should be used. Applying this principle to the Bambino Choir discs, NRV is higher than costs, because we expect to earn a profit on them, even if this profit is delayed.

However, in the case of the 'Joyful Singers' discs, net realisable value is £3.00 each, which is lower than cost of £5.00 each. Thus we will make a loss of 400 × (£5 – £3) ie £800, which, following the prudence concept we must take to the P&L as soon as it is foreseen.

Turning now to the Bach at St Thomas's discs, we see an application of *net* realisable value. The discs cost £3.50 each. While they can be sold for £4.00, this would only be after incurring further costs of £1.50 per disc. The net realisable value of each disc is therefore £4.00 less £1.50, that is £2.50 per disc. Since this is below cost, this is the figure that must be used.

SECTION 3

Tutorial notes

(1) Be careful when calculating the discounts received figure. The £30,060 paid to creditors is 90% of the normal price, so the discount is $£30,060 \times \dfrac{10\%}{90\%}$, ie £3,340.

(2) The van owned at the beginning of the year is shown at net book value. It has been depreciated for one year, so the original cost was £7,500 × 4/3 = £10,000.

BANK			
	£		£
Balance b/f	323	Trade creditors	30,060
Cash	2,770	Drawings	12,000
Trade debtors	43,210	Motor van	4,800
Capital	10,000	Rent	5,330
		Motor expenses	3,400
		Balance c/d	713
	56,303		56,303
Balance b/d	713		

CASH			
	£		£
Balance b/f	25	Bank	2,770
Trade debtors	8,340	Motor expenses	600
		Drawings (bal fig)	4,961
		Balance c/d	34
	8,365		8,365
Balance b/d	34		

MOTOR EXPENSES			
	£		£
Bank	3,400	Balance b/f	174
Cash	600	Profit and loss	4,035
Balance c/d	209		
	4,209		4,209
		Balance b/d	209

MOTOR VAN(S)			
	£		£
Balance b/f	7,500	Depreciation charge (P&L)	
Bank	4,800	$£(10,000 \div 4) + (4,800 \div 4 \times {}^4/_{12})$	2,900
		Balance c/d	9,400
	12,300		12,300
Balance b/d	9,400		

RENT AND INSURANCE

	£		£
Balance (insurance) b/f	180	Balance (rent) b/f	250
Bank	5,330	Profit and loss	5,060
		Balance (insurance) c/d	200
	5,510		5,510
Balance (insurance) b/d	200		

MATERIALS USED

	£		£
Balance b/f	1,530	Profit and loss	33,910
Purchases	33,980	Balance c/d	1,600
	35,510		35,510
Balance b/d	1,600		

TRADE CREDITORS

	£		£
Bank	30,060	Balance b/f	3,650
Discounts received		Purchases (bal fig)	33,980
($£30,060 \times {}^{10\%}/_{90\%}$)	3,340		
Balance c/d	4,230		
	37,630		37,630
		Balance b/d	4,230

TRADE DEBTORS

	£		£
Balance b/f	1,550	Bank	43,210
Work done	52,000	Bad debts	480
		Cash (bal fig)	8,340
		Balance c/d £(2,000 – 480)	1,520
	53,550		53,550
Balance b/d	1,520		

DRAWINGS

	£		£
Bank	12,000	Capital	16,961
Cash	4,961		
	16,961		16,961

SOLUTION TO TRIAL RUN
CENTRAL ASSESSMENT 2

DO NOT TURN THIS PAGE UNTIL YOU HAVE
COMPLETED TRIAL RUN CENTRAL ASSESSMENT 2

SECTION 1

Task 1

See extended trial balance on Page 321.

Task 2

(a) *Depreciation*

Delivery vans: £(12,800 − 3,520) × 20% = £1,856
Equipment £22,800 × 10% = £2,280
Total depreciation = £4,136

(b) *Interest*

£30,000 × 6% = £1,800
∴ £600 accrued interest is receivable.

(c) *Bad debts*

	£
Debtors control account balance	41,600
Debt written off: M C Millar	2,460
	39,140

Provision for doubtful debts required
= 5% × £39,140 = £1,957 ∴ reduce current provision of £1,980 by £23.

(d) *Stock*

The damaged chairs must be valued at the lower of cost and net realisable value.

		£
Cost (£230 × 4)		920
NRV:	selling price (£190 × 4)	760
	less repairs	40
		720

∴ Reduce stock by £(920 − 720) = £200
Closing stock is £(58,394 − 200) = £58,194

(e) *JB Office Supplies*

This payment has not in fact been made, so the original entry must be reversed.

DEBIT	Bank overdraft	£1,260	
CREDIT	Creditors control a/c		£1,260

(f) *Insurance*

Premium prepaid = £260 × 6/12 = £130

(g) *Rent*

Total rent payable = £200 × 12 = £2,400
∴ £200 must be accrued

Account	Trial balance Debit £	Trial balance Credit £	Adjustments Debit £	Adjustments Credit £	Profit and loss a/c Debit £	Profit and loss a/c Credit £	Balance sheet Debit £	Balance sheet Credit £
Purchases	170,240				170,240			
Sales		246,412				246,412		
Purchases returns		480				480		
Sales returns	670				670			
Opening stock	54,200				54,200			
Salaries	30,120				30,120			
Rent	2,200		200		2,400			
Insurance	360			130	230			
Delivery vans	12,800						12,800	
Provision for depreciation: delivery vans		3,520		1,856				5,376
Equipment	22,800						22,800	
Provision for depreciation: equipment		5,760		2,280				8,040
Bad debts	2,700		2,460		5,160			
Provision for bad debts		1,980	23					1,957
Debtors control account	41,600			2,460			39,140	
Creditors control account		33,643		1,260				34,903
Drawings	10,522						10,522	
Capital		83,171						83,171
Bank overdraft		348	1,260				912	
Cash	568						568	
VAT		2,246						2,246
Bank interest received		1,200		600		1,800		
Bank deposit account	30,000						30,000	
Suspense account		20						20
Accruals				200				200
Prepayments			130				130	
Depreciation			4,136		4,136			
Bank interest owing			600				600	
Closing stock (P&L)				58,194		58,194		
Closing stock (B/S)			58,194				58,194	
Provision for bad debts (adjustment)				23		23		
SUB-TOTAL	378,780	378,780	67,003	67,003	267,156	306,909	175,666	135,913
Profit for the year					39,753			39,753
TOTAL	378,780	378,780	67,003	67,003	306,909	306,909	175,666	175,666

Task 3

See extended trial balance on Page 321.

Task 4

See journal below.

Note. These journals clear the suspense account, as shown in the ledger account.

SUSPENSE ACCOUNT

	£		£
Debtors control a/c	60	Balance on TB	20
Sales	570	Discounts	250
		Purchases	360
	630		630

JOURNAL		Page 1
Details	**£**	**£**
(a) DEBIT Suspense a/c	60	
CREDIT Debtors control a/c		60
Being receipt from debtor not recorded in control a/c		
(b) DEBIT Discounts received		
DEBIT Discounts allowed	125	
CREDIT Suspense account	125	
Being correction of double entry and correct account for discount allowed		250
(c) DEBIT Purchase a/c	360	
CREDIT Suspense a/c		360
Being correction of purchases day book transposition		
(d) DEBIT Suspense a/c		
CREDIT Sales	570	
Being correction of undercast in sales day book		570

SECTION 2

1 (a) *Book value of van at sale*

		£
Cost		6,000
Accumulated depreciation	1.11.93 - 31.10.94 = £6,000 × 20%	1,200
		4,800
	1.11.94 - 31.10.95 = £4,800 × 20%	960
		3,840
	1.11.95 - 30.4.95 = £3,840 × 20%	384
Book value at date of sale		3,456

(b) *Disposals account*

MOTOR VANS DISPOSAL ACCOUNT

	£		£
Vans: cost	6,000	Motor vans: provision for depreciation £(6,000 – 3,456)	2,544
		Cash	3,200
		Profit and loss a/c	256
	6,000		6,000

2   The argument in favour of including the advertising costs in the calculation of profit for the year ended 31 October 1997 is based on the *accruals concept*. The costs of advertising will be 'matched' with the associated revenues of the service. (However, the prudence concept might dictate that the costs should be written off against current profits if there is no guarantee that the consultancy will be profitable.)

3 (a) Decreased by £250
   (b) Decreased by £360

4 (a) *Sales for October*

   (2 + 4 + 6) × £50 = £600

   (b) *Cost of goods sold for October*

	£
Sale 13.10.95: Cost = 2 × £30	60
Sale 18.10.95: Cost = 4 × £30	120
Sale 30.10.95: Cost = 4 × £30	120
	364

   (c) *Closing stock*

	£
10 at £32	320
10 at £31	310
	630

5   This statement is not true because fixed assets must be depreciated over their useful economic lives. The periodic depreciation charge passes through the profit and loss account as an expense, thus reducing profit. The benefit obtained from use of the asset is thus matched against its cost.

6 (a) It excludes VAT.

   (b) SSAP 5 *Accounting for VAT* requires all figures in the accounts, in particular sales and purchases, to be shown net of VAT, where VAT is recoverable.

7

MEMORANDUM

To: Jason Brown   Ref:

From: Accounting technician   Date: 8 December 1995

Subject: *Profit and accounting rules*

There are various problems with the changes you propose to make next year to improve profitability.

(a) At the year end the cost of sales is matched with sales to calculate profit. Where stocks are held at the year end, these must be matched against future sales (under the accruals, or matching concept), and so they are deducted from the current cost of sales. You can see then that running down stocks at the year end would therefore have no impact, for example:

	Higher year end stocks	Lower year end stocks
	£	£
Purchases (and opening stock)	120,000	100,000
Closing stock	30,000	10,000
	90,000	90,000

There is no effect on profit, just a lower closing stock figure in the balance sheet, and a higher cash balance (fewer purchases made).

(b) The prudence concept states that all losses must be recognised as soon as they are foreseen. It is therefore not acceptable to 'put off' writing off a debt until the following year (when in any case it would have just as bad an effect on profit).

(c) It is not acceptable to change the method of depreciation of assets from year to year because of the consistency concept. This requires items to be treated in the same way over time in order to allow comparison between accounts from year to year.

I am afraid that the only real ways to increase profitability are to increase sales and cut costs!

8

MEMORANDUM

To: Jason Brown   Ref:
From: Accounting Technician   Date: 8 December 1005
Subject: *Sales ledger errors*

The error discovered, that £96.20 had not been posted to the account of John Pearce Furniture Ltd, will not be discovered by a trial balance because the account in question is not part of the system of accounts. It is, rather, a 'personal' account kept as a memorandum of how much an individual owes your business, along with all other such accounts in the sales ledger.

The account within the system which relates to debtors, the debtors control account, is an impersonal, summary account which shows only the *total* owed to your business by debtors.

These accounts are both posted from the same sources (such as the sales day book and the cash book), but the debtors control account postings are in total, whereas the personal accounts in the sales ledger are posted with individual transactions.

The control account balance should therefore, in theory, be equal to the total of all the balances in the personal accounts in the sales ledger. In practice, discrepancies arise, and by comparing the two totals and investigating these discrepancies, errors can be found in both types of account and thereby corrected.

This is a good way of making sure that the figure from the control account, which appears under debtors in the balance sheet, is correct, as well as ensuring that you receive the correct amounts from the individual debtors of the business.

SECTION 3

Task 1

	£
Premises	74,400
Fixtures and fittings	28,800
Stocks £(15,613 − 10,000)	5,613
	108,813
Less bank loan	48,000
	60,813
Surplus funds	1,220
Original capital invested	62,033

Task 2

CARLTON OFFICE SUPPLIES			
	£		£
Oct 95		*Oct 95*	
		Credit purchases	10,000
Nov 95		*Nov 95*	
Bank	9,800	Credit purchases	12,500
Discount received	200	Credit purchases	8,600
Bank	12,250		
Discount received	250		
Creditor c/f	8,600		
	31,100		31,100

Task 3

	£
Carlton Office Supplies	
October	10,000
November £(12,500 + 8,600)	21,100
Cash purchases £(187 + 5,613)	5,800
	36,900

Task 4

Profit for November 1995

	£	£
Sales (balancing figure)		32,125
Cost of sales		
Purchases	36,900	
Closing stock	11,200	
		25,700
Gross profit (£25,700 × 25/100)		6,425
Discounts received		450
		6,875
Expenses		
Insurance (384 × 1/12)	32	
Depreciation		
Premises (2% × £74,400 × 1/12)	124	
Fixtures (10% × £28,800 × 1/12)	240	
Computer (1/3 × £(1,402 − 250) × 1/12)	32	
Interest (£48,000 × 10% × 1/12)	400	
Postages	43	
Sundry £(52 + 61)	113	
		984
Net profit		5,891

Task 5

CASH ACCOUNT			
	£		£
Sales	32,125	Postages	43
		Cash purchases	187
		Sundry expenses	52
		Cash banked	30,408
		Drawings (bal)	1,435
	32,125		32,125

SOLUTION TO TRIAL RUN
CENTRAL ASSESSMENT 3

DO NOT TURN THIS PAGE UNTIL YOU HAVE
COMPLETED TRIAL RUN CENTRAL ASSESSMENT 3

SECTION 1

Task 1

JOURNAL		Page 1
Details	**£**	**£**
(a) (i) DEBIT Creditors control a/c	1,800	
CREDIT Purchases		1,800
Being correction of overstatement of purchases and creditors		
(ii) DEBIT Light and heat	1,201	
DEBIT Stationery and advertising	1,025	
CREDIT Purchases		2,226
Being posting of other expenses from purchases		
(b) DEBIT Creditors control a/c	47	
CREDIT Purchase returns		40
CREDIT VAT		7
Being purchase return omitted		
(c) DEBIT Sales	245	
CREDIT VAT		245
Being correction of misposting of VAT		
(d) DEBIT Creditors control a/c	54	
CREDIT Discounts received		54
Being posting of omitted discount received		

Task 2

See extended trial balance on Page 332.

Task 3

See extended trial balance on Page 332. Workings are shown below.

(1) *Depreciation*

Motor vehicles = 20% × £(60,480 − 9,800) = £10,136

Office furniture and equipment = 10% × £(26,750 − 3,170) = £2,358

Total depreciation = £(10,136 + 2,358) = £12,494

(2) *Rent*

An accrual is required as the rent expense for the year should be £1,000 × 12 = £12,000.

(3) *Stationery and advertising*

Advertising of £1,560 has been prepaid.

(4) *Stock and insurance*

The damaged stock is correctly excluded from the stock balance. The amount due from the insurance company is a debtor.

(5) *Provision for bad debts*

	£
Debtors control account balance	120,860

	£
Provision required £120,860 × 5% =	6,043
Current provision	5,620
Adjustment required	423

Task 4

See extended trial balance on Page 332.

Account	Trial balance Debit £	Trial balance Credit £	Adjustments Debit £	Adjustments Credit £	Profit and loss a/c Debit £	Profit and loss a/c Credit £	Balance sheet Debit £	Balance sheet Credit £
Opening stock	180,420				180,420			
Purchases	606,054			2,300	603,754			
Sales		840,315				840,315		
Purchases returns		2,430				2,430		
Sales returns	2,650				2,650			
Motor expenses	5,430				5,430			
Bank	20,415						20,415	
Cash	3,420						3,420	
Rent	11,000		1,000		12,000			
Lighting and heating	5,381				5,381			
Stationery and advertising	7,145			1,560	5,585			
Provision for bad debts		5,620		423				6,043
Debtors control account	120,860						120,860	
Creditors control account		100,959						100,959
Salaries	96,200				96,200			
Bad debts	7,200				7,200			
Drawings	31,600						31,600	
Discounts allowed	20,520				20,520			
Discounts received		18,454				18,454		
Motor vehicles	60,480						60,480	
Provision for depreciation: motor vehicles		12,590		10,136				22,726
Office furniture and equipment	26,750						26,750	
Provision for depreciation: office furniture and equipment		3,170		2,358				5,528
VAT		10,512						10,512
Capital		211,475						211,475
Accruals				1,000				1,000
Prepayments			1,560				1,560	
Depreciation			12,494		12,494			
Royal Insurance Company			2,300				2,300	
Closing stock (P&L)				208,540		208,540		
Closing stock (B/S)			208,540				208,540	
Provision for bad debts (adjustment)			423		423			
SUB-TOTAL	1,205,525	1,205,525	226,317	226,317	952,057	1,069,739	475,925	358,243
Profit for the year					117,682			117,682
TOTAL	1,205,525	1,205,525	226,317	226,317	1,069,739	1,069,739	475,925	475,925

SECTION 2

1 (a) Understated

   (b) Understated

			£	£
2 (a)	DEBIT	Debtors control account	705	
	CREDIT	Sales		600
	CREDIT	VAT		105
(b)	DEBIT	Bank	705	
	CREDIT	Debtors control account		705

3 (a) Disagree

   (b) SSAP 13 *Accounting for research and development expenditure* states that both pure and applied research should be written off as incurred. Only development costs relating to new products which are technically and financially feasible may be capitalised.

4 The prudence concept suggests that Julie Owens' debt of £5,000 should be provided for as it is likely that Explosives will lose the entire amount.

5 Stay the same.

			£200	
6	DEBIT	Suspense account	£200	
	CREDIT	Cash		£200

(The original credit entry should have been to cash.)

7

MEMORANDUM

To: Melanie Lancton   Ref:
From: Accounting technician   Date: 8 July 1996
Subject: *Stock valuation*

Statement of Standard Accounting Practice 9 (SSAP 9) *Stocks and long-term contracts* requires stock to be valued at the lower of cost and net realisable value (where NRV is the selling price less any further costs to be incurred to bring the stocks to a saleable condition).

Normally, the accruals concept requires the matching of income and expenditure, as you note. However, where the prudence concept and accruals concept conflict, prudence prevails (according to SSAP 2 *Disclosure of accounting policies*).

The prudence concept requires losses to be provided for as soon as they are foreseen. Here, the 'loss' is the difference between the cost and the NRV of the stock and it must therefore be written off immediately.

I hope this answers your query satisfactorily.

SECTION 3

Task 1

DEBTORS CONTROL A/C			
	£		£
1 June 1995 Balance b/f	39,470	Cash from debtors	863,740
Credit sales (balance)	872,010	Bad debts written off	2,340
		31 May 1996 Balance c/f	45,400
	911,480		911,480

Task 2

	£
Credit sales (see above)	872,010
Cash sales	147,890
Adjustment to float	100
	1,020,000

Task 3

CREDITORS CONTROL A/C			
	£		£
Cash to creditors	607,650	1 June 1995 Balance b/f	35,960
31 May 1996 Balance c/f	49,310	Purchases (balance)	621,000
	656,960		656,960

Task 4

	£	£
Sales		1,020,000
Cost of sales		
Opening stock	33,200	
Purchases	621,000	
	654,200	
Closing stock (balance)	42,200	
		612,000
Gross profit (£1,020,000 × 40%)		408,000

Stolen stock = £42,200 – £38,700 = £3,500.

Task 5

	£	£
Sales proceeds		1,360
Net book value		
Cost	4,000	
Depreciation		
10% for 66 months	2,200	
		1,800
Loss on disposal		440

Task 6

	£
Prepaid general expenses at 31 May 1995	550
General expenses paid	6,240
Owed at year end	170
Profit and loss account	6,960

SOLUTION TO TRIAL RUN
CENTRAL ASSESSMENT 4

DO NOT TURN THIS PAGE UNTIL YOU HAVE
COMPLETED TRIAL RUN CENTRAL ASSESSMENT 4

SECTION 1

Task 1

See extended trial balance on Page 337. Workings are as follows.

(a) *Depreciation*

Motor vehicles: £32,600 × 20% = £6,520

Equipment: £(48,860 – 6,620) × 10% = £4,224

Total depreciation = £10,744

(b) *Bank loan interest*

Interest for 9 months = £50,000 × 10% × 9/12
                       = £3,750

Accrued interest = £3,750 – £2,500 = £1,250

(c) and (d)

Bad debts

	£
Debtors control account balance	189,600
Debt written off: restaurant	3,400
	186,200

Provision required = 6% × £186,200 = £11,172

Adjustment required = £12,000 – £11,172 = £828

(e) *Stock*

	£
Stock at cost	289,400
Reduction to NRV of 5 system £(1,200 – 1,000) × 5	(1,000)
Damaged system	(200)
	288,200

(f) *Advertising*

DEBIT	Advertising	£2,250
CREDIT	Accruals	£2,250

(g) *Rent*

Rent for year = £2,100 × 12 = £25,200

∴£27,300 – £25,200 = £2,100 is prepaid

DEBIT	Prepayments	£2,100
CREDIT	Rent	£2,100

(h) *Cash withdrawn*

DEBIT	Cash	£5,000
CREDIT	Bank	£5,000

(i) *Credit note*

DEBIT	Creditor's control account	£2,900
CREDIT	Purchases returns	£2,900

Task 2

See extended trial balance on Page 337.

Account	Trial balance Debit £	Trial balance Credit £	Adjustments Debit £	Adjustments Credit £	Profit and loss a/c Debit £	Profit and loss a/c Credit £	Balance sheet Debit £	Balance sheet Credit £
Sales		1,200,000				1,200,000		
Purchases	667,820				667,820			
Sales returns	96,570				96,570			
Purchases returns		52,790		2,900		55,690		
Opening stock	301,840				301,840			
Debtors control account	189,600			3,400			186,200	
Cash	1,200		5,000				6,200	
Bank	25,300			5,000			20,300	
Creditors control account		95,000	2,900					92,100
Provision for bad debts		12,000	828					11,172
Bad debts	10,100		3,400		13,500			
Discounts allowed	6,320				6,320			
Salaries	103,030				103,030			
Drawings	26,170						26,170	
Rent	27,300			2,100	25,200			
General expenses	14,310				14,310			
Capital		121,860						121,860
VAT		22,600						22,600
Bank loan		50,000						50,000
Interest on bank loan	2,500		1,250		3,750			
Advertising	11,450		2,250		13,700			
Motor vehicles	32,600						32,600	
Provision for depreciation: motor vehicles		4,100		6,520				10,620
Equipment	48,860						48,860	
Provision for depreciation: equipment		6,620		4,224				10,844
Prepayments			2,100				2,100	
Depreciation			10,744		10,744			
Loan interest owing				1,250				1,250
Other accruals				2,250				2,250
Closing stock (P&L)				288,200		288,200		
Closing stock (B/S)			288,200				288,200	
Provision for bad debts (adjustment)				828		828		
SUB-TOTAL	1,564,970	1,564,970	316,672	316,672	1,256,784	1,544,718	610,630	322,696
Profit for the year					287,934			287,934
TOTAL	1,564,970	1,564,970	316,672	316,672	1,544,718	1,544,718	610,630	610,630

SECTION 2

1 Under the materiality concept it is acceptable to write off such items to revenue rather than capitalise them. Such a small amount depreciated over the life of the calculator would have no real impact on the balance sheet or the profit and loss account.

2 This balance represents the amount owed to Castle Alarms by HM Customs & Excise. Over the quarter Castle Alarms' VAT inputs (purchases) have been higher than its VAT output (sales) and so it can reclaim the excess VAT.

3 Finance lease only.

4 (a) No.

 (b) Errors of omission are not detected by a trial balance. Both the debits and credits in the trial balance are understated by £235.

5 The total charge represents deprecation charged plus/minus the loss/profit on disposal.

	£
Depreciation (£10,450 – £4,100)	6,350
Loss on disposal (£4,100 – £3,000)	1,100
Total charge to capital	7,450

6 Stock should be valued at the lower of cost and net realisable value (NRV).

	£
List price	2,400
Less 20% discount	(480)
Plus delivery charge	10
Value in accounts	1,930

7 (a)

DEBIT	Purchases (£40 × 20)	£800	
DEBIT	VAT (£800 × 90% × 17.5%)	£126	
CREDIT	Creditors		£926

 (b)

DEBIT	Creditors	£926	
CREDIT	Discount received (£40 × 10% × 20)		£80
CREDIT	Cash		£846

8

MEMORANDUM

To: Andrew Hallgrove   Ref: Bank balance and profits
From: Accounting Technician   Date: XX/XX/XX

The profits of a business do not represent its cash flows because of the use of *accrual accounting*. Under this method transactions are recorded, not when cash is received or paid, but when revenues have been earned or costs incurred. This means that a company can make a large sale, recording a substantial profit, but the customer may not pay immediately. The amount owing is recorded as a debtor to the business, but the cash has yet to be received.

The business may have a large amount of stock at the year end. The cost of this stock will not be matched against revenue (ie affecting profit) until the following period but, if the stock has been paid for, the business's bank balance will be adversely affected.

The bank balance will also reflect purchases of fixed assets for cash, whereas profit will only be affected by the smaller impact of depreciation.

I hope these explanations are satisfactory.

SECTION 3

Task 1

	£	£
1 September balance paid in		50,000
Payments		
Fixtures and fittings	22,500	
Stock	47,300	
Rent	9,000	
Insurance	480	
General	220	
		(79,500)
		(29,500)
Balance c/f		
Bank	10,000	
Cash	500	
		(10,500)
Loan from bank		40,000

Task 2

Business assets at 30 September 1996

	£
Fixtures and fittings	22,500
Stock	47,300
Prepayments	
Rent (£9,000 × 5/6)	7,500
Insurance (£480 × 11/12)	440
Bank	10,000
Cash	500

Task 3

TRADE CREDITORS

	£		£
Discount received	1,250	Balance b/f	-
Cash paid	20,250	Purchases on credit (bal fig)	24,900
Balance c/f	3,400		
	24,900		24,900

Task 4

Statement of net profit for October 1996

	£	£
Sales (£20,000 + £2,400)		22,400
Cost of sales		
Opening stock	47,300	
Purchases	24,900	
	72,200	
Closing stock (£55,000 + (£2,000 × 70%))	(56,400)	
		15,800
Gross profit		6,600
Discount received		1,250
		7,850
Expenses		
Wages	2,400	
Depreciation: fixtures and fittings (20% × £22,500 × 1/12)	375	
Bank interest (£40,000 × 12% × 1/12)	400	
Stationery	320	
General expenses	500	
Rent (£9,000 × 1/6)	1,500	
Insurance (£480 × 1/12)	40	
		(5,535)
Net profit		2,315

SOLUTION TO TRIAL RUN
CENTRAL ASSESSMENT 5

DO NOT TURN THIS PAGE UNTIL YOU HAVE
COMPLETED TRIAL RUN CENTRAL ASSESSMENT 5

SECTION 1

Task 1

	Debit £	Credit £
Entries from purchases day book		
Purchases	20,400	
VAT	3,570	
Creditors control account		23,970
Entries from sales day book		
Debtors control account	35,955	
VAT		5,355
Sales		30,600
Entries from sales returns day book		
Sales returns	1,200	
VAT	210	
Debtors control account		1,410
Cheques issued		
Creditors control account	5,000	
Bank		5,000

Task 2

See extended trial balance on Page 343.

Task 3

For entries on the extended trial balance: see Page 343.

(a) *Depreciation*

Motor vehicles: £22,400 × 20% = £4,480

Fixtures and fittings: £(140,000 – £6,000 – £65,000) × 10% = £6,900

Total deprecation = £11,380

(b) *Interest*

Interest due = £150,000 × 6% × 6/12 = £4,500

Bank interest owing = £4,500 – £3,750 = £750

(c) *General expenses*

Prepaid £2,400 × 4/6 = £1,600

(d) *Stock*

Valued at cost = £198,650

Insurance proceeds:

DEBIT	Regis Insurance	£420	
CREDIT	Purchases		£420

(e) *Insurance*

DEBIT	Insurance	£60	
CREDIT	Bank		£60

(f) *Provision for bad debts*

	£
Existing provision	6,000
Provision required (£272,400 × 5%)	13,620
Additional provision	7,620

Account	Trial balance		Adjustments	
	Debit	Credit	Debit	Credit
	£	£	£	£
Share capital		600,000		
Premises	360,000			
Fixtures and fittings (F and F) at cost	140,000			
Provision for depreciation (F and F)		65,000		6,900
Purchases (£972,140 + £20,400)	992,540			420
Sales (£1,530,630 + £30,600)		1,561,230		
Salaries	206,420			
Sales returns (£23,200 + £1,200)	24,400			
Purchases returns		17,350		
General expenses	74,322			1,600
Insurance	16,390		60	
Bad debts	7,506			
Provision for bad debts		6,000		7,620
Debtors control account (£237,855 + £35,955 - £1,410)	272,400			
Creditors control account (£121,433 + £23,970 - £5,000)		140,403		
Stock at 1 June 1996	188,960			
Bank (£65,200 - £5,000)	60,200			60
Bank deposit account	150,000			
Bank interest received		3,750		750
Motor vehicles (MV) at cost	22,400			
Provision for depreciation (MV)		3,800		4,480
VAT: credit balance (£24,720 - £3,570 + £5,355 - £210)		26,295		
Profit and loss		91,710		
Prepayments			1,600	
Depreciation			11,380	
Regis Insurance			420	
Closing stock (P&L)				198,650
Closing stock (B/S)			198,650	
Provision for bad debts (adjustment)			7,620	
Bank interest owing			750	
TOTAL	2,515,538	2,515,538	220,480	220,480

SECTION 2

1

		£
	Total from listing of balances	274,189
(a)	Add error in customer balance (£484 – £448)	36
(b)	Subtract customer balance listed twice	(1,490)
(c)	Subtract discount misposting × 2	(200)
(d)	Subtract goods returned	(135)
		272,400

2   (a)   Profit would increase under LIFO.

     (b)   The consistency concept would prevent the basis for valuation of stock being changed.

3   (a)   No.

     (b)   The cost of the asset shown in the balance sheet should be the full cost of bringing the asset to its present location and condition. SSAP 12 *Accounting for depreciation* requires this treatment, so that self-built assets of this nature are treated in the same way as finished assets purchased. If the company had brought a competed office building, the labour cost would be taken into account in the purchase price asked.

4   Trial balance.

5

MEMORANDUM

To: Jackie Brown   Ref: VAT
From: Accounting Technician   Date: XX/XX/XX

You have raised two queries regarding the VAT which began to appear on invoices from Arun Divan Ltd just recently.

(a)   Although Electronics World Ltd pays more money to Arun Divan for the CD racks, profit is not affected because Electronics World Ltd can claim the VAT back from HM Customs & Excise on its next VAT return. The money will therefore be recouped either by a refund of VAT or a reduction in the VAT owed. The purchase is recorded net of VAT, so that VAT is not charged against profit.

(b)   This statement is true, for the same reasons given above. It is, in effect, the other side of the same coin as in (a).

You can see from this that, as far as VAT is concerned, the only person or body who pays VAT is the final consumer (not registered for VAT) and the only person or body who gains from VAT is HM Customs & Excise (ie the government). The profitability of a company may be affected, but only to the extent that, for a final consumer, goods which have no VAT charged on them (or which are zero-rated) will be cheaper (and so more attractive) than goods with VAT charged on them.

I hope that this has cleared up your misunderstanding.

SECTION 3

Task 1

Total sales: year ended 30 April 1997

	£
Private bank account	
Balance b/f	-
Drawings (£200 × 12)	2,400
Balance c/f	600
Cheques from Electronics World	3,000

ELECTRONICS WORLD LTD

	£		£
Balance b/f	-	Cash received (business a/c)	17,600
Sales (bal fig)	25,000	Cash received (private a/c)	3,000
		Balance c/f	4,400
	25,000		25,000

Task 2

Selling price for 1 pair speaker stands

500 pairs sold for £25,000

$$\therefore \text{Price per pair paid} = \frac{£25,000}{500} = £50$$

Task 3

Cost of materials for 1 pair speaker stands

$$\text{Cost per pair} = \frac{£50}{2} = £25$$

Task 4

Cost of goods sold

Total = £25.00 × 500 = £12,500

Task 5

Purchases

JOHNSON MATERIALS LTD

	£		£
Cash paid	12,000	Balance b/f	-
Balance c/f	1,500	Purchases (bal fig)	13,500
	13,500		13,500

Task 6

Stock valued at cost at 30 April 1996 = £25.00 × 120 = £3,000

Task 7

Capital invested on 30 April 1996

	£	£
Assets		
Tools and equipment	3,000	
Less depreciation (£3,000 × 20% × $^9/_{12}$)	(450)	
		2,550
Van	4,800	
Less depreciation (£4,800 × 10% × $^6/_{12}$)	(240)	
		4,560
Stock		3,000
Bank		4,250
		14,360
Rent owed		(100)
Capital		14,260

Task 8

Rent to 30 April 1997

	£
1 May 1996 - 31 October 1996 (£100 × 6)	600
1 November 1996 - 30 April 1997 (£120 × 6)	720
Rent for year	1,320

ORDER FORM

Any books from our AAT range can be ordered by telephoning 0181-740 2211. Alternatively, send this page to our Freepost address or fax it to us on 0181-740 1184.

To: BPP Publishing Ltd, FREEPOST, London W12 8BR   **Tel: 0181-740 2211**
                                                                 Fax: 0181-740 1184

Forenames (Mr / Ms): _____

Surname: _____

Address: _____

_____

Post code: _____

Please send me the following books (all editions are 8/97 unless otherwise stated):

		Price Interactive Text £	Price Kit £	Quantity Interactive Text	Quantity Kit	Total £
Foundation						
Unit 1	Cash Transactions	9.95		....		....
Unit 2	Credit Transactions	9.95		....		....
Unit 1 & 2	Cash & Credit Transactions Devolved Ass'mt		9.95		....	....
Unit 1 & 2	Cash & Credit Transactions Central Ass'mt		9.95		....	....
Unit 3	Payroll Transactions (9/97)	9.95		....		....
Unit 3	Payroll Transactions Devolved Ass'mt (9/97)		9.95		....	....
Unit 20	Data Processing (DOS) (7/95)	9.95*		....		....
Unit 20	Data Processing (Windows)	9.95		....		....
Units 24-28	Business Knowledge	9.95		....		....

		Tutorial Text	Workbook	Tutorial Text	Workbook	
Intermediate						
Units 4&5	Financial Accounting	10.95	10.95	....	....	....
Unit 6	Cost Information	10.95	10.95	....	....	....
Units 7&8	Reports and Returns	10.95	10.95	....	....	....
Units 21&22	Information Technology	10.95*		....		....
Technician						
Unit 9	Cash Management & Credit Control	10.95	8.95	....	....	....
Unit 10	Managing Accounting Systems	10.95	6.95	....	....	....
Units 11,12&13	Management Accounting	16.95	10.95	....	....	....
Unit 14	Financial Statements	10.95	8.95	....	....	....
Unit 18	Auditing	10.95	6.95	....	....	....
Unit 19	Taxation (FA 97) (10/97)	10.95	8.95	....	....	....
Unit 23	Information Management Systems	10.95	6.95	....	....	....
Units 10,18&23	Project Guidance		6.95		....	....
Unit 25	Health and Safety at Work	3.95**		....		....

* Combined Text

**Price includes postage; this booklet is an extract from Units 24-28 Business Knowledge (Interactive Text)

Postage & packaging:

UK: £2.00 for first plus £2.00 for each extra book.   ....

Europe (inc ROI): £4.00 for first plus £2.00 for each extra book.   ....

Rest of the World: £6.00 for first plus £4.00 for each extra book.   ....   _____

                                                                      Total   _____

I enclose a cheque for £ _____ **or charge to Access/Visa/Switch**

Card number | | | | | | | | | | | | | | | | |

Start date (Switch only) _____ **Expiry date** _____ **Issue no. (Switch only)** _____

Signature _____

REVIEW FORM & FREE PRIZE DRAW

All original review forms from the entire BPP range, completed with genuine comments, will be entered into one of two draws on 31 January 1998 and 31 July 1998. The names on the first four forms picked out on each occasion will be sent a cheque for £50.

Name: _____   Address: _____

_____

_____

How have you used this Workbook?
(Tick one box only)

☐ Home study (book only)

☐ On a course: college _____

☐ With 'correspondence' package

☐ Other _____

Why did you decide to purchase this Workbook? *(Tick one box only)*

☐ Have used complementary Tutorial Text

☐ Have used BPP Texts in the past

☐ Recommendation by friend/colleague

☐ Recommendation by a lecturer at college

☐ Saw advertising

☐ Other _____

During the past six months do you recall seeing/receiving any of the following?
(Tick as many boxes as are relevant)

☐ Our advertisement in *Accounting Technician* Magazine

☐ Our advertisement in *PASS*

☐ Our brochure with a letter through the post

Which (if any) aspects of our advertising do you find useful?
(Tick as many boxes as are relevant)

☐ Prices and publication dates of new editions

☐ Information on Workbook content

☐ Facility to order books off-the-page

☐ None of the above

Have you used the companion Tutorial Text for this subject? ☐ Yes   ☐ No

Your ratings, comments and suggestions would be appreciated on the following areas

	Very useful	Useful	Not useful
Introductory section (How to use this Workbook, etc)	☐	☐	☐
Coverage of elements of competence	☐	☐	☐
Practice exercises	☐	☐	☐
Devolved assessments	☐	☐	☐
Central assessments	☐	☐	☐
Trial run central/devolved assessments	☐	☐	☐

	Excellent	Good	Adequate	Poor
Overall opinion of this Workbook	☐	☐	☐	☐

Do you intend to continue using BPP Tutorial Texts/Workbooks?   ☐ Yes ☐ No

Please note any further comments and suggestions/errors on the reverse of this page

Please return to: Neil Biddlecombe, BPP Publishing Ltd, FREEPOST, London, W12 8BR

REVIEW FORM & FREE PRIZE DRAW (continued)

Please note any further comments and suggestions/errors below

FREE PRIZE DRAW RULES

1   Closing date for 31 January 1998 draw is 31 December 1997. Closing date for 31 July 1998 draw is 30 June 1998.

2   Restricted to entries with UK and Eire addresses only. BPP employees, their families and business associates are excluded.

3   No purchase necessary. Entry forms are available upon request from BPP Publishing. No more than one entry per title, per person. Draw restricted to persons aged 16 and over.

4   Winners will be notified by post and receive their cheques not later than 6 weeks after the relevant draw date. Lists of winners will be published in BPP's *focus* newsletter following the relevant draw.

5   The decision of the promoter in all matters is final and binding. No correspondence will be entered into.